HANDMADE FOR KIDS

HAND-MADE FOR KIDS

BY
BERRI INOUE

ST. MARTIN'S/MAREK
NEW YORK

Design by Holly Johnson at the Angelica Design Group, Ltd.

Library of Congress Cataloging in Publication Data

Inoue, Berri.
  Handmade for kids.

  Includes index.
  1. Textile crafts. I. Title.
TT699.I56 1983   746 83-9663
ISBN 0-312-35855-5

First Edition

10 9 8 7 6 5 4 3 2 1

To Bree, Kale, and Micah,
whose loving looks and humorous antics
make me laugh and create with joy

CONTENTS

Acknowledgments   ix

Preface   xi

1 TOOLS, MATERIALS, HINTS, AND TECHNIQUES   1

2 STUFFED ANIMALS GREAT AND SMALL   9
Daddy Kitty and Junior   9
Baby Bears   11
Draft Stopper Cats   13
Fluffy Ducks   16
Little Elephants   19
Hildy Hedgehog and Baby   21
Kara Kangaroo and Baby   23
Mice with Tote and Cheese   26
Stacy Stegosaurus   29

3 TOYS   33
Bean Bags and Carry Bag   33
Bird Mobile or Crib String   36
Costume for Collector Doll or Rag Doll   38
Cloth Rag Doll   44
Dog Hand Puppets   47
Finger Puppets   49
Rainbow Balls   50
Rupert Rabbit Puppet   52

4 CHRISTMAS WITH KIDS   55
Angel Ornaments   55
Braided Wreath   58
Calico Boxes   60
Lamb Ornaments or Toys   63
Patchwork Potholders   65
Country Patchwork Stockings   67
Calico-Covered Photograph Frames   71
Baby Stripe Stockings   75
Walnut Mice   77

5 TO WEAR AND CARRY   80
Baby Bibs   80
Child's Knapsack   81
Train and Heart Smocks   85
Heart Patch Tote   87
Child's Rainbow Tote and Pillow   91

6 COZY BEDWARMERS   93
Heart Quilt   93
Kaleidoscope Quilt   98
Appliqué Blankets   102
Sleeping Bag   105
Lamb Pajama Bag   107
Child's Rainbow Coverlet   113
Plaid Wool Coverlet   115

Patterns   117

ACKNOWLEDGMENTS

My great appreciation goes to Christopher Gowell, who patiently co-illustrated this book with me.

A note of thanks to Neal Chaves for his technical assistance in photography and to Sandra Koski for her precise sewing on several projects.

Special thanks to Sharon Lang-Grannan whose friendship and zest for life served as a constant reminder that what we make with our hands, we make out of love.

Loving thanks to Moosie, who kept my spirits kindled throughout.

And lastly and mostly I thank Naoto with all my heart, not only for his photographs and assistance in mechanical drawing, but for his driving confidence and loving arms at the end of a long day.

PREFACE

This book is a collection of original designs developed for the *Better Homes and Gardens* Crafts Club. Each project was created so that people who love to use their hands can have a chance to learn new techniques, gain experience, and create something absolutely delightful. Whether it be a huge stegosaurus that makes kids squeal and laugh, or a beautiful, warm quilt in your favorite colors, it will have a special touch that only you could have added.

There are projects for every level of ability, including a few for kids to make themselves. However, it is not the complexity or size of the design that makes the finished piece a favorite. I recall one snowy Christmas when a little white mouse was the chosen friend to be carried around all day amongst the new store-bought gifts.

Handmade for Kids is for all of us who still have some childhood left within and those of us who delight in color, fabric, dimension, expression, and sharing. Create because you enjoy the process of making as well as seeing kids giggle and glow. I wish you the very best success in your creative adventuring and hope that the projects I share here will offer the sense of personal satisfaction that comes from creating gifts for your loved ones.

HANDMADE FOR KIDS

1

TOOLS, MATERIALS, HINTS, AND TECHNIQUES

I am passing on these guidelines and timesavers so that you may construct these new furry friends, warm quilts, and other calico delights with as little frustration and the greatest excitement possible. Making mistakes is part of learning, but there is so much to learn that a little help in the beginning will only bring you further toward your goal. At times your tried and true methods will be better for you. Nonetheless, I urge you to read through the next few pages. If you can gain any insight at all that will enable you to create with your hands in a more enjoyable way, the purpose for writing this book will have been realized.

TOOLS AND MATERIALS

You will already have many of the following tools and materials in your sewing or crafts space. If you love to work with your hands, you will want to collect supplies and accessories which make it easier to complete pieces with accuracy while at the same time increasing your skills. Not all of the tools are required for every project, but you may be tempted to create something you would not ordinarily make by having the proper implements within reach. Try to keep your tools in a basket or on a designated shelf as a carpenter would, so they are handy when you need them.

Dowels. Long knitting needles, paintbrush handles or chopsticks are useful for turning pieces right side out. Push bits of stuffing in a little bit at a time so it does not lump. First, tightly stuff the corners and appendages like hands, feet, and ears. Sometimes a knitting needle or chopstick can be used to push out thick corners on quilts or bedwarmers.

Dressmaker's pencils. Dressmaker's pencils, tracing wheel, paper, and/or tailor's chalk in several colors are needed for marking dots on dark and light fabric. Also recently on the market is a fabric marker (light blue in color) that can be used for marking, easily removed by misting with water. This is a wonderful tool for tracing features as well as marking clearly.

Felt. Many of the animal designs require felt for the faces. If you enjoy making designs of this nature, keep pieces of red, black, white, and tan felt in stock.

Glue (for gluing felt and calico boxes and frames). A white glue such as Elmer's or Sobo is excellent. Do not use rubber cement.

Hole punch. Instructions on making animals with felt features often refer to a "hole punch." This is done with a standard-sized hole punch and is very accurate and quick for making black pupils in any quantity.

Iron. Especially on old appliances, keep the bottom plate clean so it will slide easily and not soil fabrics. Always press on the wrong side of the fabric when possible.

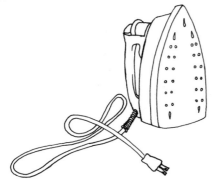

Masking tape (or Scotch Tape® for joining and tracing patterns).

Needles (for hand sewing seam openings, body parts, or felt pieces). Also, have several larger-sized tapestry needles size 18 through 26 for embroidery and tacking.

Pencils. Have several sharp ones with erasers on hand. They always seem to be hiding.

Rulers. I use a variety of sizes from 6-inch to 48-inch for tasks ranging from small feature placement to pattern making. I prefer metal rulers, but a wooden ruler with a metal edge is fine.

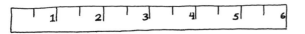

Scissors. A sharp pair of 7- or 8-inch scissors can be one of your most valuable tools. Ginghers or Wiss are of excellent quality and will last a lifetime if cared for properly. A good pair of shears will easily cut several layers of fabric at one time and help you to maintain crisp accuracy throughout your work. Some craftspeople have two pairs of scissors, one specifically for cutting fabric, as paper tends to dull the blades more easily. I have my very best scissors marked with a piece of tape around the handle so no one would dare use them for anything but fabric (and there is often that temptation).

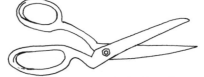

Scissors. A smaller pair of 5 inches is very helpful but not absolutely necessary for cutting small features. I much prefer one 7-inch pair of excellent quality than two sizes that are only mediocre in workmanship.

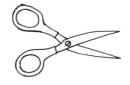

Straight pins. Although a bit more expensive, I find the ones with the little colored balls on the end to be exceptionally sharp and easy to handle and see.

Seam ripper (just in case you make an error). I always find it easier if I can rectify a mistake quickly rather than moan over something that is obviously incorrect.

Sewing machine. A machine with a zigzag stitch is convenient and certainly much faster than hand sewing but almost all of the designs can be assembled with hand stitching. An embroidered chain stitch can replace machine zigzag.

Tape measure. This is especially good for measuring your children for sizing.

Thimble. It can be useful for hand stitching or quilting.

Tracing paper. You need tracing paper or thin paper through which you can see patterns and marking. Sometimes a good-quality tissue paper works well because it is available in large sizes and will save on piecing paper together for big patterns. You may wish to transfer patterns to brown packaging paper or shopping bags (the flat kind from department stores is better than grocery bags), for patterns that will be used time and time again.

T-Square or triangles are optional, but very helpful for making both rectangular and square patterns accurately.

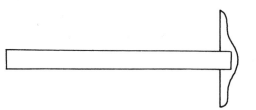

Workspace and time. You need a clean area you can call your own for a certain length of time. It should be large enough that you can make patterns, assemble, and sew without feeling cramped or rushed. The actual space requirement will depend on the size of the project.

NOTIONS

Bells. Bells give your animal friends dignity as well as a musical dimension. Depending on the finished size of your piece, a bell anywhere from ¼ inch to 1 inch may be used. Be sure they're sewn on very securely, as little children love to tug on them.

Polyester fiberfill and batting. This is non-allergenic, inexpensive, and easy to work with. You may also use a cotton filling or batting; although more difficult to locate, it is natural and warmer when used for a bed quilt.

Polyester satin ribbons. These may be washed and pressed with a *warm* iron on the back of the ribbon. They come in a large variety of widths and colors.

Thread. It is worth investing in quality thread if you are willing to put hours of time and love into your work. A cotton-covered polyester thread is fine. I enjoy using Swiss-Metrosene thread, which is of very good quality and available in an excellent variety of colors.

NOTES ON FABRICS AND ACCESSORIES FOR SAFETY AND DURABILITY

- Use fire-retardant fabrics whenever possible.
- I always use 100-percent cotton calico or solid fabrics, but poly-cottons can be substituted if you wish. Make sure all fabrics are dye-fast. This can be done by machine washing before you begin.
- Use a good quality medium- to heavy-weight felt for facial features and feet.
- Glued-on felt does not wash particularly well. To make toys washable, stitch felt on and gently hand wash with soap and water. Remove bells and ribbons first.

HOW TO MAKE PATTERN PIECES

All of the patterns are given full-size at the back of this book, starting on page 117. The page number for patterns for each project is designated in the directions.

A. To trace the patterns directly from the book, place tracing paper or tissue over book pattern and trace with a smooth pencil line. Paper should be held down with masking tape to prevent shifting while you work. Trace all placement lines, including where to place on fabric fold, darts and dots. Be sure to label what the piece is, how many you want to cut, and from what fabric.

If you plan to make many of the same design and wish to make patterns on brown packaging paper or cardboard, you can use one of several methods.

1. Tape tracing paper to a large sunny window or a glass coffee table that you can put a light underneath. Tape brown paper on top and trace over pattern. If your brown paper is very heavy you might have to darken your original lines with a black marker.
2. A second method is to tape your tracing paper pattern to brown paper and cut around it as you would on fabric.

3. Another technique, particularly good if you want a cardboard pattern for tracing, is to cut out your originally traced patterns, place them on the cardboard and trace around the edges.

B. Some of the patterns are very large and pieces must be joined together as you trace (if you have large enough tracing paper) or taped together afterwards in order to complete the full-size pattern. The sides that are to be joined or traced back to back are clearly noted by corresponding letters or instructions. Each will also have a diagram of what the finished pattern should look like and where it is pieced together.

C. Some patterns are symmetrical in shape and only half of the pattern is actually given.

To make a full pattern you can:
1. Trace all around shape, including fold line.
2. Turn paper over. Match up fold line and trace on back side of paper. You will be able to see through both sides of your transparent paper as you cut.

or

1. Trace the half pattern, including the fold line.
2. Fold paper exactly on fold line.
3. Pin the two layers of paper together adequately to prevent shifting and cut out both layers. You have probably done this as a child with hearts.

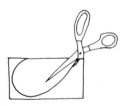

On the pattern it will be noted, "Fold here for full-size pattern." This does not mean the pattern should be put on fold when cutting fabric. That will be noted on the pattern piece by "Place on fabric fold" and it is not necessary to make a full-size pattern

(when placing a half pattern on fabric fold). This particular term and technique is used when cutting (1) fabric piece only, because it is very difficult to cut accurately more than one full-size fabric piece at a time when placing pattern on a fabric fold.

D. Some pattern pieces are simple squares and rectangles. The measurements for these are given with the pattern pieces as well as noted under pattern requirements in the directions. A square or T-square is useful in making these, but if you do not have one available, a piece of paper or cardboard that has been cut square will be fine.

1. To begin, draw (2) lines perpendicular to each other. Measure from point *a* to point *b* and mark the bottom measurement. Measure from *a* to *c* for the side measurement.

2. Place a square on bottom line *ab* and measure the same distance from point *b* to point *d* as from *a* to *c*. Join points *d* and *c*. This should measure exactly the same as *b* to *a*. Remember to label this piece as to what part it is and how many to cut.

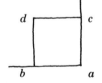

In several instances a rectangular piece will have to be joined to a larger curved pattern that you have already traced (as in the smocks and stockings). The directions will say, "add 8″ × 10⅝″ piece to the top of joined stocking bottom pieces #1 and #2."

4

HINTS BEFORE YOU STITCH

1. If you are making a design that will eventually be washed, always pre-wash all fabric for shrinkage before you begin working.

2. Iron all fabric before pinning patterns or drawing measurements on back side in pencil.

3. Cut out paper patterns completely before pinning to fabric. Use plenty of pins when pinning patterns to fabric.

4. There will be many projects you will want to make in quantity. The best way to do this is the assembly line method. Make a list of the number of each piece you will need. Multiply the quantity of finished items times the pieces required for each part. When assembling, sew or glue all of one step at the same time. For example, if you are making four potholders, sew all of the corner triangles together for all of the potholders. You would sew sixteen corners as your first step.

5. *Mark all dots and darts before removing patterns.* One of the simplest methods to use in marking fabric pieces is the tailor's tack. With a threaded needle go through the pattern and fabric, leaving at least 1½ inches on either side.

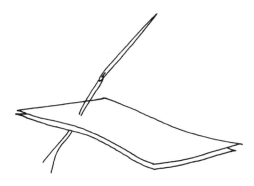

Clip thread. When removing patterns, cut the thread between fabric pieces (if marking more than one piece at a time) and pull it through so ¾ inch remains on either side of the fabric. You may also use a dressmaker's tracing wheel and tracing paper or tailor's chalk for marking dots on the outer edge of a pattern.

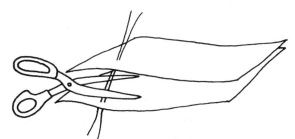

6. *Tracing feature placement onto fabric.* When tracing facial features or placement from pattern onto fabric, a sharp pencil will always suffice. However, a fabric marker now available at many fabric stores that washes out with a misting of water (you may have to ask for it) corrects mistakes simply and results in a very clean look. Pencil lines can be washed out with soap and water if they show on your final piece. To see more easily when tracing, your pattern can be taped to a sunny window and fabric taped tightly over so it will not stretch.

7. Sometimes it is helpful to have pieces labeled on the back. Tailor's chalk or a dressmaker's pencil is ideal for this. If you do not have these items on hand, you can use a pencil on light fabrics or masking tape lettered with a permanent marker for dark fabrics or velour.

8. Most sewing machines have a measurement gauge etched into the plate beneath the needle. Usually a straight stitch presser foot is ¼ inch from the needle to the right-hand edge of the presser foot. If your plate has no gauge, tape a piece of accurately lined paper (marked in ⅛-inch increments) onto the plate so that you will have an exact measurement of ¼ inch to the right of where the needle enters.

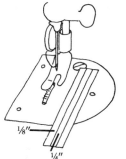

9. *How to use fabric fuser (stitch witchery):*
   a.) To save time and maintain accuracy, pin and cut out all pieces with fabric fuser be-

hind fabric. Sometimes the fuser is thin and difficult to handle; cut this way, it is exactly the same size as the fabric and is more manageable.

    b.) Put fabric fuser on wrong side of calico and place in desired position on background. Do not use pins. Place a damp pressing cloth over pieces and press with a warm iron for 5 to 10 seconds. Do not move iron back and forth. If pieces are not fused completely, press again for several more seconds.

10. *Hints for working with fur:*

    a.) When cutting out fur pieces pin wrong side of pattern to wrong side of fur. It is much easier to cut, and pattern will not slide with nap.

    b.) You should usually cut just one layer of thick fur at a time, but I have found that with very sharp scissors and a few extra pins it is possible to cut two layers. You must remember to hold scissors vertically so that the bottom piece will not come up short.

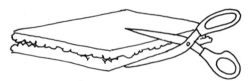

    c.) When pinning fur pieces always push all edge fur to inside (this will be the right side). This makes it easier to guide the back side for seam allowance and also achieves an unnoticeable joining on the right side.

    d.) If some of the fur is caught in the seam, pull it out later with a pin.

11. When sewing with velour, use extra pins when pinning patterns to fabric or sewing two pieces together. This will help alleviate curling and stretching.

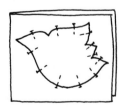

TIPS AND TECHNIQUES FOR SEWING

1. Backstitch at the beginning and end of machine-sewn seams. This is not as crucial when using the assembly line method in patchwork construction.

2. Remove pins as you machine stitch so you don't sew over them and run the risk of damaging your needle.

3. Sew with a ¼-inch seam unless otherwise indicated. Some projects that are small and/or made with thick fur are sewn with a ³⁄₁₆-inch seam to make them less bulky for turning.

4. You may want to baste rather than use pins when assembling very small pieces.

5. Use small machine stitches when assembling tiny pieces. I use 12 to 15 stitches per inch when sewing average-size shapes.

6. Trim threads as you go.

7. Press patchwork seams to one side. This is much stronger than in opening seams as in dressmaking.

8. Double sew curved seams that may eventually weaken.

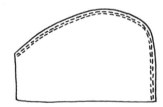

9. Clip curves carefully where noted. Try to snip close to the seam, but be sure not to cut it. If you do cut it by mistake, sew another seam, making sure there is enough margin from the snipped area. This seam should be double stitched for reinforcement. The shape may be altered slightly, but that is much better than not being able to complete a design for lack of the same fabric.

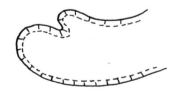

10. Use matching thread for topstitching and sewing felt to faces. Handstitch features and turning holes with a tiny invisible slip stitch.

11. *Ease seam.* An ease seam is one that usually begins from a folded edge. It does not start with a ¼-inch seam, but actually begins right on the fold and "eases" into the allowance from the fold, making a smooth transition from fold to seam allowance.

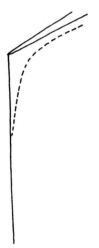

12. *Appliqué and zigzag hints.*

a.) I find the easiest method of machine appliqué is with the use of fabric fuser (see pp. 5–6). After the desired piece has been fused in place, zigzag with a wide zigzag stitch. I usually set my dials on 8 for length and approximately 2¾ on the zigzag width guide. As well as a wide enough stitch, the key to long-lasting appliqué is to use the outside edge of the piece you are applying as a sewing guide. All of the stitching should be on the piece being appliquéd, *not* half on the background fabric. Practice slowly going around curves before attempting a detailed design.

b.) All of the appliqué projects in this book have been done by machine and with the use of fabric fuser. However, if you wish to appliqué by hand and without fabric fuser, add a ³⁄₁₆-inch seam allowance to all appliqué patterns. Fold this seam allowance in, clipping a bit at curves when necessary, and sew with a tiny stitch. Hand appliqué is very lovely and delicate. A machine zigzag topstitch gives a more distinct, crisp outline of shapes.

c.) If you are appliquéing by machine without the use of fabric fuser, baste pieces in place first to prevent shifting as you work.

FINISHING TOUCHES

• Glue pompoms and felt pieces on faces of projects intended for older children. Glue and sew for young children. Later, test glued-on pieces to make sure they are secure. You might want to touch up around the edges for extra strength.

• When using glue for felt features, apply a small amount so it will not soak through. Wait until it becomes tacky before pressing it to a larger surface. If it does soak through, you can glue another layer of the same felt piece on top of it.

• To tack patchwork pieces (sometimes called tufting), thread needle with embroidery floss or yarn and do not knot it. Pull thread from the back to the front of the quilt, leaving 1¼ inch or more of thread in the back. Go right back through the quilt, as close as you can to where you just came up (⅛ inch). Tie a square knot in the back and trim embroidery floss to 1 inch or desired length. Sometimes tufting is done from the front to the back so that the floss or yarn shows on the front. The more you tack throughout the piece, the more securely the top will be held in place.

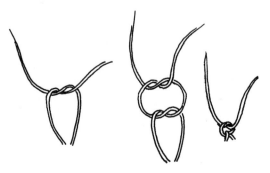

• Giving something that is handmade is so very special that it sometimes deserves a little tag or label that answers the question, "Who made this beautiful quilt or adorable dinosaur?" Personalized "Hand-made by You" or "Created Especially With You in Mind" labels can often be ordered at fabric stores or from the back pages of craft and needlework magazines. In this day of large companies cranking out thousands of machine-made items, I find nothing as special as knowing who made a lovely gift that will be cherished and passed down through generations. If the project lends itself and there is room, sometimes your name or initials and date can be embroidered in the corner.

8

2
STUFFED ANIMALS GREAT AND SMALL

DADDY KITTY AND JUNIOR

Sometimes you need a project that can be completed from start to finish in an afternoon. Daddy and Junior Kitty are just this. They have only two basic pattern pieces and the faces may be glued if they are intended for a child past the age of chewing facial features. Even stitching the felt requires little time. The arms are especially designed for hugging, and the bell absolutely delights babies.

Daddy or Junior is also a perfect project for a curious child to assist in making or create alone.

Materials

Daddy Kitty

Body, 20″ × 24″ fur
Felt, black, 4″ × 4″; white, 4″ × 2½″; red, 2″ ×
2″; gray, 1½″ × 2″; yellow, 2½″ × 1½″
Ribbon, red, ½″ × 30″
Bell, gold, 1″

Junior Kitty

Body, 15″ × 7″ fur
Felt, black, 4″ × 4″; white, 3″ × 2″; gray, 1″ ×
1½″; red, 2″ × 2″; yellow, 1½″ × 2″
Ribbon, red, ¼″ × 20″
Bell, gold, ¾″

Patterns (see page 117)

Body (2), fur*
Arms (4), fur, (2) left, (2) right
Heart (1), red felt
Nose (1), gray felt
Bottom nose (1), black felt
Mouth (1), black felt
Eyes (2), yellow felt
Pupils (2), black felt
Whiskers (6), black felt
Mask (1), white felt

* Note the direction of the fur nap when cutting body pieces.

Assembly

1. Glue or stitch felt facial features according to placement or as desired. Refer to placement on body pattern. If cat is intended for a small child and you are stitching by hand, first glue features down so they will stay in place while you work. Glue itself will hold quite well and after it dries you can retouch edges if necessary. Glue or appliqué heart in same manner. A child's name may be embroidered on heart before applying.

2. With right sides together, sew both arms, leaving open where indicated. Clip curves carefully. Turn inside out. Pin arms to front, ¾ inch from neck according to placement, and overlap ⅛ inch beyond body. Baste in place.

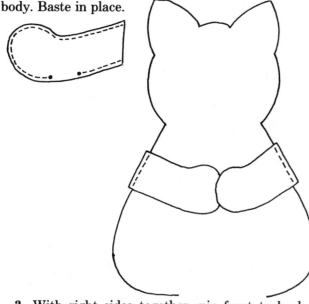

3. With right sides together, pin front to back. Stitch all around, leaving open where indicated on

body and feet on Daddy. Arms should be towards inside. Leave open on head and feet where indicated on Junior.

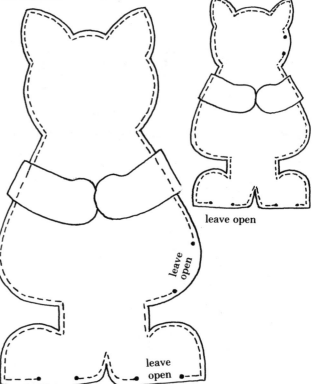

leave open

leave open

leave open

4. Clip ears and curves. Turn inside out through hole in body or head. Begin with feet. *Pull very gently* on face. If fur is very thick, enlarge opening slightly.

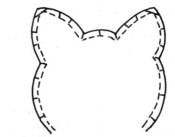

5. Stuff ears only, through body or head hole. A long pencil or knitting needle is necessary to push stuffing up. Topstitch through both thicknesses of fur on bottom of ear by machine or by hand. If you sew tightly, stitches will not show.

6. Do not stuff body yet. Sew through both thicknesses of fur, across top of legs and down between legs in same manner as ear stitching.

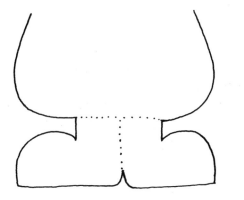

Stuff legs through feet holes. Stuff body through body or head hole. Do not overstuff. Stuff arms and legs more firmly than body. Sew up holes.

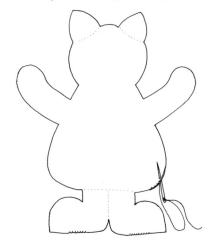

7. Tie ribbon around neck and sew bell securely in center of bow.

BABY BEARS

"It's time for baby bear to go to sleep," whispers a little voice.

If by chance you already have a big bear, maybe you should have a baby bear as well. These furry 6-inch friends are extremely quick and easy to construct. They make wonderful surprises peeping out of a stocking on Christmas morning, and are still around years later with that well-loved look about them.

Materials (for each bear)

Body and head, 30″ × 5″ brown or tan fur
Eyes, 1″ × 2″ black felt; 1″ × 2″ white felt
Nose, 1″ × 1″ tan or black felt
Mouth, 1″ × 1″ red felt
Stuffing, polyester fiberfill
Satin ribbon, ½″ × 20″, color of your choice

Patterns (see page 121)

Body front (1), Body back (2), Head front (2), Head back (1), Head back (1), Ears (4), from fur fabric

11

Mouth (1), red felt
Eyes (2), white felt
Pupil (2), black felt
Nose (1), black or tan felt

LAYOUT

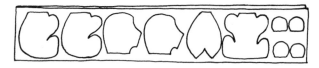

Assembly

As this is a small project with thick fabric, sew with a ³⁄₁₆-inch seam throughout.

1. Fold back of head in half with right sides together. Stitch opening from ³⁄₁₆ inch at bottom to dot to make a dart.

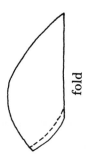

2. With fur sides together, match bottom of head front to seam just sewn in head back. Pin at bottom and top. Ease around curve as you sew to dot at top of head. This is a small piece so you will have to lift your presser foot several times to turn it if sewing by machine. Leave ³⁄₁₆ inch unsewn at bottom and top of head back (see dots on head back and head front pattern pieces). Pin and sew other side in same manner.

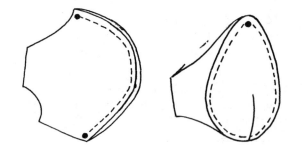

3. Sew front face together to neck edge. Clip curves. Turn inside out.

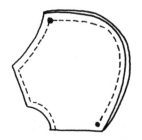

4. With right sides together, pin the two body back pieces between dots, leaving neck open. Sew between dots.

5. Open the two body back pieces up to fur side of arms and legs. Place fur side of body front on top, matching arms and legs. Pin and sew all around, leaving neck open. Check other side to be sure the stitches have not missed fur edges. Clip curves. Turn inside out.

6. Sew around ears, leaving bottom open. Clip curves. Turn inside out.

7. Stuff head and body firmly. Turn neck in ³⁄₁₆ inch on head and ³⁄₁₆ inch on neck of body, and sew together securely by hand. Fold in bottom of ears and sew in place.

8. Glue black pupil to white of eye. Glue or sew all facial features in place. See photo on page 00 for placement. Tie ribbon in a bow around neck.

DRAFT STOPPER CATS

Because of its usefulness and warm, snug expression, the draft stopper kitty seems to attract an enthusiastic response. Although the kitty is an ideal energy saver for a child's room, kitchen, or living room (fabric can be matched to decor), its tail may be shortened for a toy.

Materials

 Calico fabric of your color choice, ⅔ yard
 Bridal satin, pink, 6″ × 6″ (*press backside only*)

 Satin ribbon (cream color), 30″ × ⅝″ wide
 Bell, gold, 1″
 Stuffing, polyester fiberfill and rice or sand for
  tail (optional)

Patterns (see page 122)

 Body (2), calico
 Front legs (4), calico
 Head back (1), calico
 Stomach (1), calico
 Ears (2), calico, (2) pink satin
 Side face (2), calico

Front face (1), calico
Lower foot (4), calico
Eyes (2), white felt
Pupils (2), green felt
Nose (1), pink felt, (1) brown felt
Mouth (1), red felt, (1) tan felt
Whiskers (6), black felt
Tail end (1), calico

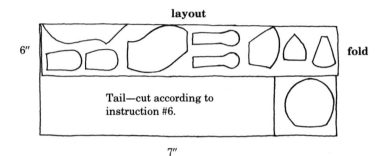

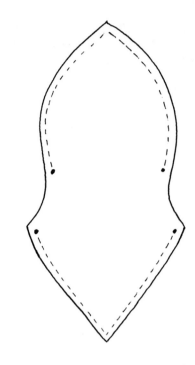

Assembly

1. With right sides together, sew front legs all around, leaving top open. Sew back lower feet all around. Clip curves. Turn inside out. Press.

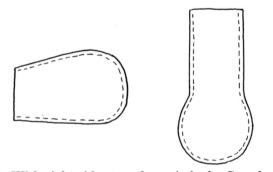

2. With right sides together, pin body. Sew down back, leaving opening for tail. With right sides together, pin front stomach piece to body pieces. Sew all around, leaving open where indicated.

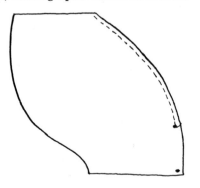

3. Sew side face pieces together at front seam. Press open. Pin front face to one side. Sew down, leaving ¼ inch unsewn at nose end. Sew other side in same manner.

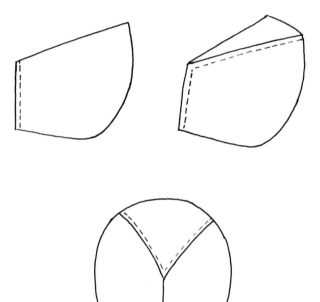

4. Make dart in head back. Press to one side. Pin to head front, matching at edges (not center seam). Sew all around, leaving bottom open.

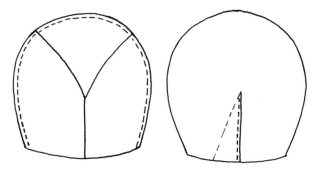

5. With right sides together, sew pink satin ear to calico ear. Leave bottom open. Trim tip. Turn inside out and press. Fold and press unsewn bottom in ¼ inch.

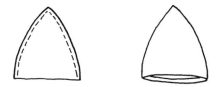

6. To make tail, measure door or window where cat is going to block the draft. Subtract 6 inches for cat. With a yardstick measure 6¼ inches wide by 30¾ inches or desired length. Add ½ inch to your measurement for seam. This will give you a 30-inch tail and 36-inch draft stopper. Fold tail fabric in half. Put 6¼-inch tail end pattern on fabric and cut around one end. Stitch down side and over end. Use an ease seam to fold. Clip curve. Turn inside out.

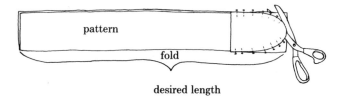

7. Separately stuff head, body, feet, and front legs with polyester fiberfill, and tail with rice or sand if desired. Pin securely and handstitch head to body. Ribbon will cover seam later. Fold open seam on

body/stomach in ¼ inch and put back legs in approximately ⅜ inch. Stitch by hand with small stitches.

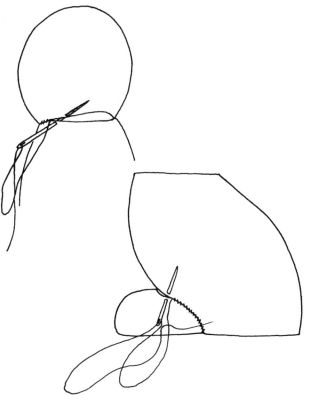

8. Pin front legs in place. Edge should touch body/stomach seam. Sew with legs up. Fold legs over so raw edges will be covered by legs. Tack down securely so cat will stand. Insert tail in hole left open for it (fold body seam in ¼ inch). Put tail seam on bottom. Sew stuffed tail in place.

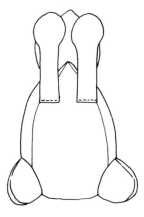

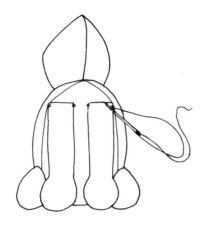

9. Facial features may be glued or sewn in place by hand if it is intended as a toy for a young child. See the photograph and illustration on page 13 for placement. Use a thin strip of brown felt to make mouth. Tie ribbon around neck. Sew bell to ribbon securely. Sew ears in place, approximately ⅛ inch in front of head seam.

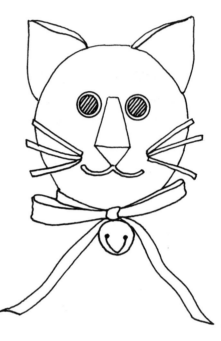

FLUFFY DUCKS

Mrs. Duck puts on her bonnet, calls Mr. Duck and friends, and goes out for a walk. Maybe they will go to the store, or a neighbor's, or just waddle and quack around your bedroom. They each need a name, a hug, and a squeeze, but it's easy for kids to give things like that. Fluffy ducks share lots of love in return.

Materials

Duck body, 13″ × 8″ yellow, white, or black sherpa fur or a smooth lightweight fur

Wings, 9″ × 4″ yellow or brown felt

Feet, 4″ × 2″ dark orange felt

16

Eyes, 2″ × 1″ black felt, 2″ × 1″ white felt
Beak, 2″ × 1″ light orange felt
Bonnet, 6″ × 6″ main color calico, 4″ × 4″ calico
  for brim, and 1¼″ × 18″ of brim calico for tie
White glue for eyes

Patterns (see page 125)

Where (2) of a piece is indicated, fold fabric in half
so you will have a right and a left.

  Body (2), fur (make sure nap is going in proper
    direction)
  Wings (4), yellow or brown felt
  Feet (2), dark orange felt
  Beak (1), light orange felt
  Eyes (2), white felt
  Pupils (2), black felt (use a hole punch)
  Main bonnet (1), calico
  Brim (2), calico
  Tie (1), calico (make pattern 1¼″ × 18″, or draw
    on back of fabric with pencil)

Assembly

1. With right sides together, pin right and left side
of body. Sew all around, leaving 1½ inches open on
bottom for turning. Clip curves carefully. Turn inside out. Stuff with fiberfill or beans. Stitch up hole.

2. Fold beak in half and sew in place. Make black
eye pupil with hole punch. Glue or sew to white of
eye. Glue or stitch in place on head.

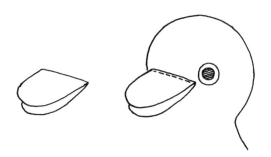

Put two wing pieces together and pin. Topstitch
around with a ⅛-inch seam, leaving a small opening
for stuffing. Without cutting threads from sewing
machine, stuff wing with a small amount of batting
and continue stitching to close opening. Sew wings
securely in placement desired on side of duck.

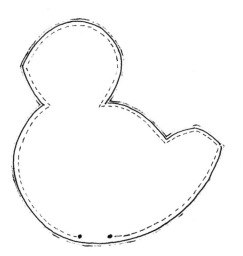

Overlap feet slightly and sew well in place on bottom. Each duck will take on its own delightful personality as the placement of features varies slightly.

3. To assemble bonnets, pin right sides of brim together and sew around front outside curve. Clip curves. Turn inside out and press.

4. Gather calico all around circle of main bonnet piece until it fits comfortably on duck's head (about 3 inches in diameter). With right sides together, pin one edge of brim to gathered bonnet and stitch in place. Turn in remaining edge ¼ inch and pin. Sew by hand later.

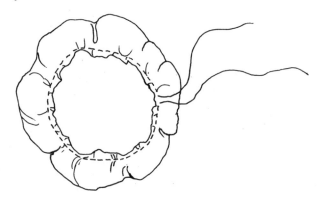

5. Fold tie in ¼ inch on both sides and iron. Fold this ironed piece in half and press again. Unfold to sew to bonnet. Mark center of tie at 9 inches. With right sides together, pin ¼ inch of first fold onto unsewn gathered back edge of bonnet, up to beginning of brim. (Center tie on bonnet back.) Baste in place. Fold tie in toward ironed folds and pin on inside of bonnet.

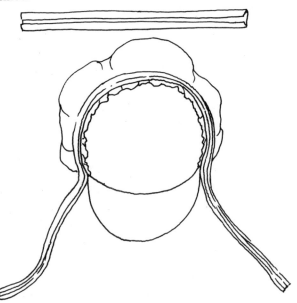

6. Fold tie ends in to finish off raw edges. Sewing very close to folded edges, stitch down tie string, across where it is pinned to gathered back, and down remainder of tie string.

Handstitch inside of brim at gathering.

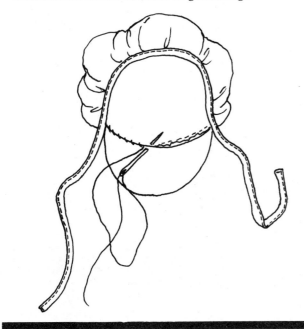

LITTLE ELEPHANTS

Baby elephants are a perfect clutch toy for a young child and require a minimum of time and skill to complete. Older children enjoy having a family of elephants. I often find them riding around in someone's pocket dressed in a vest, hat, scarf, or socks made from small calico scraps.

Materials

Elephant, 20″ × 9″ calico, corduroy, terry, or velour
Eyes, 2″ × 1″ black felt, 2″ × 1″ white felt
Heart, 3″ × 2″ contrasting-color calico
Ribbon, 18″ of ⅝″ satin ribbon
Fabric fuser, 3″ × 2″

Patterns (see pp. 125 and 127)

Body (2), calico
Head (2), calico
Ears (4), calico
Heart (1), calico of contrasting color

Eyes (2), white felt
Pupils (2), black felt

Assembly

These are ideal to make in quantity with the assembly line method.

1. Before removing pattern from fabric, mark neck hole, heart placement, and ear placement with thread on head. To appliqué heart on front of body, place fabric fuser heart behind calico heart. Center on body front. Place a cloth on top and press with a warm iron for 5 to 10 seconds. If fabric lifts or fuser shows around the edges, press again for several more seconds. Zigzag all around heart.

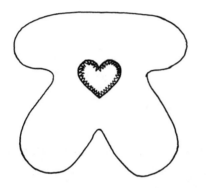

2. With right sides together, sew back to front, leaving hole open for neck. Clip curves carefully. Turn inside out.

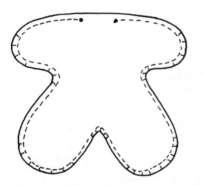

3. Sew ears together, leaving hole open for turning. Clip curves. Trim corners. Turn inside out. Press, making sure opening is pressed in an even ¼ inch from seam. Place ear on head where indicated. Rounded part of ear should face trunk. Pin. Sew with an ⅛-inch seam. Pin top and bottom of ear to

itself so it won't be accidentally sewn when stitching head.

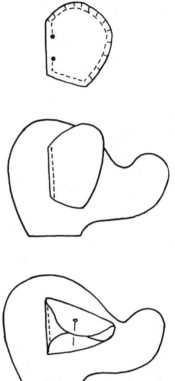

4. With right sides together, match head pieces and sew around slowly so that curves are smooth. Leave bottom open. Clip all around trunk. Turn inside out.

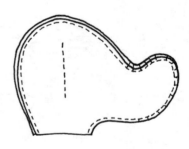

5. Stuff body and head. Fold open neck and bottom of head to inside, ¼ inch or what is needed to fit head in desired place. The head should sit right on the body and not have a wobbly neck. Match center front to trunk seam. Sew securely by hand all around with a small, tight stitch.

6. Glue or stitch black pupil to white of eye. Glue or stitch in place (see photograph for placement). Tie ribbon in bow around neck.

HILDY HEDGEHOG AND BABY

Hildy is a lovable, huggable little creature that seems to magically come alive. I find youngsters biting her on the nose, then squeezing her thick fur. She has often traveled to the grocery store peering out of a tote bag, delighting fellow shoppers. She is simple to make, yet becomes a treasured prize among animal friends.

Materials

Hildy

Body, 10″ × 14″ thick brown, gray or black fur
Head and Underside, 17″ × 6″ brown velour or corduroy
Feet and Pupils, 5½″ × 5½″ black felt
Eyes, 2″ × 1″ white felt

Baby

Body, 8″ × 5½″ fur
Head and Underside, 11″ × 3½″ brown velour
Feet, 4″ × 4″ black felt
Eyes, 2″ × 1″ white felt

Patterns (see page 128)

Body (2), fur
Head (2), velour
Underside (1), velour
Feet (4), black felt
Eyes (2), white felt
Pupils (2), black felt
Nose (1), black felt
Mouth (1), black felt (optional)

Fur Layout

It is very important to place the body pieces properly on the fur. Mark which direction the nap is going on the wrong side of the fur. Use chalk or pins to form arrow. Place body patterns so nap is going from neck to tail, and so tops of back pieces almost touch each other.

To cut a right body and left body piece, first cut with pattern face up, then flip pattern over. Pin to wrong side of fur with plenty of pins. When you cut, the fur will shed slightly. Collect shedding around cut pieces before you sew.

FUR LAYOUT

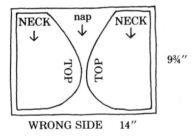

Assembly

1. Pin right sides of fur body together. When pinning, push fur to inside (right side). This will make it easier to sew and the seam in the fur won't show. Sew with a ¼-inch seam from bottom to neck.

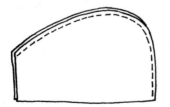

2. Pin right sides of head together. Sew around to dot on bottom, leaving neck and remainder of bottom open. Clip curves. Turn right side out.

With right sides together, match seam on head with seam on body and pin neck edges together. Again, push fur to inside. Sew. Turn right side out.

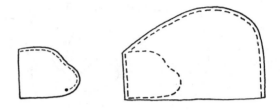

3. Measure 1¾ inch in from back seam and neck edge on bottom (1¼ inch from back seam and 1 inch from front seam on baby hedgehog). With feet pointing up, pin to right side of fur. Do the same on other side. Sew in place with ⅛-inch seam. Turn inside out.

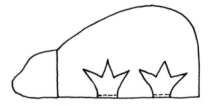

4. Pin right side of underside to right side of fur and head, matching center dot with center seam on body. Sew all around, leaving open between feet on one side. Turn right side out and stuff firmly, making underside flat. Stitch up opening.

5. Hand sew black pupil to white of eye, and sew where desired on face (see photograph for placement).

The closer the eyes are together, the sillier she looks. Sew on felt nose and mouth or use black embroidery thread to indicate mouth lines. If fur is stuck in center seam, pull it out gently with a pin.

KARA KANGAROO AND BABY

Kara and her baby require slightly more time to complete than animals like Hildy Hedgehog and Fluffy Ducks, but the effort is worth it. The lifelike sculptured form of this big kangaroo gives her maker an excellent opportunity to create detailed dimension from a flat piece of fur. Done one by one, the steps are not difficult, and the exciting result is a furry hippity-hopper that will come alive in a child's arms.

Materials (for Kara and baby)

Bodies, 16″ × 30″ dark fur
Stomachs, 24″ × 11″ light fur
Pouch lining, 7″ × 10″ muslin
Facial features, 2″ × 2″ black felt, 2″ × 1″ white felt

Patterns (see page 130)

Kara

Body (2), dark fur
Stomach (1), light fur
Pouch (1), light fur, (1) muslin
Feet (4), dark fur
Arms (2), light fur, (2) dark fur
Thighs (2), light fur

Ears (2), light fur, (2) dark fur
Nose (1), black felt
Eyes (2), white felt
Pupils (2), black felt

Baby

Body (2), dark fur
Stomach (2), light fur
Pouch (1), light fur, (1) muslin
Ear (2), dark fur
Nose (1), dark fur
Eyes (2), black felt

LAYOUT FOR DARK FUR

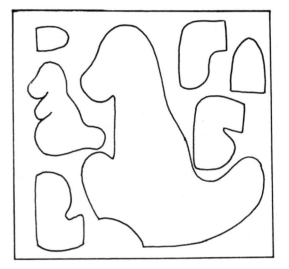

Assembly (for Kara)

1. With right sides together, sew muslin pouch lining to fur pouch at top only. Fold over so wrong sides are together and iron across top. Pin. Baste all sides and topstitch ⅛ inch from top edge.

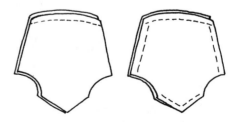

2. With muslin of pouch to fur of front, sew pouch to front. Match at corners and baste raw edges to-

gether with ⅛-inch seam. Leave top open. Pocket will not lay flat when edges are sewn.

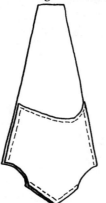

3. With right sides together, sew thighs to front/pouch piece.

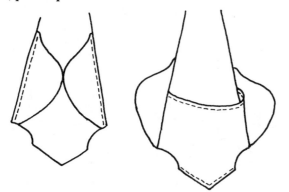

4. With right sides together, sew body from neck dot to tail dot. Leave back open between double dots. Clip curves carefully.

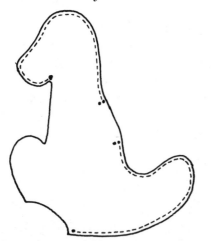

5. With fur sides together, match front (pouch and thigh) piece to body. Sew from bottom of thigh to top of neck. Be sure top of front piece stays to the

wrong side. Leave ¼ inch unsewn at top of neck front for turning. Reinforce neck stitching. Clip to dot.

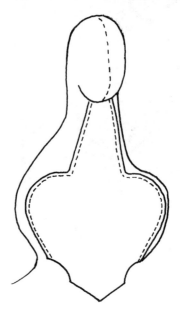

6. Match base of front to tail and sew. Leave leg holes open. In order to stitch so that tail isn't caught, sew one side up to tail, take out of sewing machine, and push tail to side just sewn. Stitch other side. Turn inside out.

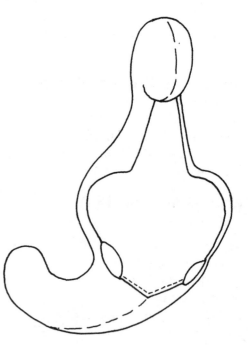

7. With fur sides together, sew one light piece and one dark piece of arm together (light fur will go to inside). Sew all dark fur feet in same manner. Clip curves. Turn inside out. Stuff firmly.

8. Stuff body firmly. Tail and thighs can be stuffed slightly more loosely. Sew arms up with a running stitch underneath several times. Then fold over and stitch securely on edges.

9. Push foot into foot hole. Turn seam on body in ¼ inch and stitch around very securely by hand.

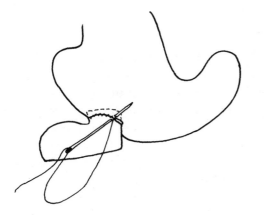

10. With right sides of one dark and one light ear piece together, sew around with a ³⁄₁₆-inch seam, leaving bottom open. Clip curves. Turn inside out. Fold bottom in ⅛ inch. Sew in place by hand. Stitch securely on edges.

11. Glue black felt pupil onto white of eye. Stitch facial features in place (see photograph for placement). With white thread stitch a "twinkle in the eye."

Assembly (for Baby Kangaroo)

Use a ³⁄₁₆-inch seam throughout.

1. Sew muslin to pouch in same manner as Kara. Topstitch ⅛ inch from top edge.

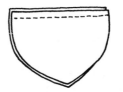

2. With right sides together, sew baby stomach down center seam. Open and pin pouch in place.

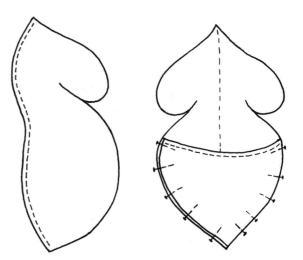

3. With right sides together, pin and sew all around body from neck to base of tail. Leave open between double dots on back.

first pinch wrong sides together at base. Sew in place by hand.

5. Glue and/or sew on facial features.

4. With right sides together, sew stomach in place in same manner as Kara (step #5). Clip curves carefully. Turn inside out and stuff. To sew baby's ears,

MICE WITH TOTE AND CHEESE

For some time these mice in their own tote with cheese have traveled the countryside far and wide with us. Each has a name, its own personality, and a place to snuggle at the end of a long day.

I often find one perched on a bookshelf or by the bedroom door "scampering" for safety. The short fur is better for younger children, who might suck on long fur.

Materials

Body, 6″ × 14″ or 7″ × 12″ long or short fur (long fur should not be too thick)

26

Ears, 3″ × 6″ pink velour
Eyes, 2″ × 2″ black felt for pupils
Pompoms, (2) ¼″ white, (1) ¼″ pink
Macrame cord or thick yarn, ⅜″, 8″ long
Tote, 18″ × 13½″ canvas, brown
Letters, 8″ × 3″ calico for M, I, C, and E
Fabric fuser, 8″ × 3″
Cheese, 15″ × 5″ yellow velour or corduroy
Beans or polyester fiberfill

Patterns (see page 135)

Mouse bottom (1), fur
Mouse sides (2), fur
Mouse ears (2), fur, (2) velour
Cheese top and bottom (2), velour
Cheese sides (2), velour
Cheese back (1)
Letters (1) each of M, I, C, and E, calico; (1) each of M, I, C, and E, fabric fuser
Pupils (2), black felt (use a hole punch)

Assembly (for Mice)

Mice are quick and ideal for making in quantity. Instructions are for the assembly line method.

1. Cut 8 inches of cord for tail. Knot end. Sew tail securely at base of bottom, going back and forth several times to make secure.

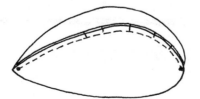

2. With right sides together, sew top of mouse side pieces together to dots. Clip curve.

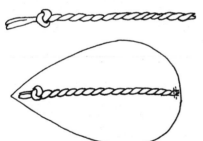

3. With right sides together, pin mouse bottom to body, tucking tail inside so it won't be caught while sewing. Sew all around, leaving 2 inches open on end.

Be sure fur is pushed to inside. Clip nose. Turn inside out.

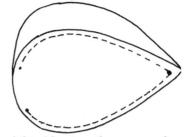

4. With right sides together, sew velour to fur ear. Use lots of pins so velour won't stretch. Clip curves carefully. Turn inside out.

5. Stuff with beans or polyester fiberfill. Fold seam of opening in ¼ inch and stitch. Fold bottom of ears in ¼ inch and hand stitch in place securely (see photograph for placement). Glue black felt pupil to white pompoms. Glue eyes and nose in place. If nose does not adhere, stitch and glue. Do not overglue. The nose should be sewn on securely for children who might bite it.

Assembly (for Tote)

1. From your 18-inch by 13½-inch piece of canvas, cut off a 2-inch by 18-inch strip for handles. An 11½-inch by 18-inch piece should remain. From the top, measure 3½ inches down and 2⅝ inches in from the sides. Mark lightly with pencil. Put fabric fuser behind calico letters and space properly. Place a cloth over letters and press with a warm iron for 5 to 10 seconds. If letters lift, press again for several more seconds. Zigzag around letters.

2. Fold canvas in half, with wrong sides together, and sew edges with an ⅛-inch seam. Clip corners. Turn inside out. Sew edges again with a ¼-inch seam. Called a French seam, this will not ravel. You can also use a regular seam and zigzag raw edges.

fold

3. Match edge seam to center of bag bottom. Crease bottom so you can see center. Mark ends in pencil according to guide, and sew across twice. Turn right side out.

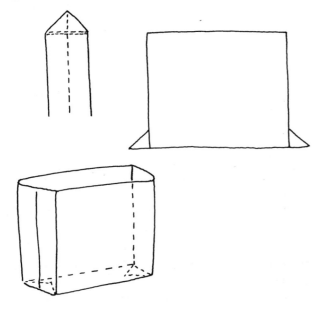

4. Fold edge of handle in ¼ inch on both sides, then fold handle in half. Pin. Sew close to edge. Cut in half to make two handles. Fold top of bag over ⅜ inch, then ½ inch. Put handles in place 3 inches from each side. Topstitch around at ½ inch and also at ¼ inch if you wish.

Assembly (for Cheese)

Use plenty of pins when working with velour.

1. With right sides together, sew side to top. Leave ¼ inch unsewn at each end. Sew other side in same manner. Sew bottom to sides in same manner as top, leaving ¼ inch unsewn at ends.

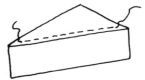

2. Sew down front of cheese where sides meet. Sew on back of cheese in same manner as other pieces. Leave 1½ inches open as illustrated. Clip corners. Turn inside out. Stuff with polyester fiberfill. Sew up seam.

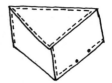

Back leg inside (2), green velour
Back leg outside (2), green velour
Front leg inside (2), green velour
Front leg outside (2), green velour
Mouth (1), orange velour
Spikes (2) each of (10) sizes, blue velour (fold fabric in half to be sure to get one left and one right), (2) each of (10) sizes purple velour (instructions as above)
Back foot bottom (2), blue velour
Front foot bottom (2), blue velour
Tail spikes (8), purple velour

STACY STEGOSAURUS

From around the corner peers Stacy. Three-year-old Kale is close behind, communicating in dinosaur language. His eyes are alive with fantasy as he feeds her some dinosaur raisins.

Stacy appeals to anyone who wants a humorous friend. Surely, there is nothing so comforting (or unusual) as taking a nap with a two-foot-long velour stegosaurus.

Materials

Instructions are written for a green stegosaurus with purple and blue spikes. Substitute your own colors and make a note on the pattern pieces you trace.

    Body, ¾ yard velour, 56″ wide, green or color of your choice

    Spikes, ½ yard each of two secondary colors, 56″ wide, blue and purple or your color choice

    Tongue, 2″ × 3″ velour, pink or orange

    Eyes (2), white 1″ pompoms, (2) black ⅝″ pompoms

    Stuffing, about 1 lb. of polyester fiberfill

Patterns (see page 137)

    Body (2), green velour
    Bottom (1), green velour

Cutting and Layout

1. Join six separate body pieces to form one large piece. You will need a 29″ × 11″ piece of paper. (See page 137 for pattern joining hints.)

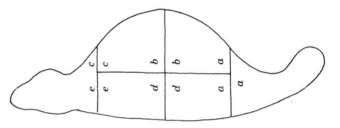

2. Join three bottom pieces to form one long piece.

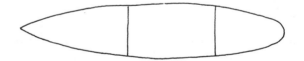

3. Join two pieces to form back leg inside and two pieces to form back leg outside.

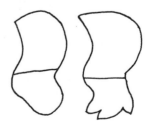

LAYOUT FOR GREEN

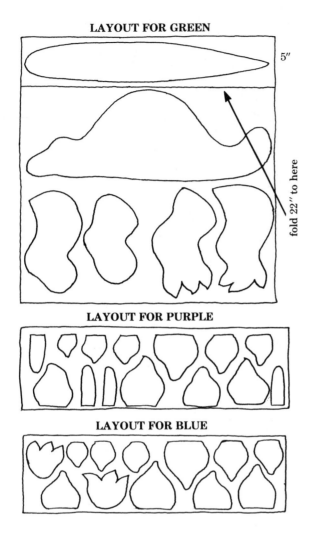

5″

fold 22″ to here

LAYOUT FOR PURPLE

LAYOUT FOR BLUE

With the right side of one body piece facing up, pin corresponding spike numbers in place. (Every other spike should have the same color facing up.) Do the other body piece in same manner, but start with the opposite color facing up first (see photograph for finished look of spikes). Pin securely in place. Sew with a ¼-inch seam along spikes.

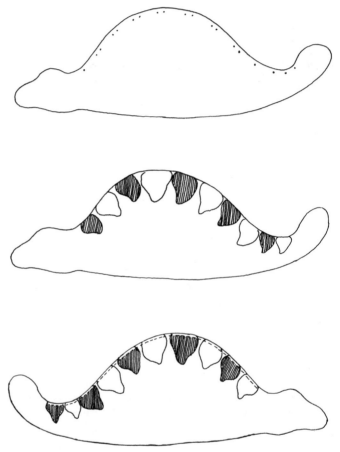

Assembly

1. After cutting out spikes as indicated on layout you should have two of each secondary color, a right and a left. With masking tape or tailor's chalk, number each one on the back. With right sides together, pin corresponding number of opposite color (blue to purple). Sew around, leaving bottom and space between dots open. Clip points and curves. Turn inside out.

2. Mark spike placement on body dots with thread, tracing paper and wheel, or tailor's chalk.

3. With right sides together, pin body pieces. Match spikes, head and tail. Sew from dot on tail to dot on nose, making sure spikes are sewn on securely.

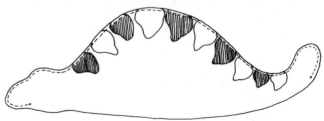

4. With right sides together, pin bottom to body, matching rounded mouth end and pointed tail. Sew from mouth dots to tail and back again, leaving open where indicated.

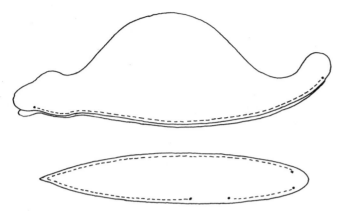

5. Fold mouth in half and, with right sides together, pin to body nose and to unsewn section of bottom. Sew with ⅛-inch seam. Clip curves. Turn inside out.

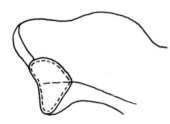

Stuff body and sew hole by hand. Stuff spikes through remaining opening and stitch with small stitches and matching thread. Stuff tail spikes, fold open ends in ¼ inch, and sew in place. Reinforce edges of mouth if necessary.

6. Match curves and dots of inside and outside front legs. Sew to dots on foot and leave open between dots on top. Sew with a ³⁄₁₆-inch seam. Do not turn inside out. Match front foot piece to front leg and pin with plenty of pins. Sew all around, lifting presser foot and moving main leg out of the way at side seams. Clip curves carefully. Turn inside out. You can pull toes out with a pin. Sew back legs together in same manner. Stuff legs firmly. You might want to reinforce by hand where foot meets leg seam. Leave ⅜ inch unstuffed at leg top.

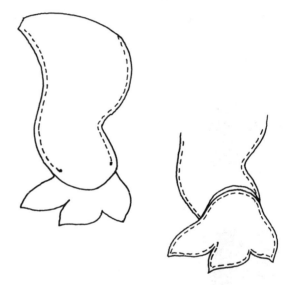

7. Pin legs in place on body (see patterns for placement). With legs up, sew across by hand securely. Use a double seam.

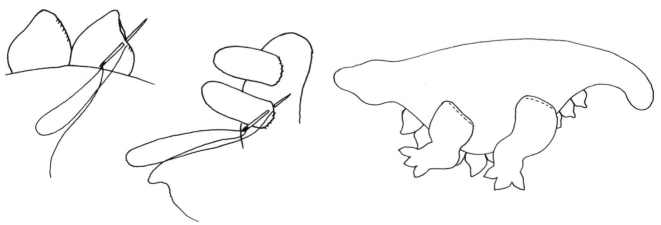

Fold legs down. Tack well at edges and at bottom so she stands steadily. It is not necessary that the legs be stiff. Where the feet bend at ankles, it looks like she's walking.

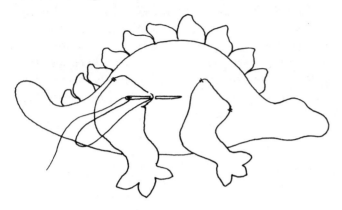

8. Glue black pompom to white. Glue eyes in place on face (see photograph for placement). Stitch down later if you wish.

3

TOYS

BEAN BAGS AND CARRY BAG

A small child loves to explore the colors, dimension, feel, and tossing possibilities of bean bags. Over and over the bags are tossed, making a new design every time they land. It's even a game just to put them back into their own special carrying bag. Older children toss them into cans or boxes at varying distances, and they are perfect for jugglers of all ages.

Materials (for eight bean bags and drawstring carrying bag)

26″ × 10″ navy blue or other main color velour or corduroy
14″ × 6″ velour or corduroy of eight contrasting colors: pink, light blue, green, cream, yellow, orange, red, purple or rust
17″ × 12″ muslin lining
48″ of heavy string or cord for bag, cut in half
Beans or rice for filling

Patterns with rainbow balls (see page 156)

1. Make a 2½-inch by 12-inch pattern for bag strips. Mark a dot 2 inches and another 2½ inches from the top. Cut (1) bag strip in each of eight colors. You may want to include one of the main colors and leave out one of the contrasting colors.

2. Make an 8½-inch by 12-inch pattern for bag lining. Cut (2) from muslin piece.

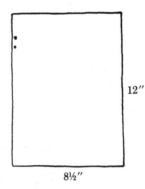

12″

8½″

3. Trace or draw a 2-inch by 4⅜-inch pattern for bean bags.

4. Cut (16) of navy or main color.
5. Cut (2) each of eight contrasting colors.
6. Fold in half and cut two or four at once.

Assembly

1. For each bean bag you will need two rectangular pieces of navy and two pieces of a contrasting color. Lay the contrasting color across the navy with right sides together. Sew a ¼-inch seam and leave ³⁄₁₆ inch unsewn at both ends of the seam. Sew the second two rectangles in the same manner.

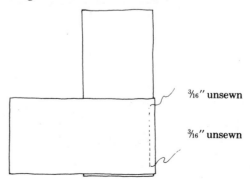

³⁄₁₆″ unsewn

³⁄₁₆″ unsewn

33

2. Join the pairs to each other as illustrated in diagrams. Open seams to match (see detail). Make sure right sides are together and leave ³⁄₁₆ inch unsewn at beginning and end of seams.

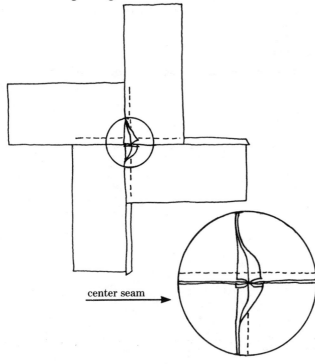

center seam →

3. Following diagram, carefully join edges with corresponding letters. Always leave ³⁄₁₆ inch open at the end of the seam so it will turn the corner easily.

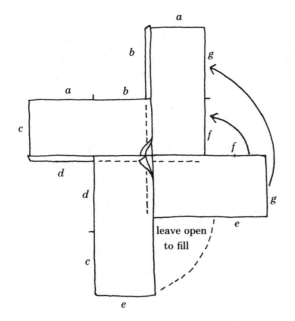

leave open to fill

4. It will be more accurate to sew from an unsewn seam into a sewn seam.

sew from here to already sewn seam

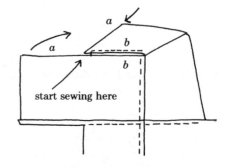

start sewing here

5. Sew up all but one side. Turn bag inside out and fill with beans or rice. Use a small whipstitch to close.

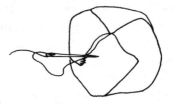

6. In assembling the carry bag, you may create your own order of colors or follow the spectrum I have chosen. Use plenty of pins if using velour, as it is more difficult to sew a straight line on a longer piece. Assemble and sew two pieces made up of four strips each.

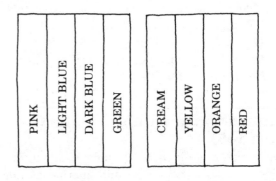

PINK | LIGHT BLUE | DARK BLUE | GREEN   CREAM | YELLOW | ORANGE | RED

7. Put the two four-strip pieces together on the right sides. Match up the seams on the bottom. Pink should be opposite red and green should be opposite cream. Sew around three sides, leaving space open between dots. Clip corners and turn inside out. Sew muslin pieces together on three sides, leaving top open. Do not turn inside out. Put lining inside velour bag and push all the way down to bottom. Turn both velour and muslin inside out together (so muslin is on outside).

8. Tie ends of 24-inch strings together, forming two loops. Fold top of bag, muslin and velour, over toward muslin ¼ inch, and pin. Put loops of string around bag 1 inch down from fold and push one loop of string on each side through space you have left open.

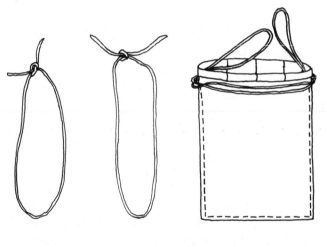

Fold velour and muslin over 1⅛ inches towards muslin and pin. Pin string to top of bag so it will not be in the way while sewing. Turn right side out and sew all around with invisible thread or color of your choice at 1 inch.

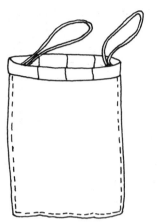

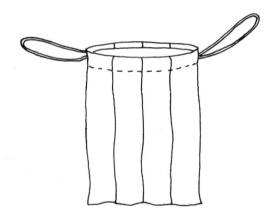

BIRD MOBILE OR CRIB STRING

This design can be used to create something for someone of almost any age—the crib string for an infant, the mobile for a baby, older child, or even an adult. The cloud can go with the mobile or hang separately. Try to use strong colors and form a bold spectrum. Children will study the birds for hours as they fly with just the slightest air movement. This can be a fascinating way for them to experience color and motion.

Materials (for either mobile or crib string)

Birds

Bodies, 10″ × 8″ piece of velour in each of the following colors: navy blue, light blue, purple, red, yellow and green (velveteen may be used in place of velour)

Eyes, 2″ × 3″ black felt, 2″ × 3″ white felt (a hole punch is very helpful)

Dowel, ⅛″ × 48″, cut into three 14″ pieces, for mobile only

Heavy colored string, 3 yards, for hanging mobile only

¼″ blue satin ribbon, 1 yard for crib string only

Stuffing, polyester fiberfill

White glue

Satin Cloud

9″ of ⅝″ satin ribbon in six colors: yellow, green, blue, purple, red, orange

16″ × 9″ white bridal satin or white felt

24″ string for hanging

Patterns (see page 145)

Birds. With right sides together, fold fabric in half to cut a right and left of each color. Mark dots and eye on bird with thread or sharp pencil. Remove pattern; pin as is, ready for sewing.

Cloud. Fold fabric in half to cut one right and one left piece.

If you are going to make both the crib string and the mobile, it is easier to make them at the same time so you won't have to change thread color as often.

Assembly

1. Pin birds with right sides together. Sew all around, leaving 1½ inch open on bottom. Carefully clip close to dots. You might want to restitch some of these spots after clipping. Turn inside out. Pull beak and wing tips out with pin, or gently push from inside with capped pen or paintbrush.

2. Stuff firmly, but don't overstuff so that bird loses shape. Close opening by hand sewing with matching thread.

3. Use a hole punch to cut out eyes, 12 white dots and 6 black dots for each mobile or crib string. Cut black dots in half, then trim corners off. Glue black to white, then white to bird. See placement on pattern.

4. For crib string, arrange in spectrum or as desired. Sew beaks to tails. Cut ¼-inch ribbon into two 18-inch pieces and sew to either end.

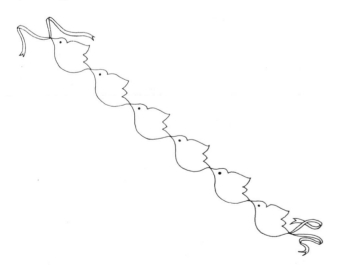

5. For mobile, spread the three 14-inch sticks an even distance apart. Glue and tie with heavy thread in the middle. Let dry. Cut 12-inch threads so birds hang 6 inches from stick. String birds at balancing point. Hang in spectrum or as desired.

6. With right sides together, sew around satin cloud from dot to dot. Carefully clip at curves. Turn inside out. Stuff. Fold in ¼ inch at ribbon placement and pin ribbons ½ inch into cloud (note: if necessary, satin ribbons should be pressed with a warm iron only). With white thread and small running stitches, sew in place, making sure ribbons hang straight. If necessary, trim ribbons so they are straight across. Put a tiny bit of white glue on ribbon edges to prevent fraying.

COSTUME FOR COLLECTOR DOLL OR RAG DOLL

The calico country doll costume will fit most 15-inch collector dolls. Porcelain doll kits consisting of head, hands, and feet may be purchased at doll stores and from mail-order companies that carry a variety of dolls from different time periods, and of varying quality.

The costume is not particularly hard to construct, but one must bear in mind that several of the pieces are quite small. It's these special detailed touches, however, that make this apron-frilled costume so dear to doll lovers young and old.

Materials

Dress, 22″ × 20″ calico
Apron, 12″ × 44″ bleached muslin
Shoes and lamb, 9″ × 8″ black felt
Lace for apron, 17″ × 2″ wide
Scalloped eyelet for apron, 14″, already ruffled, 1″ wide
Stocking tubing for collector doll, 8″ of ⅝″ wide; for rag doll, 10″ of 1″ wide (optional)
Bloomer lace, 11″ of ⅜″ wide
Elastic, 24″ of ⅛″; 27″ for rag doll
Small snaps (2)

Tiny doll buttons (2)
Lamb, 4¼″ × 4″ sherpa fur, tiny bit of batting
Fabric fuser for heart appliqué (optional)

Patterns (see page 146)

Make rectangular patterns with pencil and ruler for each of the following pattern measurements.

Upper apron piece, 16½″ × 5″ (1), muslin
Lower apron piece, 16½″ × 2½″ (1), muslin
Apron strap, 14″ × 2⅛″ (1), muslin
Apron band, 11″ × 3″ (1), muslin
Dress skirt, 8½″ × 8¼″ (2), muslin

The following patterns appear on pp. 146–49.

Dress top front (1), calico
Sleeve (2), calico
Dress top back (2), calico
Heart (1), calico, (1) fuser (optional)
Collar (2), calico
Shoe sole (2), black felt
Shoe top (2), black felt
Shoe straps (2), black felt
Hat (1), calico, (1), muslin
Bloomers (4), muslin
Lamb body (1), sherpa fur
Lamb legs (1), black felt
Lamb head (2), black felt
Head piece (1), fur
Ears (2), black felt

Assembly

1. To make bloomers, sew down center seam of two pieces to form front piece. Press. Sew back piece together in same manner.

2. With right sides together, sew back bloomer piece to front bloomer piece at one side seam. Fold top over ⅛ inch, press, then fold again at ¼ inch.

Press and hem with a ³⁄₁₆-inch seam. Sew 8 inches (8½ inches for rag doll) of elastic along this hem stitching. To sew elastic, put on inside of stitching and sew a couple of stitches on sewing machine to hold it. Stretch elastic to end and sew, holding tension as you go. Sew other side seam.

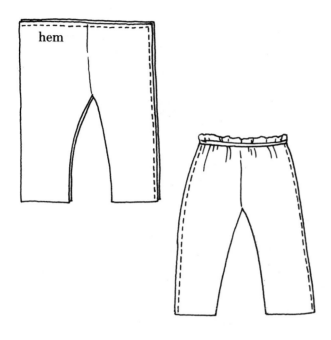

3. Hem bottoms in same manner as top. Cut 11 inches of ³⁄₈-inch lace in half. Topstitch thin lace in place so half of it hangs below hem. With right sides together, sew inside of legs.

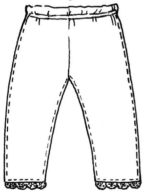

4. To gather dress skirt, sew with large machine stitches ⅛ inch from top on edge that measures 8¼ inches. Gather both dress skirt pieces to the same size as top front piece, 5¾ inches. Spread gathering evenly, leaving ¼ inch on ends ungathered. With right sides together, pin top front to gathered edge. Use plenty of pins. Sew across.

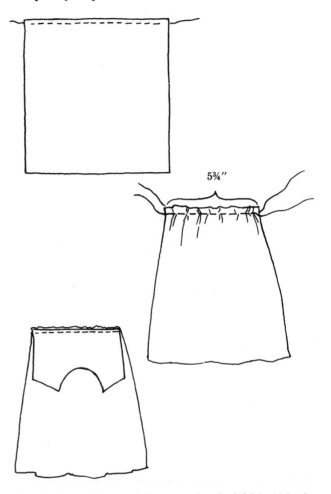

5. To hem side *a* of dress top back, fold in ⅛ inch, then fold again at ³⁄₁₆ inch. Hem with a ⅛-inch seam. Pin back pieces in same manner as front, lapping one side over the other. Gathering should measure 5¾ inches.

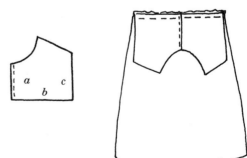

6. To hem sleeves, turn in narrow end ⅛ inch, then ¼ inch. Stitch hem on sleeve. Draw a pencil line ¾ inch in from edge on wrong side of fabric. Stretch and sew 2½ inches (3 inches for rag doll) of elastic, leaving ⅛ inch from edges without elastic. Hold tightly at both ends as you did previously.

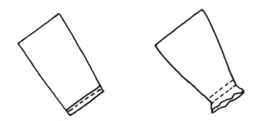

7. With right sides together, sew shoulder seams. Press. Match arm dot with shoulder seams and pin arm to top front and top back. Sew. Match front to back at gathering seams and down arms. Sew up side seams and down arms. Clip curves under arms. Turn inside out and press seam. To hem bottom of dress, fold in ³⁄₁₆ inch, and fold again at ¼ inch. Topstitch on machine or hem by hand.

8. With right sides together, slowly sew collar around outside and straight edges. Clip curves. Turn inside out. Press. With right sides together, sew bottom edge to neck opening. Match at finished back edge. Clip curves. Fold top piece in ¼ inch and sew by hand, pushing seam allowance to inside, making a clean edge.

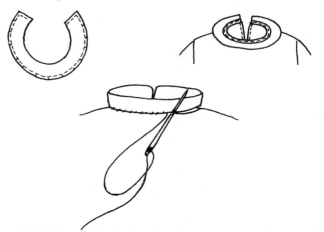

9. To hem one long edge of upper apron piece and top and bottom of lower apron piece, fold over ³⁄₁₆ inch, and fold again at ¼ inch. Press and sew at ³⁄₁₆ inch. Pin wide lace so it overlaps ¼ inch over hem on both pieces. Topstitch in place.

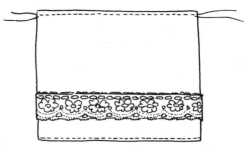

Hem sides as you did on bloomers. Gather top to 9½ inches, leaving ¼ inch ungathered at edges (to gather, sew at ⅛ inch with large machine stitches).

10. Fold apron band in half and sew ends together. Clip corners. Turn inside out. Fold strap in half. Sew down long side with a ¼-inch seam and one end with ⅛-inch seam for easy turning. Turn inside out and press. Sew ruffled scalloped eyelet to bottom of folded edge of strap, ⅛ inch from edge, so eyelet binding is on bottom. Cut in half.

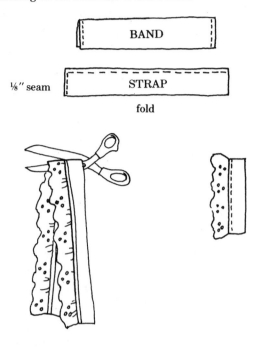

BAND

⅛″ seam   STRAP

fold

11. Pin one thickness of right side of apron band to wrong side of gathered apron bottom. Band will overlap ¼ inch on either side. Sew with gathered side up to guide folds. Fold unsewn side of band in ¼ inch and press. Put straps in under pressed edge as illustration indicates. Topstitch at ⅛ inch and on front folded edge. Be sure straps are pinned in straight.

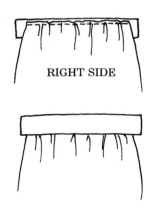

RIGHT SIDE

Press straps up and topstitch in place. Topstitch a second time ⅛ inch from first stitching.

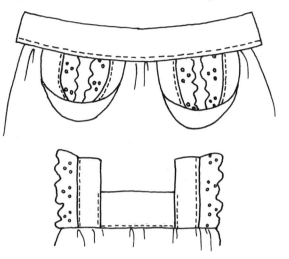

12. Place heart in center of apron between straps, approximately ⅜ inch from each edge. Iron with fabric fuser behind or tack down by hand. Slowly zigzag around in place or, if you prefer, chain stitch around with embroidery floss. Sew snap in back to close apron.

13. To make hat, mark placement (by tracing) for elastic with marking pen or pencil on white muslin. With white top thread and calico-colored bottom, pin right sides of hat together. Sew all around, leaving a 2-inch opening on bottom. Clip curves. Turn inside out. Sew up hole. Press.

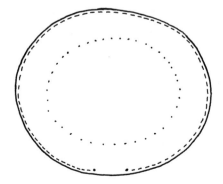

Cut 8 inches (9½ inches for rag doll) of elastic. Sew around on marking, pulling gently as you go. Cut off excess of about 1 inch.

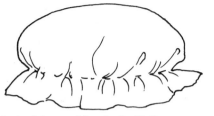

14. Cut stocking tubing in half. Sew one end with a ³⁄₁₆-inch seam. Hem top by spreading second and third fingers between stocking, and stretching while sewing folded-over edge. Go in and out loosely.

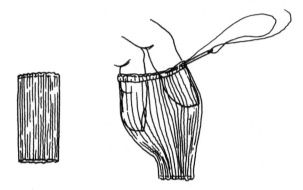

15. Topstitch very close to felt edge of shoe top and straps. For collector doll with small feet, sew top to sole by machine or hand all around, easing around curves. (There will be ¼″ overlap in the back.) Lap flaps over one another in back, making slightly smaller on top of shoe.

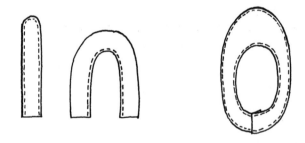

Sew securely by hand. Cut strap to desired length. Sew strap by hand to outside of shoe. Sew button on side of shoe so it will stay on tightly. Make tiny slit in felt strap and put button through. This can be stitched or touched with a bit of glue as the shoe should slip on and off with the strap tacked in place. You can also make a loop of embroidery thread or thin elastic and attach it to strap end if you want to put the strap end off and on the button frequently.

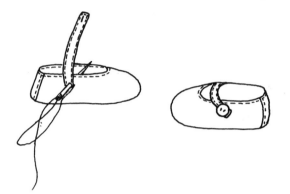

For rag doll shoes, topstitch close to edges and proceed as for collector doll shoes, but sew shoe top all around without lapping and joining back. Attach strap as in instructions above. If the doll is for a young child you may want to sew the shoes to the foot or use a black suede fabric that is more durable than felt.

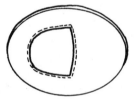

16. To make little fur lamb, fold edges of leg piece in ¼ inch on both sides. Then fold this piece in half and sew down one side, giving you a thick ¼-inch piece. Cut in half.

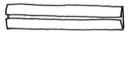

With a ³⁄₁₆-inch seam, sew head piece on one curved side.

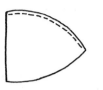

With right sides together and a ³⁄₁₆-inch seam, sew head to 3⅛-inch side of fur.

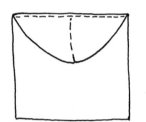

Fold legs in half and attach to one side of fur, ½ inch from back end and on head/fur seam (flip head felt to right side first).

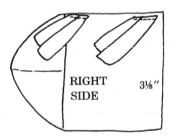

RIGHT SIDE

3⅛″

Sew head bottom and tail end. Turn inside out. Stuff head and body. Sew legs and rest of body by hand. Trim fur head piece to fit around head. Glue ears under head piece. Glue head piece in place, just slightly over body fur. Make white eyes with thread or felt and a black pupil of thread or marker. Stitch mouth and nose with embroidery floss if desired. Sew a small piece of elastic on body for hanging on doll's arm.

Soles (2), body fabric
Body (2), body fabric
Eyes (2), black felt

Assembly

1. With pencil or wash-out fabric marker, trace facial features onto head of one of body pieces. You can tape fabric and pattern to a window, or a glass coffee table with a light underneath. Embroider mouth and nose with a small chain stitch in red and light orange embroidery floss (I used three strands). Glue felt eyes in place. Stitch down to hold securely and embroider five black eyelashes on top of felt.

2. Sew foot to leg piece. You should have two left and two right. Sew a right and left leg piece together, leaving opening at bottom and 1½ inches in middle of leg back.

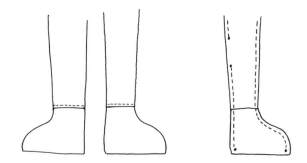

With right sides together, slowly sew sole to foot (you might want to sew by hand). Clip curves on sole and ankle and turn inside out.

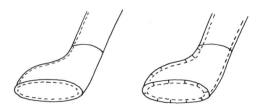

CLOTH RAG DOLL

Somehow these simple cloth rag dolls find a place in everyone's heart. It seems that mine grew up with me, and it remains forever in my memory of my childhood room.

This rag doll can be made to look just like a present-day best friend or a lovely calico-dressed doll from the past. It's such fun to choose your own fabrics and hair design. Truly, the gift of a handmade rag doll from someone you love is never to be forgotten.

Materials (for body; see collector doll costume that also fits rag doll)

Body, ½ yard unbleached muslin or brown body color fabric

Face, 1″ × 1″ black felt for eyes; embroidery floss, black, red, light orange

Hair, small skein of yarn depending on length of hair. Check to see if you have any small balls of yarn left over from larger projects. A kinky black yarn is used for black doll.

Stuffing, polyester fiberfill

Patterns (see page 150)

Arms (4), body fabric
Legs (4), body fabric
Feet (4), body fabric

3. Sew arms together, leaving opening at top. Clip curves and turn inside out.

Clip curves. Turn inside out.

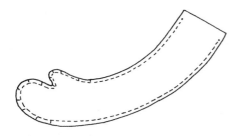

4. On front (face) side of body, pin legs ⅜ inches in from sides. Toes should be pointing toward face. Pin legs together and then to middle so they are not in the way when sewing. Baste tops of legs. With right sides together, pin back to front of body. Sew all around, leaving 2 inches open on side of body.

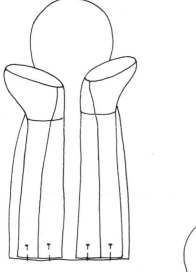

5. Stuff legs, body and arms firmly, leaving 1 inch unstuffed at top of arms. Fold top of arms in and close open ends by hand or machine stitching.

leave 1″ unstuffed

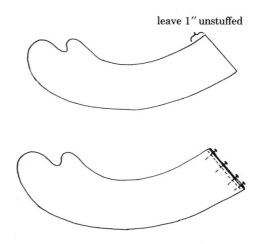

Sew arms to shoulders 6¾ inches above hip so arm can move up and down.

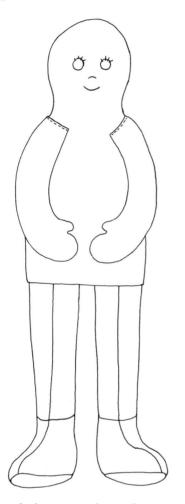

6. For long hair, cut a piece of corrugated cardboard 6½ inches by 6½ inches, and one that measures 2¼ inches by 3 inches.

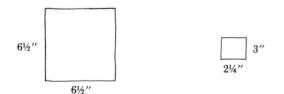

With 4-ply yarn (color of your choice), wind around the 6½-inch by 6½ inch cardboard approximately 100 times (more with a thinner yarn). Cut this yarn at one end. Make a "tape" of scrap fabric that measures ¾ inch by 5¾ inches. Spread yarn ½ inch from end and sew down middle with thread of matching

color. Use crease from where it was wound around board as a guide.

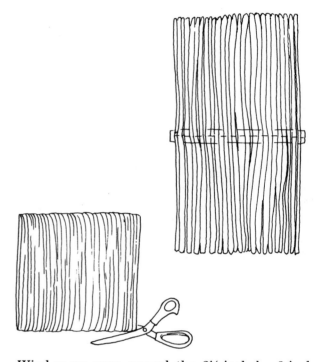

Wind more yarn around the 2¼-inch by 3-inch piece 25 times. Cut at one end, keeping it folded in half. Sew to a ¾-inch by 5-inch "tape" on folded edges. These are the bangs. Pin bangs in place. Fold ½-inch ends of tape under. Pin long hair over sewn folded edge of bangs and down back. Make adjustments with pins. Sew hair securely in place. Individual strands can be sewn in to cover seams if necessary. Hair can be put in pigtails, braids, or loose, and trimmed to desired length.

For black doll's hair, make a 5½-inch board for winding yarn rather than the 6½-inch board as above. If yarn is thick and kinky, wind about 70 strands and sew it to a 5½-inch by ¾-inch tape. All methods of assembly are the same as for long hair instructions.

DOG HAND PUPPETS

Dog puppets are easy, fast, and fun to make. Each takes on its own silly character when you vary eye or nose placement. Carry it around in your purse or bag for when you really need to "pull a rabbit out of a hat."

Materials

Body, ears, 13″ × 15″ piece of sherpa fur or other lightweight fur

Mouth, 7″ × 8″ velour or corduroy, pink or orange

Eyes, ⅝″ white pompoms (2), ¼″ black pompoms (2)

Nose, 1″ black pompom (1)

Ears, 8″ × 6″ calico, color of your choice

Patterns (see page 152)

Body piece #1 (1), Body piece #2 (1), Body piece #3 (1), fur

Mouth (1), velour or corduroy

Ears (2), fur (a right and a left), (2) calico (right and left)

FUR LAYOUT

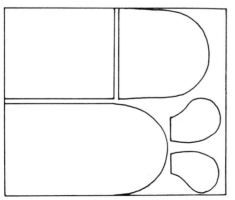

Assembly

1. Fold bottom in ¼ inch on piece #1 and piece #2 and topstitch ⅛ inch from edge.

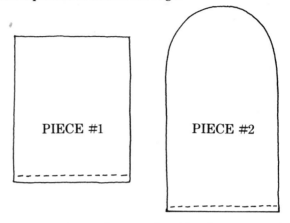

2. With right sides together pin piece #1 to piece #3. Stitch.

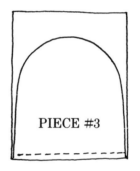

Match right ear calico to right ear fur, and left ear calico to left ear fur. Pin with right sides together and sew around, leaving top end open. Clip curves. Turn inside out and press. Fold top raw edges in ¼ inch and press.

3. Measure up 1⅛ inch from edge on head seam (seam between piece #1 and piece #3). Topstitch ear with calico side up. Do other side in same manner. Pin them together at center so they will be out of the way when sewing.

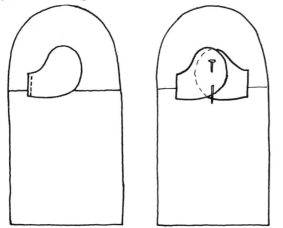

4. With right sides together, pin back to front (piece #2 to pieces #1 and #3). Stitch sides up to head seam.

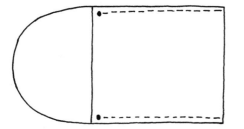

With right sides together, put mouth in place, matching center dot. Sew all around with velour or corduroy side up (it's easier). Turn inside out. If you want lower jaw slightly smaller for a little hand, stitch inside seam already sewn.

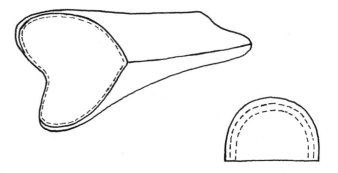

5. Tack ears in place at edges. Glue black ¼″ pompom to white. Glue eyes and nose in place. Touch up with glue later if necessary to make very secure. If the dog puppet is intended for a very young child who may chew the nose, that part should be sewn on.

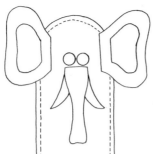

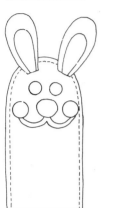

FINGER PUPPETS

Finger puppets are a terrific rainy day project for kids 4 and up (with a little help from you). They also make lovely ornaments and party favors.

These designs are just a stepping stone for what busy hands will eventually create. It is a delight to watch wild-colored monsters and ladies with flowing yarn hair evolve from this basic pattern and scraps of felt.

Materials (to make all 8 puppets)

Gray felt, 4″ × 10½″
Medium brown felt, 4″ × 10″
Yellow felt, 4″ × 6½″
White felt, 4″ × 6″
Light pink felt, 4″ × 6″
Light orange felt, 4½″ × 5″
Green felt, 4″ × 4″
Black felt, 3″ × 3″
Dark brown felt, 3″ × 3½″
Dark orange felt, 3″ × 3½″
Dark pink felt, 3″ × 3″
Olive felt, 2″ × 2″

Red felt, 1″ × 2″
White glue (Elmer's or Sobo is excellent)
Yarn, floss, sequins (optional for your own creations)

Patterns (see page 154)

1. The basic puppet pattern is used for all puppet bodies. When making several it is easier if you make a pattern out of heavy paper. Instead of pinning thin

49

paper to each piece of felt, you can trace around your cardboard pattern with a fabric marker or pencil.

2. The suggested colors and quantities required for each puppet are given on pattern pages.

3. Larger pattern pieces can be cut out and pinned or traced around with a marker. The very small pieces should be copied onto the felt with a marker or sharp pencil. If you cannot copy them, put a piece of carbon paper between the pattern and felt. Use a ballpoint pen and work on a hard surface.

4. Wherever it says "punch eye," eyes are exactly the same size as a hole punch. If you have a punch and do them all at once, you can save time. If not, just cut the small circles freehand and match up the best-looking pairs.

Assembly

1. Sew two body pieces together with an ⅛-inch seam by machine or by hand.

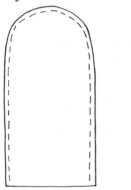

2. For placement of the pieces use the photograph and illustration. Apply glue generously with a toothpick, but don't soak the felt with glue.

3. You may want to sew large pieces that hang off of body, such as trunk, ears, beak and wings, to prevent their being pulled off. After pieces have been glued you can touch up around felt edges for extra strength.

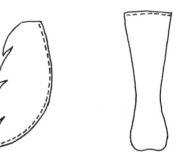

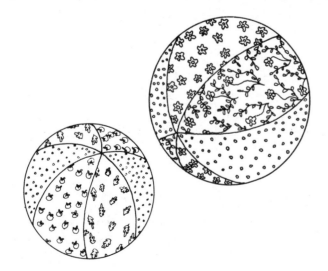

RAINBOW BALLS

Sometimes I wonder what I will ever make with those tiny, beautiful scraps that I love and save for years. Rainbow balls borrow from that scrap collection so that I may finally enjoy those precious pieces in a finished toy. The smallest balls are ideal for infants to hold and a bell can be sewn inside to add a little jingle. They can also be hung from a crib or playpen, and of course kids love to roll them on the floor and toss them to one another.

As there is only one pattern piece for each size ball, young children can enjoy choosing fabrics and pinning and cutting the shapes. After it has been sewn, they can stuff it and proudly admire it.

Materials

You will need six pieces for each ball. Balls can be made of three contrasting colors. Cut (2) of each (see red, white, and blue ball); or six shades of one color (see brown); or a rainbow assortment.

Patterns (see page 156)

For each ball cut (6) pieces measuring:
  5″ × 11″ of pattern A for large ball
  3½″ × 9″ of pattern B for medium ball
  3″ × 7½″ of pattern C for small ball
  Polyester fiberfill for stuffing

Assembly

1. Arrange pieces in the order you wish them to show on your ball. With right sides matching, sew two together, leaving ¼ inch unsewn at top and bottom. Sew a third piece to the two pieces already sewn.

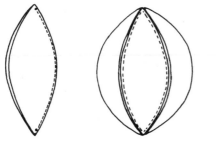

2. Assemble the three remaining pieces in the same manner, leaving ¼ inch unsewn at top and bottom. Put the two halves together, matching tips. Sew one side. On second side, sew down halfway. Leave 1½ inches open for stuffing. Sew the rest of the curve. Clip all curves. Turn inside out. Stuff very firmly. Blind stitch opening.

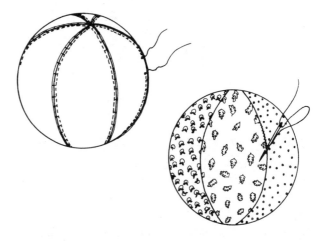

3. If you want to make a "jingle ball," put a bell in a small container (a film container is perfect). Stuff ball a little more than half full. Put container in middle of ball and continue stuffing around so container is not near edge.

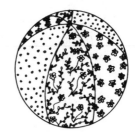

RUPERT RABBIT PUPPET

Micah squeals with delight as Rupert's arms hug her head. She holds up his carrot to feed him (after first tasting it herself), and laughs when he takes it. With a little help he starts dancing, his ears flopping magically. In a twinkling, he's pulled toward the tiny face for a loving kiss on the nose.

Rupert can also be a star in a puppet show given by older children. He does very well in the part of a bunny rabbit.

Materials

Body, 20″ × 22″ dark fur
Stomach, 10″ × 10″ light fur (includes tail)
Ear lining, 5″ × 6″ pink felt
Eyes, 2″ × 1″ black felt, 2″ × 2″ white felt
Head stuffing, 7″ × 11″ scrap fabric or muslin

Patterns (see page 157)

Back (1), dark fur
Stomach (1), light fur
Foot (2), dark fur (1 right, 1 left)
Arms (2), dark fur (1 right, 1 left)
Tail (2), light fur
Ears (4), dark fur (2 left, 2 right)
Ear lining (2), pink felt
Head stuffing (2), muslin
Nose (1), tan or pink felt
Pupils (2), black felt
Eyes (2), white felt

Mark all dots with thread before removing pattern pieces.

52

Assembly

1. On front left ear and front right ear, pin pink felt to fur. Topstitch felt close to edge. With right sides together, sew front ears to back ears. Clip tips, turn inside out. Pin bottom raw edges together. Baste.

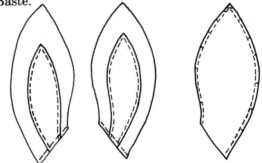

2. On back piece, cut fur between dots. Put ear on outside and push basted bottom through slit to inside, ¼ inch beyond slit. Pin very securely. Sew from ⅜ inch on either side of slit with ease seam (see page 7 for ease seam hints). Stitch a second time for extra strength.

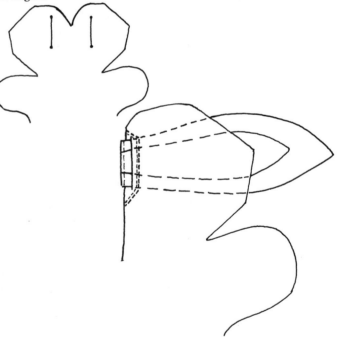

3. With right sides together, pin head as far down as neck (large dot). Push ears towards the back to keep out of the way of stitching. Top of head may be slightly bunched when pinned, but by keeping tension in front and back while sewing, you can achieve a straight seam. Pick presser foot up at sharp corners to turn. Use ease seam to begin from fold side (see detail in illustration).

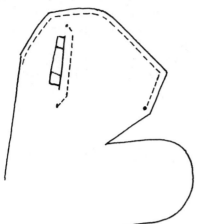

4. With right sides together, pin feet from bottom to double dot on stomach. Pin arms from double dot to neck (single dot). They should overlap slightly in the middle. Sew arms and feet in place.

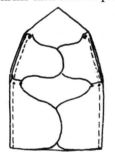

5. When pinning back to front, again make sure ears are stuffed well into head. Start pinning bottom edge of foot with back facing up so it will "curve" into the front. Keep stomach/arm seams open and match dots at neck.

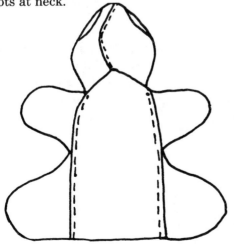

6. Leaving bottom open, sew all around with stomach side up. When you reach neck (point *b*), lift pressure foot and turn head so light-colored stomach is on top. Lift presser foot again at top of neck (point *a*) to keep stomach on top. Be sure ears are not in the way while stitching. Clip carefully at neck corners.

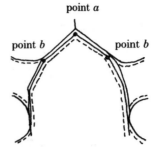

7. Fold bottom over towards inside ⅜ inch. Stitch close to fold with a ³⁄₁₆-inch seam.

8. To stuff head, sew two head lining pieces together, leaving bottom open. Turn inside out and stuff. Sew up bottom. Push into puppet head and stitch into place in front. Fingers should go behind stuffing.

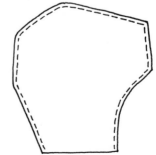

9. Cut out facial features. Handstitch them all into place (see photograph). Give Rupert a twinkle in his eyes by stitching white thread over and over three times, towards top of eye. A little snip of tan or red may be used for a mouth.

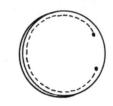

10. With right sides of tail together, stitch pieces all around, leaving 1½ inches open. Turn inside out and stuff. Sew opening closed and handstitch on back side, 1½ inches from bottom. Tack ears to stand up straighter if desired.

Rupert's Carrot

Materials

    Orange felt, 4½″ × 7″
    Green felt, 1½″ × 1¼″

Patterns (see page 160)

    Carrot (1), orange felt
    Leaves (1), green felt

Assembly

1. Fold orange felt in half and stitch long, curved side. Turn inside out, pushing point out with a dull pencil. Stuff firmly, leaving ⅜ inch unstuffed at top.

2. Make (7) slits in green felt rectangle, leaving ⅜ inch uncut at bottom. Taper slits slightly.

3. Gather around carrot top by hand, ⅛ inch from edge. Roll green "leaves" up and push inside gathered top. Pull thread tightly and stitch back and forth until green felt is sewn in securely.

4
CHRISTMAS WITH KIDS

ANGEL ORNAMENTS

Add a unique and special touch to calico angel ornaments by choosing hair colors and designs that strongly resemble folks you know. Choose someone's favorite color for a dress, or write their initials and date on the songbook.

These tiny dolls do require a few minutes of patience, and even though their parts are ideally sewn with the assembly line method, you may want to complete them one at a time. When all is done and they hang sweetly swinging on the tree, smiles will be brought to the faces of those whose lives they touch.

Materials (for each angel)

Dress, sleeves, 4″ × 12″ calico, color of your choice

Wings, 11″ × 4″ white bridal satin (If making six at a time, you will need a 12″ × 18″ piece. See layout on pattern pages.)

Hair, 2½ yards of yarn, color of your choice

Half-star, 2″ × 2½″, pink or yellow felt

Face, hands, feet, muslin, 8″ × 6″

Lace, 8″ × ⅜″ wide

Candle, 1″ × 2″ blue felt, tiny scrap of yellow for flame

Book, 1¼″ × ¾″ cardboard or oaktag, and solid or pretty paper to cover it

Ribbon for hanging, 8″ × ¼″ wide blue satin

Patterns (see page 161)

Body (2), calico
Wing (2), satin
Head (2), muslin
Feet (2), muslin
Hands (2), muslin
Sleeves (2), calico
Half-star (1), felt

Assembly

1. Topstitch lace to bottom of front body piece as indicated on pattern. Sew body front to body back, leaving top open.

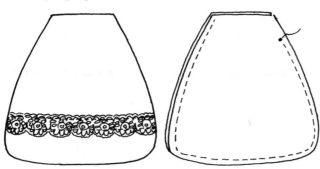

2. Sew back of feet to front of feet, leaving top open. Clip curves, turn inside out. Topstitch by machine up center.

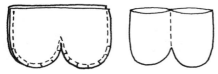

3. With right sides together, sew muslin hands to calico sleeves. Press open. Then match sleeve and hand and sew together, leaving end open. Clip curves. Turn inside out.

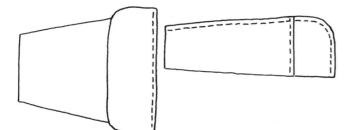

4. With fine-point, felt-tipped marker, trace face onto one muslin head piece (it is helpful to trace through a window or glass coffee table). You may want to do several until you are happy with the expression.

With right sides together, sew face to back of head, leaving bottom open. Clip curves. Turn inside out. Stuff loosely.

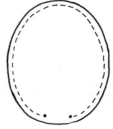

With right sides together, sew around wings, leaving bottom open. Clip curves and tips carefully. Turn inside out.

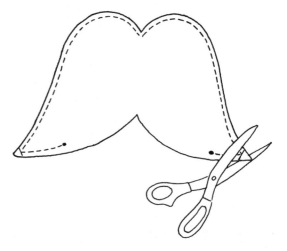

Stuff bodies, half of arms, feet and wings. A pencil, paintbrush or short knitting needle is very helpful. Sew wing closed at opening.

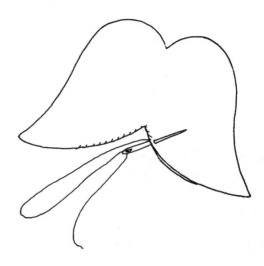

5. Fold top of body in ¼ inch and pin. Tuck head into body neck so it is below neck fold ⅛ inch or more. Sew fold and head to front securely by hand.

6. Pin arms in back, approximately ¼ inch down from shoulder (arms should be only half-filled). Raw edges will overlap in back and hands should just touch together in front. Stitch securely in place on back.

7. Fold top of feet over. Stitch in place, ¼ inch up on body back. Also, sew an invisible running stitch to tack feet to front of body.

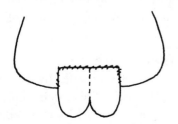

8. Sew wing in place on top and bottom. The head should rest slightly below top of wing. Glue a 2-inch piece of lace around each wrist, where hand meets sleeve.

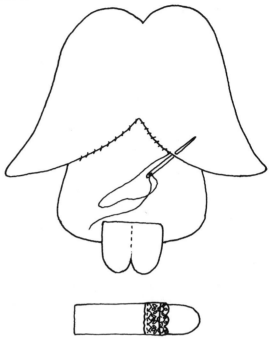

9. To make hair, fold about 90 inches of yarn in half four times (or in thirds one time) to obtain the desired length. To make bangs, sew and/or glue (4) 1-inch pieces that have been folded in half, to top of head. Sew long hair to head. After arranging, glue in spots to hold individual strands in place. Braid or tie off in ponytails; indicate barrettes with thread; or stitch a bun to the top. Create angels of people you know or use suggested hair designs (see drawings of finished angels).

10. Glue felt half-star between hair and wing. Glue any hair out of place to other hair or on to wing. Cut ribbon into (6) 8-inch pieces. Stitch ribbon onto back of star. (Fold raw ends in on back.) Reinforce with glue if necessary.

hand, back through candle to first hand. Go back and forth several times, then knot. You can also glue the candle so it won't wobble. To make book, cut a 1¼-inch by ¾-inch piece of cardboard or oaktag. Cover it with paper of your choice and write "Christmas Carols" on the right-hand side. Stitch book through cardboard to both hands.

11. To make candle, cut a ⅞-inch by 1¼-inch piece of blue felt. Put glue on one side and roll up with a tiny piece of yellow felt on one side between layers. Put aside to dry. To sew to hands, stitch from one hand through to candle, through inside of other

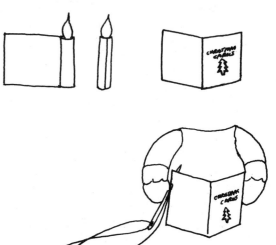

BRAIDED WREATH

Braided country calico wreaths may be made in a variety of colors and hung on entranceways or inside

year after year. You may vary the design by choosing three different, but coordinated, calicos.

Kids love to help stuff the tubes and watch it grow from a simple braid to a charming door or wall hanging. In the early part of winter, it has become a tradition for us to hang our braided wreath.

Materials

Wreath, ½ yard of green fabric or color of your choice
Bow, ¾ yard red or complementary color
Stuffing, about 1 lb. polyester fiberfill

Patterns (see page 162)

1. Cut (3) pieces of 4¾ inches by 44 inches from your green wreath fabric. This can be done by marking on the back side of fabric with chalk or fabric marker and a long ruler, or by making a newspaper pattern 22 inches by 4¾ inches and pinning it to fabric that is folded in half.

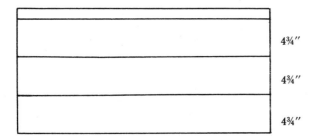

2. Cut (2) pieces #1, bow fabric; (2) pieces #2, bow fabric; and (1) piece #3, bow fabric.

Assembly

1. Fold the wreath strips in half lengthwise, with right sides together, so that they measure 2⅜ inches by 44 inches. On all three strips, sew the long, open side with a ¼-inch seam. At one end of the strip sew close to the edge for 1 inch with a big stitch. This will make it easier to turn inside out. Using a long thin tool such as a knitting needle, paintbrush, or dowel, turn the three strips inside out by placing dull end on sewn corner and pushing through.

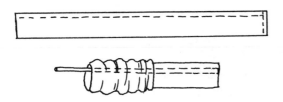

2. After the strip is inside out, you can take out the stitches from the sewn corner. When stuffing strips, it is easier to fill from both sides. Pack it quite tightly, using your long tool again. When the strips are filled, pin or baste at both ends so you won't lose stuffing.

3. Baste stitch the three filled tubes at one end. Braid tightly until there are eleven evenly braided twists (see photo).

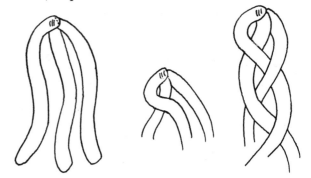

4. Form into a circle with braid side up. Pin ends to beginning of tubes at corresponding end or at back where it fits tightly and won't show. Your wreath may have to be more tightly braided or may need another twist to come out evenly. Shape wreath so it looks symmetrical, and securely stitch by hand. Don't worry too much about stitches showing; the bow will cover most of the joined seams.

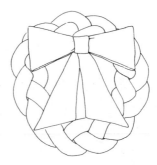

5. With right sides together, sew all sides on piece #1 and piece #2 of bow, except where indicated to leave open. Fold piece #3 lengthwise and sew long edge only. Trim corners on all pieces and turn inside out.

6. Fold sides of piece #1 into center along fold line on pattern.

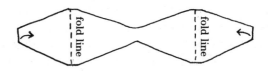

59

7. Fold piece #2 over as illustrated and place in back of piece #1. Stitch in place. Wrap piece #3 around center and stitch in back by hand.

8. Place bow on wreath, covering seams as much as possible. Tack in place at center and where arrows indicate.

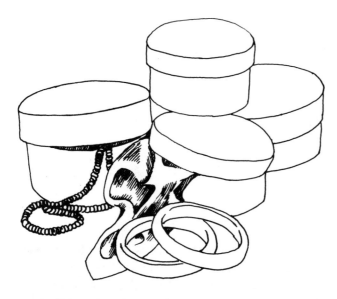

small circle. Making more than one at a time works well, because while glue is drying on one, you can be working on the other.

Materials

For 2 small boxes
Calico fabric, 14″ × 18″
Cardboard, 4½″ × 11¾″
Cardboard, 8″ × 9″

For 2 large boxes
Calico fabric, 14″ × 22″
Cardboard, 6″ × 14⅜″
Cardboard, 10″ × 11″
White glue

CALICO BOXES

Fabric-covered boxes with a padded top require no sewing, but rather an hour of simple box construction and gluing. The end result is a lovely and lasting receptacle for anyone's small (under 4 inches) treasures. To give a small gift inside one requires no wrapping paper, only a delicate ribbon and bow. The larger sizes are actually easier to make because the curves are not as acute.

With these patterns you can make four different boxes: a large oval, a large circle, a small oval, and a

½″ masking tape
Pencil and ruler

Patterns (see page 164)

Trace top and bottom oval and circle patterns onto tracing paper, cut them out, then trace around paper patterns onto cardboard with marker. For each box you will need to cut:

Cardboard top (1)
Batting (1) (trace around cardboard top pattern with marker)
Cardboard bottom (1)
Fabric top (1)
Fabric bottom (3) (use cardboard bottom pattern and trace onto fabric)

For the following side pieces make paper patterns or draw on material with ruler and pencil. See layout suggestions below.

FABRIC LAYOUT

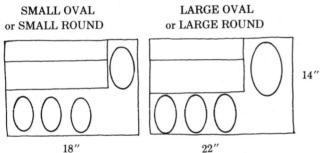

SMALL OVAL or SMALL ROUND — 18″

LARGE OVAL or LARGE ROUND — 22″

For Large Oval or Circle:
Large top side cardboard (1), 1″ × 14⅜″
Large bottom side cardboard (1), 2″ × 14⅜″
Large top side fabric (1), 14⅞″ × 2⅝″
Large bottom side fabric (1), 14¾″ × 4¾″

For Small Oval or Circle:
Small top side cardboard (1), ⅝″ × 11¾″
Small bottom side cardboard (1), 1⅝″ × 11¾″
Small top side fabric (1), 1¾″ × 11⅞″
Small bottom side fabric (1), 4″ × 11¾″

Layout Suggestions for Cardboard Side Pieces and Fabric Ironing

1. For large boxes, cut from 14⅜-inch by 6-inch cardboard: (2) 1-inch by 14⅜-inch and (2) 2-inch by 14⅜-inches. For small boxes, cut from 11¾-inch by 4½-inch cardboard: (2) ⅝-inch by 11¾-inch and (2)

1⅝-inch by 11¾-inches Note: The cardboard sides for ovals and circles measure the same.

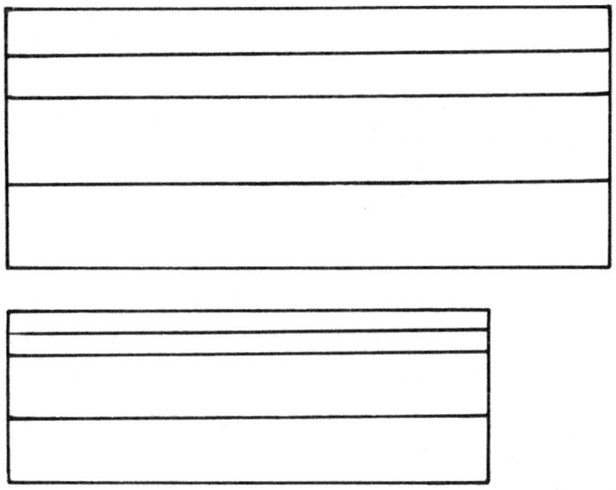

2. The fabric side pieces for the oval and circle measure the same, so if you are making two large or two small boxes you can cut two different colors at the same time.

3. For each box, fold one long edge of top side fabric in 3/16 inch to wrong side and press. Also, fold bottom side fabric piece in half with wrong sides together and press.

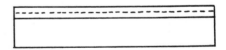

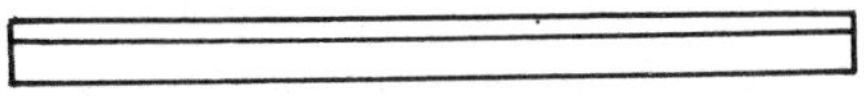

Assembly

Begin with a large box, which may be slightly easier because the curves are not so acute.

1. Cut a piece of ½-inch masking tape a little longer than a top side piece of cardboard. Put half (¼ inch) of tape on cardboard.

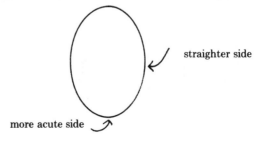

Beginning on the straighter side of the oval, bend and tape, as you go, the top side piece of cardboard around the top oval cardboard pattern. If you are making a circle, it does not matter where you start.

straighter side

more acute side

Tape will have creases on the top, but these will later be covered by batting. Put a piece of tape from outside to inside to hold where the side of the cardboard ends.

2. Put white glue all around seam on inside, and where cardboard ends. You can make a "glue spreader" with a thin scrap of cardboard. Put top aside to dry. Assemble bottom in same manner. Note: do not put tops on bottoms to dry or they may stick together.

3. When both bottom and top are dry, take off masking tape from *bottom only*. It does not have to come off of the side because the tape should be fairly smooth here.

4. Spread glue all over top and glue batting to cardboard.

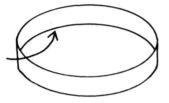

5. Notch all around top fabric piece, with approximately ¼-inch slits on small box pieces and ⅜-inch slits on large box pieces. You may need to make several slits bigger as you glue.

6. Spread glue around top side about ⅜-inch down from cardboard seam. Let dry for a minute until it is tacky. Center slitted top fabric on batting. Stretch over top (not too tightly) and hold opposite sides down with fingers at the same time.

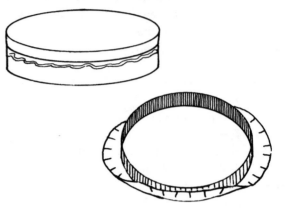

When this is dry enough to hold by itself, start pressing down slitted pieces all around. They will overlap slightly. Keep tension on the fabric, but not so tight as to lose the puff in the batting. If it buckles on the edge you can lift up a glued section immediately and adjust tension and increase the slit size. This is the most difficult part of your box. Bear in mind the fabric side piece will cover right up to the cardboard seam.

7. When top fabric is dry, spread glue all around top side of cardboard (including over notched fabric). When tacky, glue down top side fabric with *folded, ironed edge on top*. Put a touch of glue where raw edge of fabric ends. This will keep it from fraying.

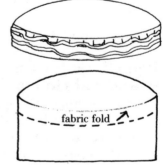

fabric fold

8. Spread glue on *inside* of top cardboard side and ⅛ inch around on top. Wait until tacky. Push fabric to inside and press all around side. Then press remaining fabric onto glued cardboard side. This should be pressed towards top/side cardboard seam.

9. Open bottom fabric that has been ironed in half. Spread glue all around outside of cardboard bottom piece. Glue bottom half of fabric to side all around. This should be easy to put on smoothly. You can actually "roll the box" onto the fabric, following the creased, ironed line. There will be a small overlap at the bottom. Spread ¼-inch glue around on cardboard bottom edge to glue down overlap. When tacky, press down all around.

10. Spread glue on inside of cardboard and ⅛ inch on bottom edge. When tacky, fold fabric in and press around until smooth as possible. Put extra glue on seam.

11. Measure cut fabric circles or ovals against inside top, inside bottom, and outside bottom. They may need to be trimmed to fit tightly. They should not overlap edges. The inside circles may need to be smaller than bottom outside. Spread glue on these cardboard areas. When tacky, press into place. Again, do not let dry with top on.

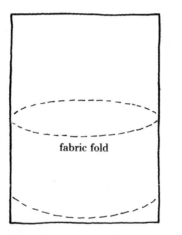

fabric fold

LITTLE LAMB ORNAMENTS OR TOYS

Fluffy little lambs with their silly, wiggle-eyed expressions are adorable when hung all over Christmas branches. Give one to a friend as a special holiday season delight. Although the finishing details require a moment of patience, the end result will be a cherished Christmas decoration for years.

Materials (for each lamb)

Note: it is quite practical to create these in quantities of 2 to 6 rather than one at a time.

63

Body, 6″ × 7″ white, black or brown sherpa fur
Head and legs, 11″ × 6″ black velour
Wiggle eyes, (2), ¼″ or white and black felt
Ribbon, ¼″ × 14″, red
Bell, ⅜″ or ½″, gold
White glue

Patterns (see page 166)

Body (1), fur
Head fur (1), fur
Legs (1), velour
Head (2), velour
Ears (2), velour
Tail (1), fur

Assembly

Thread color indications are for white lambs. Use appropriate thread color if making other than white lamb. Sew with a ³⁄₁₆-inch seam unless otherwise noted.

1. With right sides together, fold 7-inch by 1½-inch black velour leg in half lengthwise and sew with black thread and ⅛-inch seam. Use plenty of pins to hold in place. Cut into four pieces, each measuring 1¾ inch in length. (A leg measure is included in patterns.)

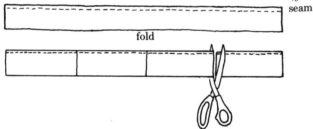

⅛″ seam

fold

2. Sew down one end of each 1¾-inch piece. Turn inside out with a pencil. Stuff hard, leaving ¼ inch at the top unstuffed. Use a pencil to push stuffing in.

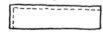

3. With right sides together, sew top of head with a ³⁄₁₆-inch seam using black thread.

³⁄₁₆″ seam

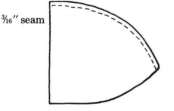

4. Mark the center of body piece where indicated with pencil or dark thread. Open head piece. Match head seam to center dot on body. With right side of head to right side of fur, sew head to fur.

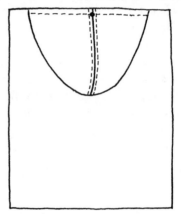

5. Fold fur in half with right sides together. Sew the rest of head and front seam of body with black thread.

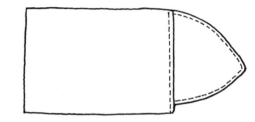

6. Change to white thread. Sew down back end of body. Clip back corner. Turn inside out. Head will look long, but another piece will later go on top. Stuff body and head firmly.

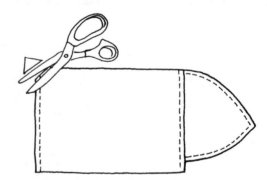

7. Sew legs onto body by hand. Be sure they are firmly stuffed. They should be sewn on two at a time, as close to the front and back as possible. Fold bottom of body in ¼ inch and stitch together as legs are sewn on. Sew legs securely, exactly to where they are stuffed. Sew tail on by hand to top of body back.

like this   *not* this

fold in ¼″

8. If necessary, trim head fur so it will fit around velour head properly. Glue ears on velour head, ap-

proximately ⅝ inch down from top center seam. Then glue head fur over ends of already glued ears. Stitch in place at bottom of neck and ears or reglue edges after several hours.

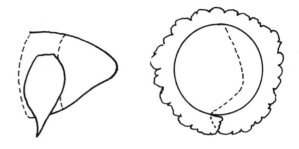

9. Glue eyes on head (see photograph for placement). Retouch later to make them extra secure. Tie 14-inch ribbon in bow around neck and push to one side. Tack in place. Sew bell on ribbon in front. For use as ornament, sew metallic thread or string through fur on back where lamb will be balanced. (See body piece for balance approximation.) To make lamb stand up, you may have to push its legs outward, into a "running" position.

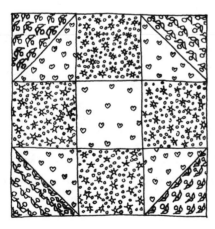

PATCHWORK POTHOLDERS

When my daughter, Bree, was three, I taught her how to pin and cut. We went through the scrap bag and cut squares and triangles until we had a stack of

each in a variety of colors. As I knew there was no time to begin any project of major proportion, we settled for potholders.

This design is included to help kids construct as well as enjoy an exercise in design and color. Don't rush; have fun turning and rearranging pieces. The potential is endless and you will be surprised how attractive the unlikely combinations chosen by a young mind can be. Perhaps later you'll want to try a scrap bag quilt of the same design.

Materials

Patchwork, lots of scraps measuring at least 3″ × 3″

Backing calico matching one of the pieces used in the patchwork, 8″ × 8″

Batting, 8″ × 8″ thick or (2) layers of medium thickness batting or blanket

Patterns (for each potholder; see page 167)

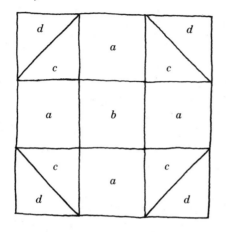

Squares (5), 3″ square; (4) of the same color (see *a* in illustration) and (1) that matches or complements the triangle colors (see *b* in illustration)

Triangles (8), cut of two different colors, (4) of each (see *c* and *d* in illustration)

Loop, 3½″ × 1⅜″, same fabric as piece *d*

Backing, 8″ × 8″ calico

Batting, 8″ × 8″, ½″ thick

Assembly

1. With right sides together, sew the *c* and *d* triangles on the long diagonal edge. Press seams to one side.

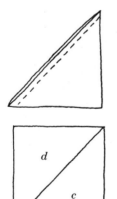

2. Arrange these pieces with the five squares as you desire. Start with the odd square in the middle and put the four matching squares on each side. Arrange remaining pieces as you wish. You can turn triangle pieces around to see what other designs you can make.

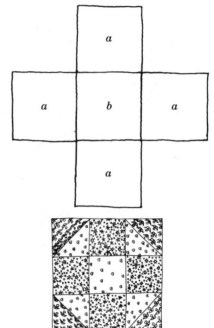

3. Sew the *c/d* piece to one side of the *a* square. Sew another *c/d* piece to the other side of the *a* square. For row two, sew *a* piece to *b* piece and *b* piece to *a* piece. Make the third row as you did the first. Then sew bottom of row one to top of row two, and bottom of row two to top of row three. (See placement diagram.) Press all seams flat to one side.

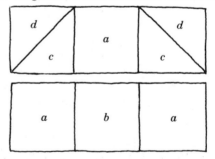

4. Fold both edges of loop in ¼ inch and press. With wrong sides together, fold loop in half and press again. Topstitch very close to edge on long side.

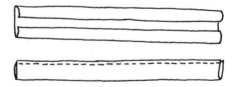

5. Pin right side of backing to right side of patchwork front. Fold loop in half and pin in between front and back on one corner. Raw ends, not loop, should stick out ¼ inch from corner. Pin batting on top of wrong side of patchwork. Sew all around, leaving 2 inches open for turning. Clip corners. Turn inside out. Fold open, turning edges in, and stitch by hand or machine.

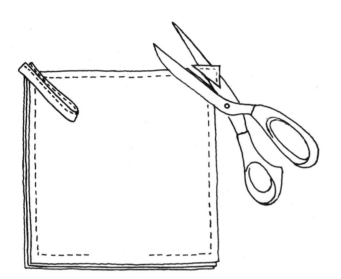

6. Quilting potholders by machine is very quick and easy, but they also look lovely quilted by hand. You can quilt ¾ inch in from edge and ¼ inch on outside of middle square, or diagonally across. To hold layers in place you may also tack at the corners or centers of squares and triangles.

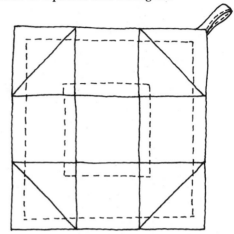

If you enjoyed making these, you might like to try the pattern on pp. 66–67 from the patchwork stocking. The patchwork piece measures exactly the same size, so you can use the backing, batting and loop measurements in this pattern.

COUNTRY PATCHWORK STOCKINGS

The traditional star pattern makes lovely potholders as well as the insert for the country stockings. It is a bit more advanced than the design for the potholder project on pp. 61–62, and might serve as a special project for an older child. For either design, the assembly line method should be used to keep pieces in order and uniform.

Materials

Stocking back and stocking front, 28″ × 22″ (total), main calico color
Muslin lining, 28″ × 22″
Batting, 28″ × 22″

Lace, 17″ × 1¾″ wide

Design insert, pieces smaller than 4″ × 4″ (see patterns and quantity required)

Tracing paper (3), 14″ × 11″ for making patterns

Patterns (see page 168)

For 8″ × 8″ star patchwork, use small calico pieces that go well together. You might want to use the main calico color as center piece *c*.

Small triangles (piece *a*), (8), calico

Large triangles (piece *b*), (4), calico

Squares (piece *c*), (4) calico outside squares and (1) calico inside square, or they can all (5) be of the same fabric

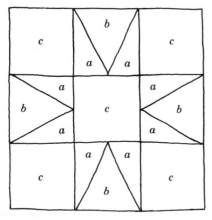

Stocking

Stocking bottom (1), main calico color

Stocking top (1), main calico color

Stocking back (1), main calico color

Lining (2), muslin, a left and right (fold fabric when cutting)

Batting (2)

1. Join stocking front bottom pattern piece #1 to stocking front bottom piece #2 to make one piece. Flip pattern over when pinning to right side of fabric so toe is pointing towards right-hand side.

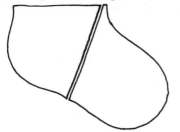

2. Make a rectangle 8 inches by 3¾ inches for front top pattern.

3. To make stocking back pattern for calico, lining, and batting, first trace stocking front bottom as pieced together in step 1. Do this so that toe is pointing toward the left-hand side, the opposite direction of the front piece. Then add an 8-inch by 10⅝-inch piece to top to make one piece. Be sure to place pattern on the right side of the fabric when cutting, to ensure toe points in proper direction.

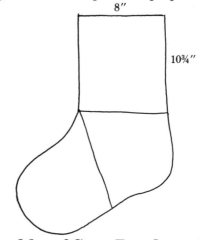

Assembly of Star Patchwork To Be Used for Stocking or Potholders

There are several ways to assemble this traditional patchwork pattern. I have found the following method to be one of the simplest. The star is actually made up of nine blocks. 1, 3, 7, and 9 are squares of the same color and size, and block 5 is also the same size. You will begin by completing blocks 2, 4, 6, and 8 (pieces *b* and *c*).

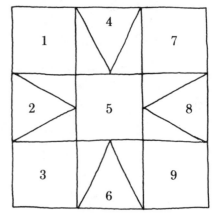

1. With right sides together, match the long side of piece *a* to piece *b*. Match at wide corner so there is a ⅜-inch overlap at the thin corner. Sew all four pieces in this manner. Trim threads. Press seams to one side, towards piece *b*.

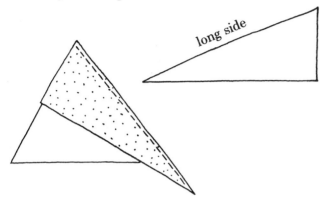

2. Again match piece *a* to piece *b* at same corner (match from pressed seam of same color). There will be an overlap at the thin point again. Press seams to one side.

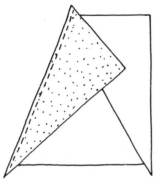

3. You should now make three strips as follows. With right sides together, first sew a piece *c* to piece *a* on both sides of block 4, and also on both sides of block 6. For the middle strips sew the remaining *a/b* blocks (2 and 8) to block 5. Press seams to one side.

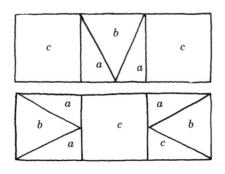

4. Match seams and sew strips together as illustrated in preceding diagram. Press seams flat.

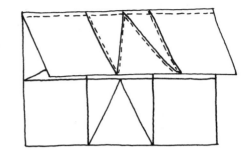

Assembly of Stocking with Star Design, from Page 68 or an Appliqué that Measures 8″ × 8″ When Finished

1. With right sides together, pin and sew bottom front to patchwork. In same manner, sew top to patchwork. Press seams to one side.

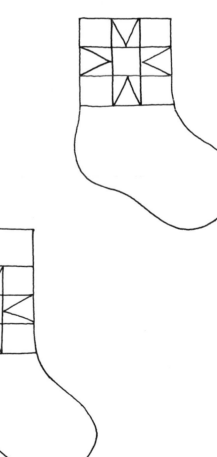

2. With right sides together, pin and sew back of stocking to completed front patchwork piece. Leave top open. Clip around all curves. Turn inside out and press.

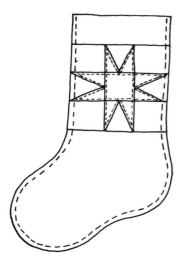

3. Trim ¼ inch off top of both batting pieces. Put batting on either side of both lining pieces. Pin in place and sew batting and lining together all around, except for top. Sew with a ⅜-inch seam to make up for width of batting. Do not turn inside out. Trim close to seam.

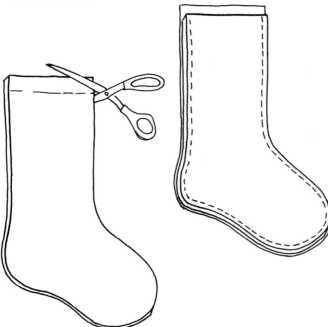

4. Put lining/batting piece inside patchwork stocking. Smooth lining all the way to toe and across

from side to side. If lining is too big (depending on thickness of batting), sew around lining again, ¼ inch in from present seam. Trim excess. Fold top of calico over ⅜ inch toward lining and fold lining over ⅜ inch toward calico on top. Pin all around.

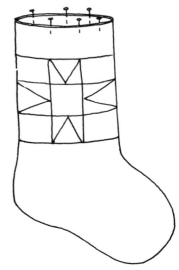

5. To make loop for hanging, fold long edges of tab over ¼ inch and press. Then fold tab in half and press. Topstitch very close to open edge. Pin in between lining and backing on top left-hand seam. Sew top all around with ⅛-inch seam.

Measure 16½ inches of wide lace if desired. Pin all around top, beginning and ending in back. Topstitch on lace close to edge.

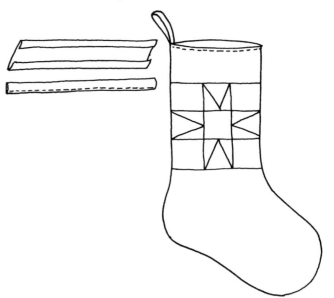

around centered oval on cardboard and cut with an X-acto or mat knife, making curves as smooth as possible. Depending on the thickness of your board and your skill this may be difficult; a precut frame kit is always easier to work from.

Calico fabric of your choice, 24″ × 12″ for single frame, 22″ × 24″ for double frame
Batting, 8″ × 6″, ½″ thick
Grosgrain ribbon, 16″ (optional)
White glue

Spring-type clothespins (8)
Scrap of cardboard to use as a glue spreader

CALICO-COVERED PHOTOGRAPH FRAMES

There is nothing that brings a smile to my face more than a picture of someone I love. I've included the instructions for these frames so that you may enhance a captured moment with lovely fabric and your personal touch. Calico frames require about half an hour of your time after you've made one, and the cost of materials is minimal. No one will ever turn one down as a gift.

Materials (for one frame)

Heavy cardboard or chipboard, or a purchased precut cardboard frame kit available at fabric or craft stores, (2) 6″ × 8″, (1) 2″ × 4¾″ for single, (4) 6″ × 8″ for a double frame*

* If you are cutting the frame yourself, use the bottom large oval cardboard patterns from the cardboard boxes shown on page 165. To cut oval, trace

Patterns

Draw measurements directly onto fabric back, or if you plan to make many frames, make paper patterns in the following sizes:

Piece A, 9½″ × 7½″, front and back
Piece B, 7¼″ × 5¼″, inside back
Piece C, 6″ × 5″, stand (single frame only)
Piece D, 7½″ × 1¾″, center strip (double frame only)
Piece E, 14¼″ × 9½″, backing (double only)

For single frame

Piece A (2), calico, (1) batting
Piece B (1), calico
Piece C (1), calico
(2) 8″ ribbons

For double frame

> Piece A (2), calico, (2) batting
> Piece B (2), calico
> Piece D (1), calico
> Piece E (1), calico
> (2) 8″ ribbons

Assembly

1. Put fabric piece A down on your work table, wrong side up. Center the backing cardboard or chipboard (the one without the oval cut) on fabric. Spread glue on opposite sides of board from edge to ¾ inch in. A scrap of cardboard is helpful to have on hand as a glue spreader. Wait a few seconds until glue is tacky. Pull fabric edges to fold tightly around board, but not so tight as to buckle board. Put glue on unglued opposite edges as before. Fold fabric as in wrapping a package, mitering corners. Glue down when tacky. Put extra glue on corners if necessary to make secure.

2. Spread uncovered section of backing with thin film of glue and when tacky, glue piece B to it. You can put a little extra glue around edges of fabric to prevent fraying. Put this piece aside to dry.

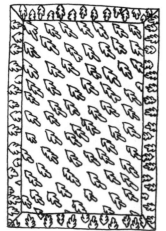

3. To cover stand (piece C) put glue on top and bottom edge to ¾ inch in. Fold edges in when tacky. Put glue on remaining cardboard. Miter corners and fold one side in. Spread glue over center part of piece just glued (where remaining other side of fabric will cover), miter corners and stretch last fabric side tightly. Put a touch of glue on edges to prevent fraying and hold securely.

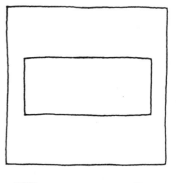

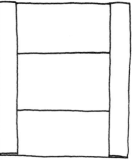

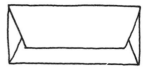

4. To cover the front, spread a thin film of glue over the oval cut (front) board. Press batting on to glue. Carefully trim away excess batting from oval opening and around edges.

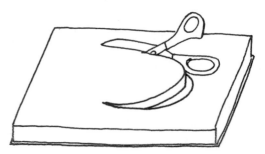

5. Lay the fabric wrong side up on your work surface and cover the front of your frame the same way you did the back.

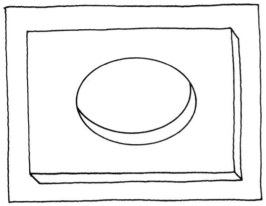

6. Trim fabric inside the oval opening, leaving ½-inch to ¾-inch allowance to turn under. You may want to draw with a pencil on fabric ½ inch in from cardboard edge before you cut. Notch with approximately 22 notches all around as shown. Spread ½ inch of glue a third of the way around oval. Wait until tacky. Pull notches on to glue and hold with fingertips until it stays. Do not pull so tightly that it puckers in front. Continue in this way all around oval. Towards the end, sometimes you can lift several notches already glued to eliminate a small wrinkle.

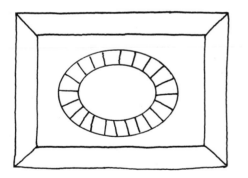

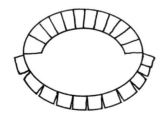

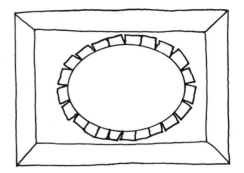

7. Put 8 inches of ribbon diagonally across one side of frame front. Glue in place in back. Spread a ½-inch line of glue around three edges of back (the side with piece B). Press the front and back together and put clothespins around to hold tightly while drying. Be sure to leave one side open for picture to slide in.

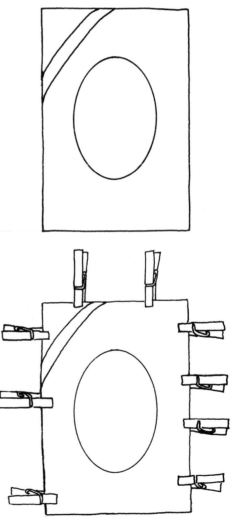

8. Spread a 1-inch bead of glue to top inside of stand and place stand on center back. When glue is completely dry, fold stand back 1 inch from top using a straight edge.

9. To make a bow with 8-inch ribbon, first cross ends. Then place middle of loop on cross. Stitch together in center by hand or machine. Glue in place on diagonal ribbon.

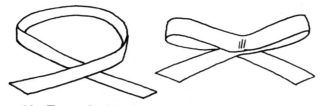

10. For a double frame, cut a 10-inch by ½-inch piece of masking tape and place on work surface, sticky side up. Put the two back pieces of cardboard on tape, leaving an ⅛-inch space between boards.

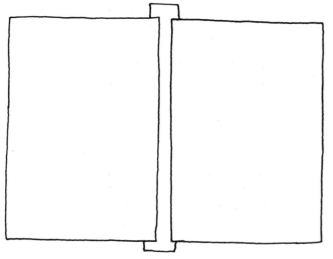

Fold excess masking tape to front side of boards. Put 7½-inch tape on front to cover remainder of seam.

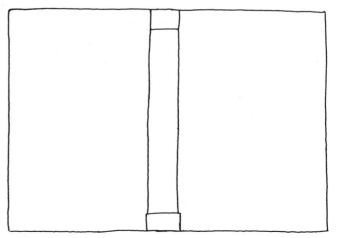

Spread glue down center and wait until tacky. Glue piece D over center seam. Continue to cover back pieces as instructed in steps #1 and #2.

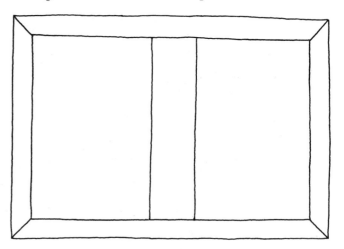

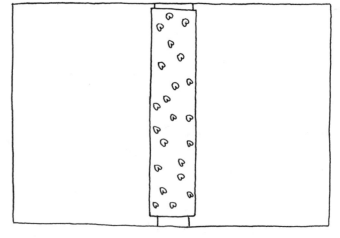

11. Follow steps #4, #5, #6, and #7, making sure there is at least ⅛ inch between two frames in the center. This will make the double frame stand nicely when folded slightly in the middle. You might want to put bows on top of oval rather than diagonally across one corner. See step #9 for bow instructions.

BABY STRIPE STOCKINGS

Baby Christmas stockings are a scrapsaver's joy. They can be made in a variety of colors and hung filled with holiday treats, on a door or chimney.

Materials

Stripes (6), calico colors from your scrap bag
Backing (1), 12″ × 10″ of a calico that will also be used on the front patchwork and loop
Lining (2), 22″ × 12″ muslin
Lace, 14″ × 1¾″ cotton lace

Patterns (see page 170)

Stripes (1), of each stripe pattern. Place pattern side up on *right* side of fabric.
Stocking back (1). Place pattern side up on right side of fabric.
Lining (2), muslin, (a right and a left)
Loop (1), 1″ × 4″ calico

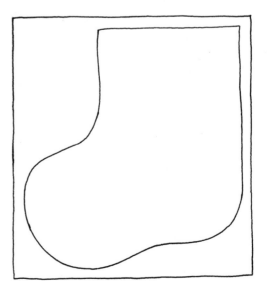

75

Assembly

1. Beginning with stripe 1 (the top left-hand corner), with right sides together, center the hypotenuse (long side) of stripe 1 on stripe 2. Stitch.

PIECE #1
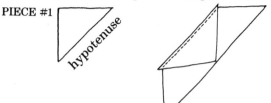

2. Center stripe 2 on stripe 3. Stitch.

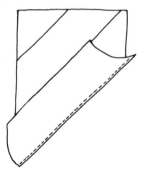

3. Match stripe 3 to stripe 4 on heel end (left-hand side). Stitch.

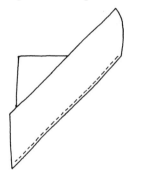

4. Match stripe 4 and stripe 5 from right-hand side. Stitch.

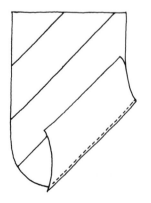

5. Match stripe 5 to stripe 6. Stitch.

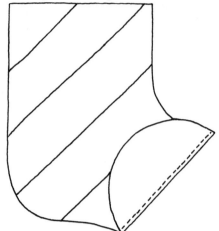

6. Press all seams to one side. With right sides together, sew stocking back to front stripe work, leaving top open. Clip curves. Turn inside out and press.

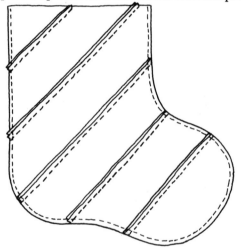

Sew lining together in same manner. Do not turn inside out.

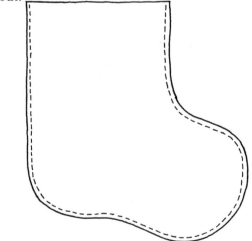

7. Put lining inside calico. Fold top of lining and calico in ⅜ inch toward each other and topstitch around at ³⁄₁₆ inch.

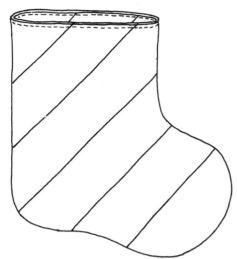

8. Pin lace around and topstitch ¼ inch in from edge. To make loop, fold edges in to wrong side ¼ inch, then fold piece in half with wrong sides together. Press. Topstitch close to edge. Sew in top left-hand corner for hanging.

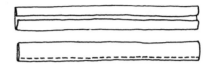

WALNUT MICE

These tiny little friends in a walnut shell seem to find some of the most loving and lasting homes. Walnut mice are the kind of project Sharon and I do 'til odd hours of the morning about a week before Christmas. By the end of our effort, new friends peer up at us, each tucked under its new calico coverlet. We begin to name them—Foxy, Droopy, Bucktooth, Smiles, Plumpy, Manx; and before we know it, we've shared them all with our friends.

Materials

Head, tail and outside ear, 2″ × 3″ gray felt
Ear lining, 1″ × 1″ pink felt

Coverlet, 3″ × 3″ scrap of calico fabric
Scrap of batting, 1″ × 1″
Black embroidery floss, three strands
Red embroidery floss or thread
Gray thread
Half walnut shell (Some nuts, such as Diamond, are pre-split and easy to break into halves. If you can't crack one in half, use a jeweler's saw to cut it.)
White glue

Patterns (see page 173)

Head piece (1), gray felt
Outside ears (2), gray felt
Inside ears (2), pink felt
Calico coverlet (1)
Batting (1)
Tail (1), gray felt

Assembly

As there are quite a few steps involved, plan to make more than one of these at a time using the assembly line method (page 5).

1. Wrap wide curved side of head piece around to make cone shape. Stitch closed with small stitches.

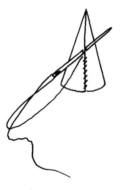

2. Hold cone so stitches are on the bottom (chin side). With black embroidery floss, go in through back of head and make eyes about ⅜ inch from pointed end with a French knot. Then go through to tip of point and make a French knot nose. With red floss make two stitches across seam about ¼ inch down from nose for a mouth.

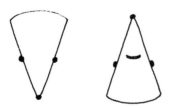

3. Glue pink lining of ear to middle of gray outside ear.

Hold bottom of ear slightly under top of head, and with tiny stitches sew ears to top of head.

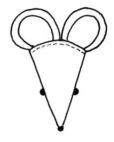

4. Place nut shell so pointed side of shell is on top. Spread glue all over inside shell except for pointed end. The head will go at the pointed end. Put felt tail into glue at center of rounded bottom, sticking straight out.

5. Fold calico fabric around batting or cotton ball and fit into shell where glue is. First fold side, then top and bottom.

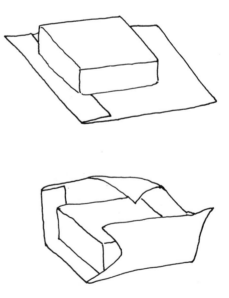

The coverlet should puff above the side of the shell a bit. You can trim the top of the coverlet with a thin piece of lace if you wish. Be sure to leave enough room, ¼ inch to ⅜ inch, for head.

6. Glue head in place by putting glue on rim of shell and back of base of ears. Ears will go over tip of

shell. If nutshell is large, you can make an optional white felt pillow and glue it under the head.

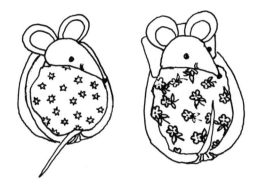

7. Sew metallic thread or matching thread to side of coverlet at balancing point for hanging.

5

TO WEAR AND CARRY

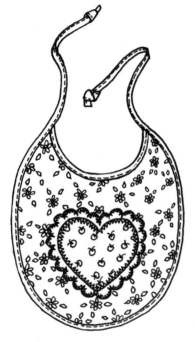

BABY BIBS

An extra bib can really save on clothes washing if you have a youngster in the house. This design lends itself to stitching in quantity, using the assembly line method. The zigzag stitching on the back makes the bib reversible, and a child's name can be hand embroidered in the center of the appliqué as a special touch. Quilted bibs make lovely shower gifts or presents for newborns.

Materials (for each bib)

Bib backing, 11″ × 9″ pre-quilted fabric (This usually has calico on both sides. You can make four bibs out of ¼ yard.)

Appliqué, 6″ × 6″ of two contrasting or coordinated fabrics that go well with your quilted background (This is an ideal place to use some of your favorite scraps.)
Fabric fuser, 6″ × 11″ (optional)
Binding, 48″ double-folded

Patterns (for each bib; see page 174)

Bib backing (1), quilted fabric
Outside heart or star (1), calico, (1) fuser
Inside heart or star (1), calico, (1) fuser

Assembly

1. With fabric fuser behind outer heart or star, place in center of bib. Measure in 1⅝ inch from each edge and 1½ inch up from bottom. Place inner heart or star on top, with fabric fuser behind. Put a cloth over the heart or star and press with warm iron for 5 to 10 seconds. If fabric lifts, press again for several more seconds.

2. Zigzag slowly around inner and outer hearts or stars with thread color of your choice. If you use white or a light color, the design can be seen on the other side, making it reversible.

3. Cut 8½ inches of binding from 48-inch length to be used for bib top. Unfold binding and pin first ¼ inch to back (first fold). Sew along this fold. Put remaining binding half to front of bib. Topstitch close to binding edge on front. Match center of remaining binding to center of bib bottom and sew around bib same manner. Knot binding ends.

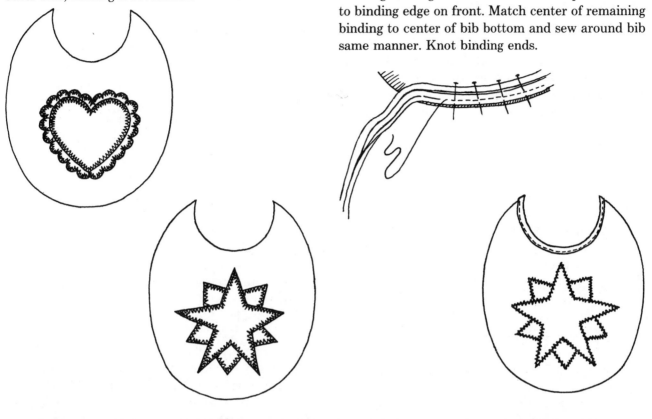

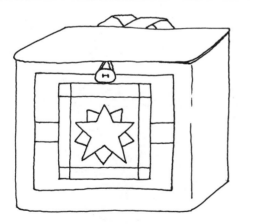

CHILD'S KNAPSACK

The backpack tote is intended for a child about 6 years or older. It is ideal for bike rides, school or a hike. Although not as rugged as a heavy-duty canvas rucksack, it holds up very well carrying moderate loads. The straps are reinforced and should be adjusted to fit the body snugly. It's also extremely nice for a mother who wants to enjoy an outing with both hands free.

Materials (all fabric is calico)

Dark brown, 1 yard
Gold, 7″ × 7″
Beige with flowers, 10″ × 11″
Green, 8″ × 6″
Rust, 8″ × 9″
Yellow for star, 5″ × 5″
Fabric fuser, 5″ × 10″

Batting, ½ yard × ½″ thick
Button, 1″ wood or your choice
Thick shoelace, 18″ dark brown

Patterns (see page 176)

As most of these measurements are straight lines and rectangles, you can cut fabric pieces from a paper pattern that you make, or simply draw the pattern measurements on the back of the fabric with pencil and ruler. A T-square is also quite helpful. The smaller patterns are given full size on page 180 under heart patch tote.

Outer star, (1) gold, (1) fabric fuser
Inner star, (1) yellow, (1) fabric fuser
(For above, see patterns on pp. 174–75 from baby bibs.)

   a. (1) green, 5″ × 5″
   b. (4) rust, 5″ × 1¾″
   c. (4) gold, 1¾″ × 1¾″
   d. (2) beige (make your own pattern, 1½″ × 7½″)
   e. (4) beige, 4″ × 2½″
   f. (2) green, 2½″ × 2½″
   g. (2) dark brown (make your own pattern, 9½″ × 2″)
   h. (2) dark brown (make your own pattern, 14½″ × 2″)
   i. (2) dark brown (make your own pattern, 14½″ × 4½″)
   j. (4) dark brown (make your own pattern, 12½″ × 4½″), (2) batting
  k. (2) dark brown (make your own pattern, 13¾″ × 12½″), (2) batting
  l. (1) dark brown (make your own pattern, 14¼″ × 13″)
   m. (4) side flaps, dark brown, (2) batting
   n. (2) back flaps, dark brown, (1) batting

Straps (2), dark brown (1) batting (make your own pattern, 20″ × 3½″)

* Here is a hint on cutting two pieces from one piece (particularly pieces *k* and *l*): First cut piece *l*, then trim pattern to *k* piece size.

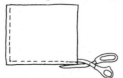

Assembly

Refer to pp. 88–89 of heart patch tote for first part of assembly instructions. You need only one star or heart patchwork for one side of knapsack. A solid piece, *l*, is used for the back of the knapsack. Appliqué star pieces in same manner as heart. Proceed through step #5 of heart patch tote instructions.

6. Pin side pieces *j* in place and sew on three sides, leaving ¼ inch unsewn at bottom seams. On bottom back side, leave 1½ inches unsewn on both sides for straps. Clip corners. Turn inside out.

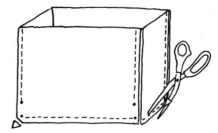

Complete steps #7 and #8 from heart patch tote instructions.

9. To make side flaps, cut (2) 7-inch pieces of shoelace so both pieces have finished ends. Save 4-inch piece for top flap. Pin 7-inch shoelace to right side of flap in center of rounded side. Shoelace should overlap seam ¾ inch. Pin other side of flap on top. Pin batting to one side. Sew all around. Double stitch over shoelace. Clip curves. Turn inside out. Sew other side in same manner.

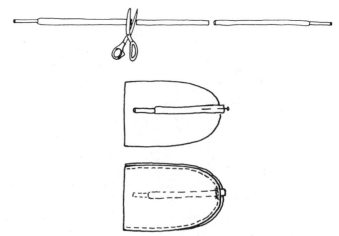

10. Pin flaps to sides of outside bag. To already pinned flaps and patchwork front, pin right sides of lining to right sides of outside bag. Sew both sides and front (with batting on bottom so it won't be caught in presser foot). Flap should be sewn between lining and outside piece. Leave all of back seam open. Flip lining to inside.

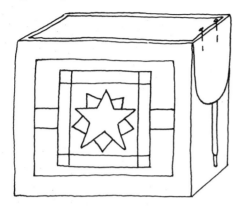

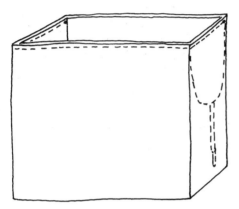

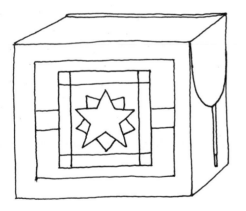

11. To make straps, fold 20-inch by 3½-inch piece in half. Cut strap batting in half so you have (2) pieces that measure 20 inches by 1¾ inches. Pin one batting piece to one side of folded strap. Sew down one end and one long side.

Turn inside out. Topstitch ¼ inch from edge.

12. To make back flap, pin back flap pieces *n* with right sides together. Then pin batting on top. At center, insert 4-inch shoelace between calico layers, extending ends to outside, ½ inch over seam. Stitch all around. Double stitch over shoelace. Clip curves. Turn inside out.

13. With bag right side out, insert straps in 1½-inch opening left at bottom back and pin at an angle. Turn inside out once more, and sew along seam line, with strap between layers. Triple stitch over straps for extra strength.

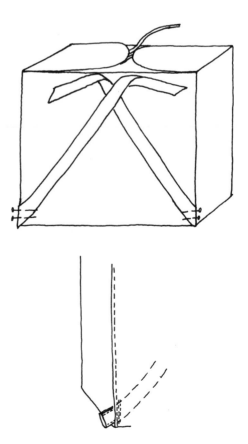

14. Sew back flap to right side of inside lining/batting (not piece *l*). Then fold piece *l* (outside back) in ⅜ inch to cover flap/lining seam and pin. Pin crossed straps securely in center of back. Insert ¾ inch or more into seam. This is where you can adjust for size.

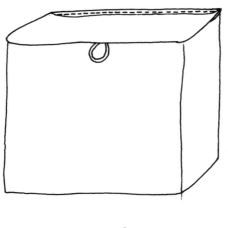

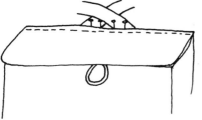

Topstitch across back, close to edge. You will have to pull straps toward you in order to sew underneath them. Sew again over strap insertion for strength.

You can sew this by hand if it is difficult to reach by machine.

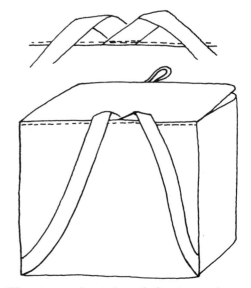

15. The star and patchwork front may be quilted by machine or by hand to hold layers together. If you wish, you can tack it at the corners where the patchwork pieces meet. Tack on back side of knapsack as well. Sew a button on center front.

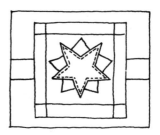

by 15¼-inch finished apron (the size of heart apron pictured, size 3–4). If you want to enlarge or reduce it, add or subtract to length of bottom piece and overall width. The train apron pictured is 1¼ inches shorter (size 2–3), so the bottom piece added to the smock was 7⅝ inches by 16¾ inches.

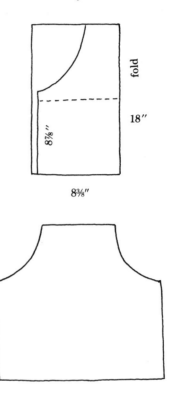

TRAIN AND HEART SMOCKS

These reversible smocks can be worn in the kitchen or at the crafts table. Stuff the pockets with art supplies, kitchen utensils, or small trucks and toys to bring a grin of delight from the young artist, chef, or inventor in your life. They make an especially practical gift that kids will wear with enthusiasm.

Materials

Smock, chintz, polished cotton or Scotchgarded® fabric, ½ yard

Calico lining, ½ yard

Appliqué pieces (Check actual sizes from pattern pieces. You can probably find most of the small pieces in your scrap bag. The largest piece needed for the train is 4″ × 4″ and the largest size needed for the heart is 6″ × 7″.)

Fabric fuser, ¼ yard

Patterns (see page 177)

Sizes are given for the heart smock that measures 16 inches by 15¼ inches when complete (sizes 3–4). If you wish to make the smock smaller or larger, see pattern adjustment below.

1. To make paper pattern for smock, fold an 18-inch by 20-inch tracing paper in half. Trace top smock pattern on upper half of paper, matching fold side where indicated. Add an 8⅞-inch by 16¾-inch measurement to bottom to give you the full-size pattern, 16¾ inches by 15⅞ inches. This makes a 16-inch

2. Make a pocket pattern that measures 3¾ inches by 16¾ inches, or draw measurements in pencil on back of fabric.

3. Make a strap pattern that measures 18 inches by 2½ inches, and one that measures 16 inches by 2½ inches.

Apron shape, (1) chintz, (1) calico

Pocket, (1) 3¾″ × 16¾″ chintz front and (1) calico lining; or, as in train smock, make front pocket 3⅛″ × 16¾″ of chintz and a 1¼″ × 16¾″ strip of lining calico for front top edging

Side straps, (2) 16″ × 2½″ chintz or calico

Neck straps, (2) 18″ × 2½″ chintz or calico

Cut appliqué pieces with fabric fuser behind. See appliqué instructions and hints on page 7.

Assembly

1. With fabric fuser behind appliqué pieces, lay out and center on polished cotton. Heart measures 3¼ inches down from top. Measure equal distance from each side. Train cloud measures ¾ inch down from top. Measure equal distance from each side. Step back and look at appliqué pieces to be sure they are straight. Fuse to backing and zigzag around each piece (refer to pp. 5–6 and 7 for fabric fusing hints and appliqué instructions).

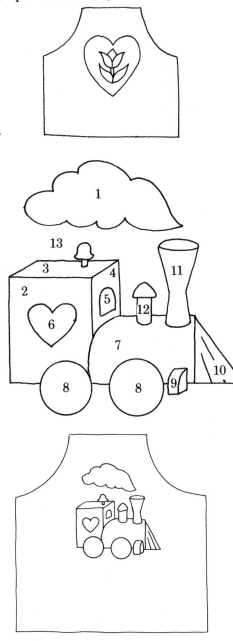

2. With right sides together, fold straps in half. Sew down one long side and 1 inch from end diagonally to point. Clip tip. Turn inside out with a long tool and press.

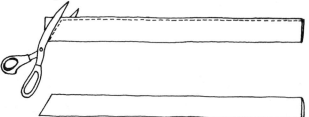

3. With right sides together, sew 1¼-inch calico strip to pocket from chintz (optional). Press open. With right sides together, pin this piece or front pocket without top edging to calico pocket lining. Stitch top edge only. Turn to right side. Press.

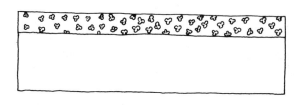

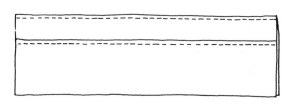

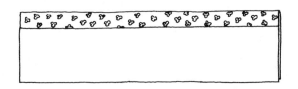

4. Pin pocket to front of chintz smock. Pin top straps ⅜ inch in from top side edge. Pin side straps ⅜ inch down from bottom of curved edge. Pin all straps together and to smock in middle so they won't be in the way when sewing.

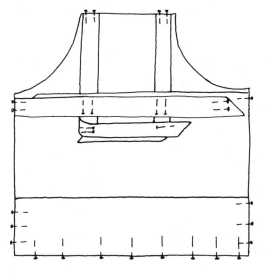

5. With right sides together, pin lining on top of front. Stitch all around, leaving 2¾ inches open 1¼ inch down on straight side (in between strap and pocket). Clip corners. Turn inside out. Fold, turning

seam in ¼ inch, and press. You can use a ½-inch strip of fabric fuser here, but also sew closed by hand with small stitches.

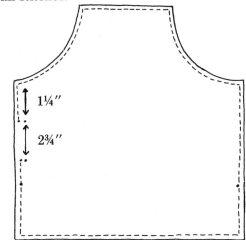

6. Press pocket flat and pin in place. Measure in and draw lines at approximately (3) 3-inch intervals, then (1) 4½-inch interval, and (1) 2½-inch interval to hold scissors, crayons, tape, ruler, glue, kitchen utensils, or small toys.

HEART PATCH TOTE

Every time I dash out of the house I grab my tote bag. Filled with snacks, extra clothes, and everyday supplies, it can be used as a diaper bag, carryall, or child's traveling tote. It's wonderful to have something so useful that is also washable and attractive. Use these same patterns to make a handsome child's knapsack (see page 81). As a time saver you can cut and sew the first part of tote and knapsack at the same time.

Materials (all fabric is calico)
Dark blue, ¾ yard
Lavender or pink, 5″ × 9″
Light blue, 10″ × 22″
Maroon, 6″ × 15″
Olive green, 8″ × 17″
Pewter or gold, 6″ × 11″
Fabric fuser, 5″ × 10″
Batting, ½ yard of ½″ thick

Patterns (see page 180)

As these measurements are all straight-lined and rectangular, you can cut fabric pieces from a paper pattern or simply draw the pattern measurements on the back of the fabric with pencil and ruler. A T-square or triangle is also quite helpful.

- *a.* (2), pewter, 5″ × 5″
- *b.* (8), olive green, 5″ × 1¾″
- *c.* (8), lavender, 1¾″ × 1¾″
- *d.* (4), light blue (make pattern, 1½″ × 7½″)
- *e.* (8), light blue, 4″ × 2½″
- *f.* (4), maroon, 2½″ × 2½″
- *g.* (4), dark blue (make your own pattern, 9½″ × 2″)
- *h.* (4), dark blue (make your own pattern, 14½″ × 2″)
- *i.* (2), dark blue (make your own pattern, 14½″ × 4½″), (1) batting
- *j.* (4), dark blue (make your own pattern, 12½″ × 4½″), (2) batting
- *k.* (2), dark blue (make your own pattern, 13¾″ × 12½″), (2) batting

Heart, (2) maroon, (2) fabric fuser

Handles, (2) dark blue (make your own pattern, 17″ × 3″), (1) batting

Fold fabric so that you will be cutting at least two at a time.

Assembly

1. With fabric fuser behind, put heart in center of piece *a* (do not pin). With piece of fabric over heart, press with a warm iron for 5 to 10 seconds. If heart lifts, press again for several more seconds. Zigzag all around with thread color of your choice. (See appliqué hints, page 7.) Repeat process with second heart and second piece *a*.

2. With right sides together, pin two *b* pieces to sides of each piece *a*. Sew seams. Press, pushing seam to one side. Pin one piece *c* to each end of remaining piece *b*. Sew and press. Pin to heart piece, matching seams. Stitch and press.

Sew piece *d* to top and bottom in same manner as previous seams.

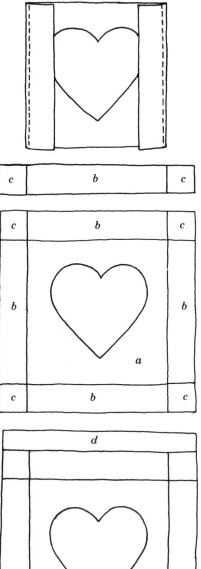

3. Sew one piece *e* to each side of piece *f*. Pin and sew this to sides of main patchwork piece.

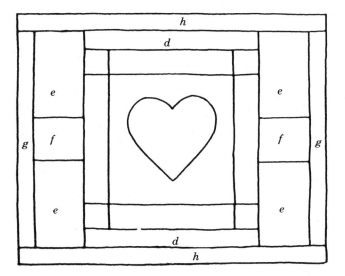

4. Pin and sew dark blue piece *g* to sides as indicated in illustration. Press. Sew piece *h* to top and bottom in same manner. Press entire piece.

5. With right sides together, pin a bottom piece *i* to patchwork piece at bottom. Stitch, leaving ¼ inch unsewn to each end. Sew second patchwork piece to other side of bottom in same manner.

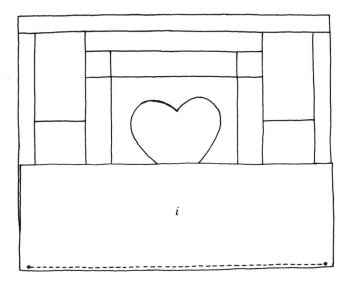

6. Pin side pieces *j* in place and sew on three sides, leaving ¼ inch unsewn at bottom seams. Clip corners. Turn inside out.

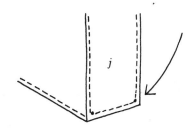

7. Trim ¾ inch off of remaining bottom *i* piece so it measures 13¾ inches by 4½ inches. The lining is smaller to make up for the thickness of the batting. Cut one piece of batting for each piece of lining, i.e., (1) bottom, (2) sides, etc. Cut only (1) handle piece of batting. Cut this piece in half so you have two pieces that measure 17 inches by 1½ inches.

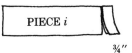

8. With batting on wrong side of each piece of lining fabric, sew piece *k* to bottom (piece *i* trimmed) in same manner as patchwork pieces. Leave ¼ inch unsewn at ends. If batting becomes caught in presser foot, trim away as you go. Sew sides, piece *j*, in same manner as previously done. Trim away any excess batting after sewn. Clip corners.

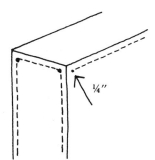

9. Put lining/batting into outside bag and push corners all the way down. Match side seams and fold top of lining and patchwork in ¼ inch and pin well.

10. To make handles, fold handle fabric in half with right sides together. Pin batting to one side. Sew down one side and one end (to turn inside out easily). Turn inside out with pencil or knitting needle. Press. Topstitch ⅛ inch from each edge. Pin handles in between lining and patchwork 3½ inches from side seam. Push handles in at least 1½ inches or desired length. Topstitch around top of bag at ¼ inch, and then again at ⅛ inch.

11. Quilt around outside of rectangle formed by pieces *e*, *f*, and *d* by machine or by hand. You can use a fairly long machine stitch and go around on the seam edge. Also, quilt the heart and any other desired pieces in the same manner. Be sure pieces lay flat and use plenty of pins to hold layers together while you sew.

12. Sew corners together securely if desired, to maintain squareness on top.

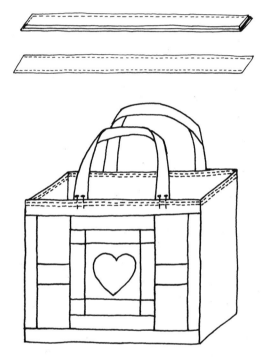

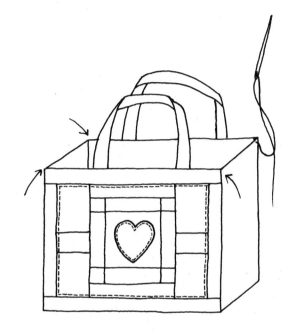

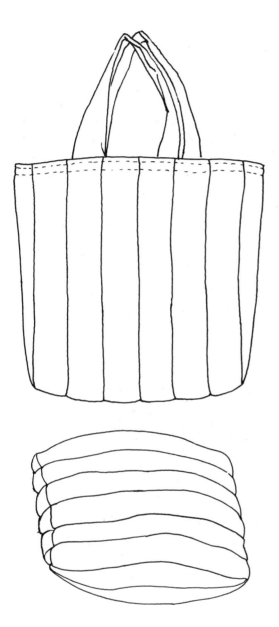

so once you've mastered the technique, a finished carryall or pillow in any size takes but a short time.

Materials

Strips, 8 solid colors—purple, dark blue, light blue, green, yellow, orange, red, and pink, 22″ × 2″. ⅛ yard of each would make two bags or a bag and a pillow.

Lining, blue or your color choice. ½ yard gives you enough for the lining, handles and the blue strip needed for the bag.

Batting, 12½″ × 22″

Patterns

Make a paper pattern that measures 2 inches by 22 inches, or rule with pencil on back of fabric.

Strips (8), 2″ × 22″
Lining (1), 12″ × 22″
Batting (1), 12½″ × 22″
Handles (2), 17″ × 3″ lining fabric, (2) 17″ × 1½″ batting

Assembly

See steps #1 through 3 of rainbow coverlet on pp. 113–14.

4. With right sides together, fold bag in half and sew sides. Do not turn inside out. Fold lining in half and sew sides with a ⅜-inch seam to account for the thickness of batting.

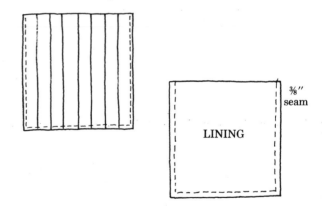

5. With right sides together at corners, match side seam (where two purple or two pink are sewn), and pin together. Draw a pencil or marker line across batting where it measures exactly 3 inches across (1½ inches on either side of seam). You will notice that this will come out exactly to the beginning of

CHILD'S RAINBOW TOTE AND PILLOW

This 11½-inch by 10½-inch rainbow tote is made with the same technique as the rainbow coverlet on page 113. The design can easily be adapted for a larger bag by varying the length and width of the strips. Calico prints rather than solid colors create an exciting effect, but you may want to keep them more unified by choosing several shades of one color rather than a wide spectrum.

Your piece becomes quilted by machine as you go,

next strip seam. Sew across line twice for extra strength. Do the same for lining, but draw line where it measures 3¼ inches across. Trim excess of corner triangle on lining and outside of bag.

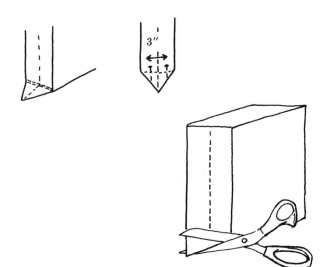

6. Turn strips and batting right side out. Do not turn lining. Put lining inside strips/batting piece. Fold tops in ½ inch and pin all around. If lining is too large, increase the lining seam size slightly near top.

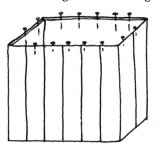

7. To make handles, fold fabric handle piece in half. Pin 1½-inch strip of batting to one side. On one end and down one long side, stitch on fabric side so batting won't become caught on presser foot. Turn inside out with long turning tool. Topstitch ⅛ inch from edge on both sides of handle.

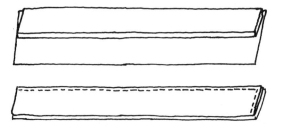

8. Pin handles ¾ inch down, in between lining and batting, on third strip in from end. Topstitch all around ¼ inch from edge, and again at ⅛ inch.

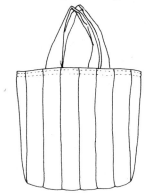

9. To make a quilted rainbow pillow, proceed as instructed through step #3 of rainbow coverlet. (You will not need a lining piece.) Then fold in half and match seams of strips at top and pin. Sew all three sides, leaving 4 inches open for turning. Clip corners. Turn inside out. Stuff and sew opening with blind stitches.

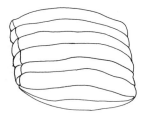

6
COZY BEDWARMERS

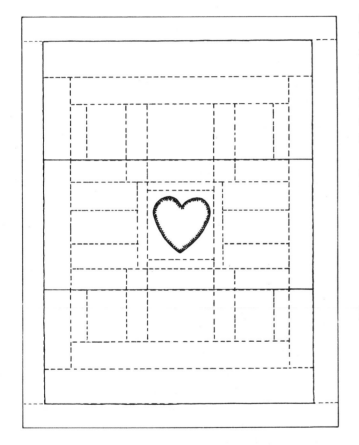

HEART QUILT

This is a wonderful project for using up many of your old and favorite scraps. Use the dimensions listed on the chart to see if you have enough yard-age. You can purchase additional fabrics to fill in what you need. It is important to take a sample of what you already have to the store to help coordinate colors and tones. The yardage in the material list is actually more than is required in many cases, but it is the minimum you could purchase at a fabric store and still obtain the necessary width for your measurements.

The heart quilt, simple to piece and quilt, is a wonderful beginner's project destined to become a well-loved heirloom.

Materials

9 calico colors
Borders and backing (pieces *h, l, m*)
Dark blue, 2¼ yards
a, g. ⅓ yard
b. ¼ yard
c. ¼ yard
d, k. ½ yard
e1, e2. ¼ yard
f. ¼ yard
i. ¼ yard
j. ⅓ yard
Fabric fuser, 10″ × 10″ (optional)
Batting (Purchase batting slightly larger than 40″ × 53″. There is usually a choice of weights; sometimes it is sold on a roll 45″ wide.)

Patterns (see page 182)

There is already a ¼-inch seam allowance in these measurements.

Piece Identification	Color	Dimensions to Cut	Number to Cut
a	lt. pewter	2½″ × 8½″	4
b	dk. green	6½″ × 8½″	4
c	purple	3½″ × 8½″	8
d	maroon	3½″ × 3½″	4
e1	lt. blue	12½″ × 2″	2
e2	lt. blue	14½″ × 2″	2
f	med. blue	6½″ × 10″	2
g	lt. pewter	4½″ × 10″	4
h	dk. blue	12½″ × 3½″	2
i	white and green	12½″ × 8½″	2
j	dk. pewter	12½″ × 11½″	1
k	maroon	34½″ × 3½″	2
l (sides)	dk. blue	42½″ × 3¼″	2
m (top & bottom)	dk. blue	39½″ × 5½″	2
back	dk. blue	52½″ × 39½″	1
heart appliqué	maroon	heart pattern 10″ × 10″	1

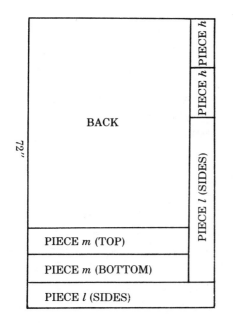

Suggested Layout of Dark Blue

As it is impossible to match your calicos exactly to the nine I have chosen, be sure they go well side by side and overall. If you change one color, you may have to change another. The best way to see how the finished quilt will look is to lay all of the calicos next to each other in the order they are to be sewn. Step back and look at them. After you cut the pieces, you can lay them out again in the same order. It is much easier to change a piece of fabric at this point, even if it is already cut, than after your quilt top has been sewn together.

How to Cut Quilt Pieces

To cut pieces for your quilt, you will need a yardstick or 48-inch ruler (a metal ruler is the best), a 12-inch ruler, and a pencil soft enough that you can see it on the back of your fabric. A T-square is also very helpful.

As you will need to cut two or four pieces of most sizes, the fabric should be folded in half so you are cutting two at a time. Before drawing the piece size on the back of the fabric and cutting, check the measurements, the number of pieces you are to cut from each color, and the best way in which to lay them out.

When fabric is folded in half, pin it so the bottom piece will not slip when cutting. Begin by drawing a line perpendicular to the edge or grain of the fabric. As all of your pieces are rectangular in shape it is very important that the sides be accurately drawn at right angles to one another.

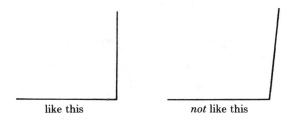

like this   *not* like this

From a starting point on your line, measure the length or width of your piece. For example, for piece *a*, 8½ inches by 2½ inches, measure 8½ inches from a point on your line. If you do not have a T-square, use a piece of paper that is cut square. Put your square or paper exactly on the line you have drawn, and draw a line perpendicular to it measuring 2½ inches. Do the same for the other side. When points *d* and *c* are connected they should measure the same as *a* to *b*.

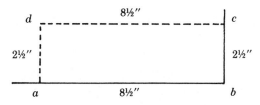

Use color photo to correspond fabrics with the letter identification of each piece, or work from a color-coded sketch of your own. Draw all needed measurements in pencil on one piece of fabric before cutting. After cutting pieces, label them in pencil on the back. Before sewing, look at the diagram of the finished quilt so you will know where each piece is to be sewn.

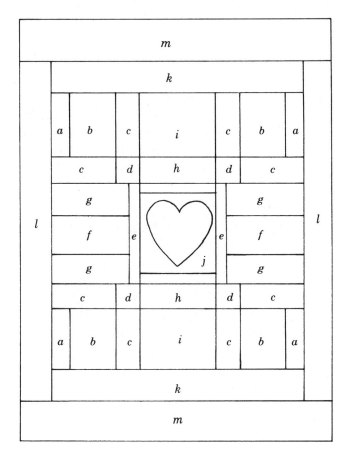

Assembly

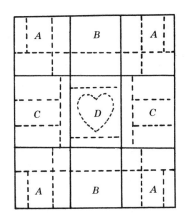

1. The quilt is made up of nine main blocks. Begin with Block A, of which there are four. With right sides together, sew piece *a* to piece *b*. Do the same for the remaining three blocks. Press seams to one side on back.

2. It is essential that you make two left A Blocks and two right A Blocks. To do this sew a piece *c* to piece *b*. Press back seam toward piece *b*. Sew unsewn piece *c* to piece *d*. Press seam towards piece *c*.

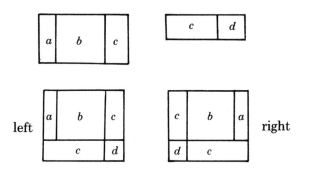

left   right

3. Match *cd* seam and *bc* seam and sew together. At this point, be sure to make two left and two right. Press seams.

4. To make Block B, sew piece *h* to piece *i*. Make two of these blocks. Press seams towards *i*.

5. To make Block C, sew piece *g* to piece *f*. Sew the other piece *g* to long side of *f*. Press seams. Sew

piece *e2* to one edge. To have a right and a left, turn other block around.

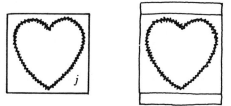

6. To complete Block D, place heart appliqué with fabric fuser behind it in the center of piece *j*. Measure in 1½ inches from sides, and ⅞ inch down from top. With a cloth over the heart, press with a warm iron for 5 to 10 seconds. If heart lifts, press again for several more seconds. Zigzag all around with color thread of your choice. If you prefer to appliqué by hand, turn heart edges under ⅛ inch and sew with tiny stitches. Sew *e1* pieces to top and bottom.

7. Sew Block A to Block B and Block B to Block A (refer to first assembly diagram). Sew Block C to D and Block D to C. Sew Block A to B and B to A as you did in row one. Sew the 3 rows together, matching seams at blocks. Sew 3½-inch strip *k* to top and bottom. Sew 3¼-inch strip *l* to both sides. Sew 5½-inch strip *m* to top and bottom.

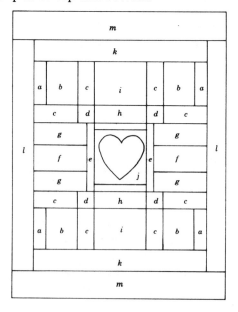

8. Cut batting ½ inch larger than quilt top. (It is always easier to trim than to patch.) In laying front and back of quilt down it is helpful to have two people to pull it straight. Trim backing calico to top patchwork if it is not exactly the same size. Place batting down on work space, then quilt top with right sides up. Then quilt back with wrong side up. Pin well. Stitch around through all three layers with batting on bottom, leaving a 9-inch hole on one side for turning. Clip corners. Trim excess batting. Turn inside out. Sew, turning hole by hand.

9. Quilt by hand or machine. The coverlet pictured is machine quilted with long stitches around the heart (on top of the zigzag stitching), ¼ inch around the blue border, and across the middle between Blocks ABA and CDC on both sides. Use plenty of pins to hold the layers in place. The quilt may also be held together by tacking (see page 7) in corners of pieces with yarn or embroidery floss. Perhaps the most lovely technique is hand quilting. You will probably want to use a quilt frame or large embroidery hoop to do this. Your name and date can be embroidered in the corner, and/or a child's name on the heart.

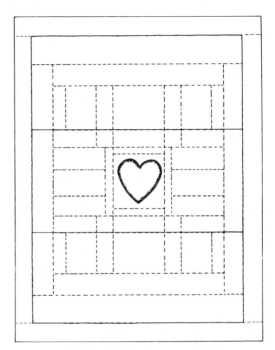

solid inside lines are quilted

97

Patterns (see page 181)

a. Light calico, 96 pieces

PIECE *a*

b. Light calico, 24 pieces

PIECE *b*

c. Dark calico, 24 diamonds cut in half so you have 48 large triangles; and muslin, 24 diamonds cut in half so you have 48 large triangles

PIECE *c*

Side borders (2), 3½″ × 50″
Top and bottom borders (2), 3½″ × 39″

LAYOUT DIAGRAM A (DARK CALICO)

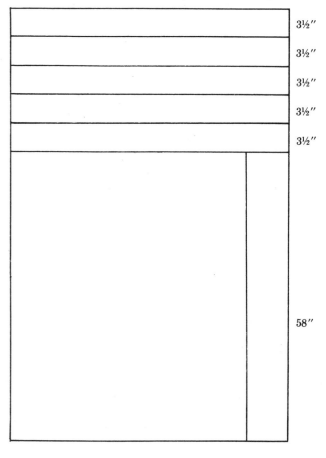

KALEIDOSCOPE QUILT

The kaleidoscope pattern may be used to make this child's quilt, or to create a single pillow or a king-size bedwarmer. Because of its warm, subtle colors, it recalls an antique heirloom. It looks particularly rich and beautiful when hand-quilted.

After keeping a small child cozy for several years, your work may also be admired and treasured as a wall hanging.

Materials (finished size: 36″ × 56″)

Dark color calico (patchwork, borders and backing), 3¼ yards
Light color calico, 1 yard
Muslin, ¾ yard
Batting, 58″ × 40″
Embroidery floss for tufting

LAYOUT DIAGRAM B (CALICO AND MUSLIN)

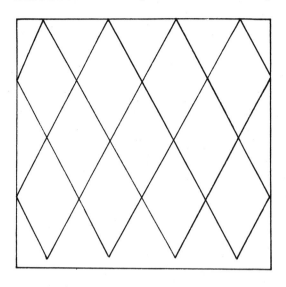

LAYOUT DIAGRAM C (LIGHT CALICO)

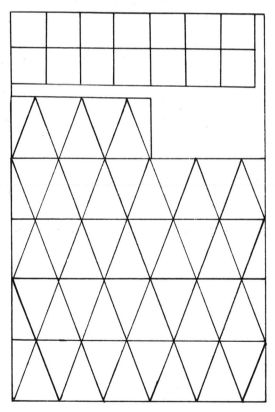

Suggestions for Layout and Cutting

1. When following the layout diagrams, pin the fabric edges to keep them straight before you lay down your pattern pieces.

2. As you will be using your patterns to cut a lot of pieces, it is a good idea to cut extra pattern pieces to maintain accuracy.

3. Lay the pattern pieces as close together as possible. You should have plenty of fabric, but in case you do make an error, there will be enough remaining to cut extra pieces.

4. One technique used in cutting large pieces of fabric such as the back and borders is to measure the length needed, fold it over square to both edges, pin, and cut the fold.

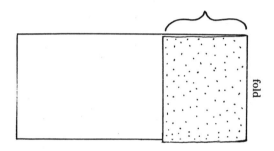

5. When all of your pieces are cut, take time to figure out how they go together before you start sewing. It makes sense to sew all of one size at one time (e.g., all of the four-cornered stars).

6. Cut 24 inches from dark piece of calico (use hint 4, above). Work with layout diagram B. Also use this layout diagram for muslin.

7. Use diagram A to cut borders and backing after you have completed patchwork. To cut long borders, use hint 4 (above) and piece one side border together.

8. With pencil and ruler, follow diagram C to cut 4½-inch strips that measure 5⁷⁄₁₆ inches in width. You may want to make a paper pattern for the strips, then cut triangles two or four at a time. This is only a suggestion. It is equally accurate to cut pieces two at a time with a pattern.

Assembly

There are several ways to assemble this kaleidoscope quilt pattern. The quilt is made up of six large squares. Each large square has four small individual squares. Begin by completing these 24 small blocks.

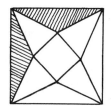

1. To create four-cornered stars, you will be working with pieces *a* and *b,* the light-colored calico squares and triangles. The "star" itself is made up of one square and four triangles. With right sides together and all edges matched evenly, sew *a* triangles to two opposite sides of *b* square. Do all 24 in this manner and press seams to one side.

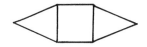

When sewing the other two *a* triangles to the square, center each triangle (ends will overlap seam ¼ inch) and sew only from stitching of pressed seam to stitching of pressed seam. There will be ¼ inch unsewn on either side of the triangle. To accurately stitch from seam, always keep the wrong side of the square facing up. Do not press seams on these triangles.

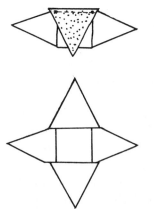

2. Each block has two dark *c* pieces adjacent to each other and two muslin *c* pieces adjacent to each other.

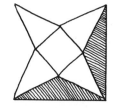

With right sides together, place a dark piece *c* on a piece *a* that overlaps another piece *a* at the corner. Match edges from the point of the triangle. With the "stars" wrong side up at all times, sew from the unpressed seam to the point. Match up and pin the other side and sew from the center to the point again. Take the second dark piece *c* and again place it on an overlapping corner. At point of triangle where the first piece *c* is already sewn, match up seams, making the second piece match evenly with the open seam of the first piece *c.* Sew from unpressed seam to point.

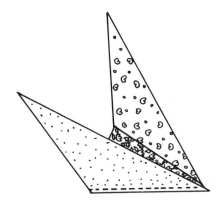

Do the two muslin *c* pieces in the same manner, sewing first the side overlapping at the corner. You will have 24 small blocks. Trim threads and press all seams flat.

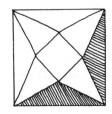

3. To assemble the six large squares, sew two of the small squares together by matching the edges of the dark *c* pieces. You will have twelve double blocks as in illustration.

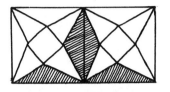

Choose pieces that match seams most closely and sew two of the double blocks together (match dark *c* pieces again). This will give you six large squares.

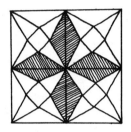

In the same manner, match muslin pieces and sew two large squares together.

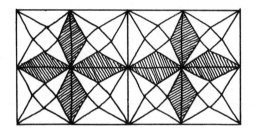

Finally, sew the three large pieces you now have. Trim thread and centers where all twelve points come together. Press these seams open. The patchwork top should measure about 33 inches by 48¾ inches.

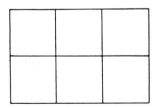

4. Long side borders are sewn on first. You must piece at least one to make it long enough (it looks best if it is pieced in the middle). Make borders a few inches longer than needed. It is always easy to trim off later. (See layout diagram A.)

Pin long borders to sides of quilt. Sew with wrong side of border piece up so you can follow a straight edge. Some of your small blocks may not match up perfectly at the side seams, and this is where you can compensate. However, be sure to have at least a ⅛-inch seam on quilt top if it is uneven. Trim off excess on side borders and press seams flat. Sew top and bottom short borders in same manner.

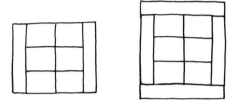

5. To assemble backing, pin right sides of quilt together with backing side up. Pin batting to wrong side of quilt back. Use plenty of pins and be sure everything lays flat. Sew with quilt patchwork side up (on borders) to ensure a straight seam. Leave 9 inches open for turning. Trim excess fabric, batting, and corners.

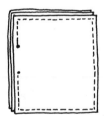

Turn inside out and lay flat. Press border edges. Pin all over to keep top, borders and patchwork in place before tufting or quilting.

To tuft, thread needle with embroidery floss and do not knot it. Pull thread from the back to the front of the quilt, leaving 1¼ inches or more of thread in the back. Go right back through the quilt, as close as you can to where you just came up (⅛ inch). Tie a square knot in the back and trim embroidery floss to 1 inch or desired length. Tuft at the corners and where all twelve points meet. You can do more or less, but the more you tuft, the more securely the top will be held in place. Various sections may also be quilted in a symmetrical pattern.

have to purchase some additional fabric to be used with them, it is nice to use old pieces that are special to you.

Train

14 different calico colors, plus velour or felt for nose (check individual pattern pieces for size and suggested color)

Kitty

13 different fabric colors, plus satin for ear (optional) (check individual pattern pieces for size and suggested color)

Binding, ½ yard of one of the fabrics that you've used in the appliqué

Blanket fabric, 30″ × 40″ or larger, gray, blue, yellow or color of your choice. Choose one of good quality as this may become a treasured possession and experience lots of loving.

Fabric fuser, 1 yard

As it is very difficult to match colors of calicos exactly to mine, you may have to make color adjustments to complement the fabrics you have on hand. Lay them next to one another before cutting to be sure they go well together. An important consideration is contrast. Generally in appliqué, you should not put dark pieces on top of a dark background, although sometimes just a tone variation or the difference in calico prints will be enough to set off the shapes and create dimension, or to tie together a busy section.

APPLIQUÉ BLANKETS

A favorite bedtime blanket is one of those beloved possessions with which few children are willing to part. Need I say more about "blanky's" condition when it is finally retired? For this reason, use a soft, good-quality blanket as a base.

Appliqué is fun, like building a colorful puzzle, and not nearly as complicated as it looks. Many fabric pieces may already be sitting in your scrap bag. You might want to personalize the train or the kitty's balloon. A special blanket won't last forever, but few belongings will share more of a child's love.

Materials

It is best to first consult your favorite calico scrap pieces before you go to the store. Although you may

Patterns (see page 183)

1. Pin all patterns with right side up to right side of fabric.

2. To save time and maintain accuracy, pin and cut all pieces with fabric fuser behind fabric. Sometimes the fuser is thin and difficult to handle; this way it is cut exactly the same size as the fabric, and is more manageable.

Assembly

1. After all pieces are cut, use small placement drawing to arrange pieces as they should look when finished. Now is the time to change a color or print if it looks a bit "off."

For Kitty, follow steps #2, 4, 5, 8.

For Train, follow steps #3, 6, 7, 8.

2. To center kitty design on a 30-inch by 40-inch blanket, measure 9½ inches in from the left side (basket side), 10½ inches from the right side (to tail), 6 inches to edge of balloons, 12½ inches up from bottom, and 11 inches from top to balloons. Mark placement tentatively with pins or pencil, then step back to see if it looks balanced. Make adjustments if desired, then mark placement again with pins, pencil, chalk, or fabric marker.

3. To center train, measure 10 inches in from the left, 10 inches in from the right, 13½ inches up from the bottom to the wheels, and 13 inches down from the top to the smokestack. Mark placement tentatively with pins or pencil and step back to see if it looks balanced. Make adjustments if desired, then mark placement again with pins, pencil, chalk, or fabric marker.

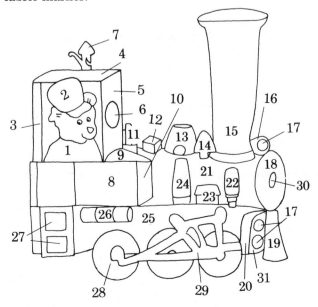

4. To appliqué kitty, trace mouth from pattern through fabric with pencil. Place facial features on brown face with fabric fuser behind fabric pieces. Fuse pieces in place (see fusing instructions). Place brown mask on head piece and fuse in place. Zigzag all around each piece with a wide zigzag stitch. Always use zigzag stitches on the top fabric piece that is being appliquéd. Do not try to sew so that half of stitching is on the background; e.g., all zigzag stitches should be on the brown face fabric, not the orange head background. Slowly zigzag slits in eyes (see eye piece and draw in with pencil first if you wish) and zigzag mouth. If you prefer, you can embroider mouth by hand. Do not make whiskers yet. I usually zigzag the facial features before putting the appliqué on the blanket. It is much easier to maneuver small pieces at this point, and if an error is made, it is much simpler to correct if not already fused to the blanket.

5. After face is completed, fuse all pieces to blanket, making sure certain pieces go under other pieces, i.e., pants under jacket, basket under left front paw, back paws under pants. All pieces should overlap one another slightly, not merely touch edge to edge. Zigzag up center of pants as you go. When all pieces are appliquéd, draw and zigzag whiskers, balloon string, and basket top (see basket pattern).

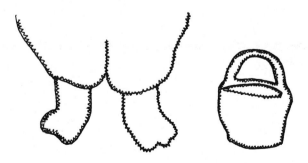

103

6. To appliqué bear trace facial features through fabric. Fuse nose in place. Zigzag eyes, around nose and ear lines, as well as mouth and neck line.

7. Place large train background pieces down first and fuse. Then apply smaller pieces on top. Make sure pieces overlap slightly when next to each other. Remember to have all zigzag stitching on the piece you are appliquéing, not the background. Around edges, stitching should be all on the calico pieces, not half on calico, half on blanket. Accent small blue and purple pieces with stitching where indicated. Use wider zigzag to accent top of smokestack. A child's name can be embroidered by hand or machine on the train side.

8. Cut (2) strips of 4½-inch by 42-inch calico binding fabric, and (2) strips of 4½-inch by 32-inch calico binding fabric. Fold and press sides in ½ inch to wrong side. Then with wrong sides together, fold and press entire piece in half. With blanket inside fold of binding, pin to top and bottom. Topstitch ¼ inch from edge. Trim ends.

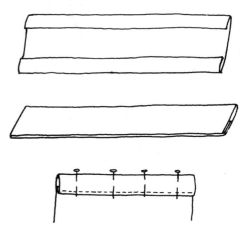

Side binding should measure 1 inch longer than blanket on either side. Pin binding to sides, all but ends. Fold ends in 1 inch, then into a triangle to miter corners on front and back. Pin. Topstitch sides ¼ inch from edge, then topstitch mitered corners very close to edge. Embroider your name and date in the corner if you wish.

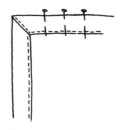

SLEEPING BAG

Roll out this cozy sleeping bag for any night away from home. Made in harvest colors from the same heart quilt pattern on page 93, this old-fashioned nighttime comforter provides a warmth not found in synthetic fabrics most often used for this purpose today. The finished size of 36 inches by 60 inches will keep any child less than 4 feet tall "snug as a bug in a rug" on a crisp or chilly evening.

Materials

Front heart patchwork, all calico fabric required for top of child's heart quilt (refer to page 181)

Backing, 2 yards calico, same color as pieces *m* and *l*

Inside lining, 3½ yards corduroy

Batting, 3½ yards of 40″ wide × ½″ thick, or two layers of a medium weight

Patterns

Cut all of the same pieces as for child's heart quilt on page 94, *except* cut sides (piece *l*) only 2 inches wide rather than 3¼ inches.

Also cut:

(1) corduroy and (1) batting, 37½″ × 53″, or same size as top patchwork

(1) corduroy and (1) batting, 37½″ × 62″ for backing

(1) calico, 37½″ × 62″ or 63″ (this extra 1″ is optional for turning over on top as a trim)

Assembly

1. After top quilt patchwork is completed, lay wrong side of pieced work on top of batting and pin down along seams where the three main strips have been joined (on the heart side of *cd, dc* pieces). Sew to batting by machine or hand. I quilted the one pictured by machine and found it helpful to have another person holding up the end of the batting so it did not become caught on the work table. Sew with a long machine stitch. Also quilt batting to patchwork around heart.

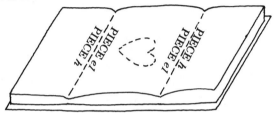

2. To machine quilt calico batting to backing, proceed as follows. With a yardstick, draw a pencil line on right side of fabric at intervals of 16 inches, 12 inches, 12 inches, 12 inches, and 10 inches (see diagram). With batting to wrong side of calico, pin along pencil lines. Sew with a long stitch as you did on front piece.

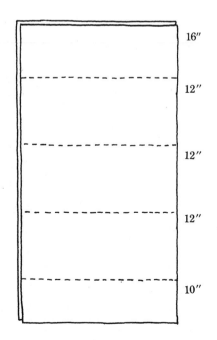

3. With right sides together and a ½-inch seam (to make up for thickness of batting), sew corduroy lining all around on three sides, leaving top open.

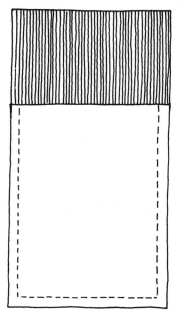

4. With right sides together, sew patchwork that is quilted to batting to back calico that is quilted to batting. Sew all around on three sides as you did for lining. Clip corners.

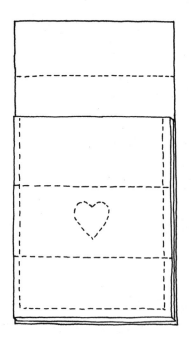

5. Turn lining right side out. With right sides together, sew top front of lining to top front of patchwork. You will have to push lining around to meet calico backing on sides. Sew sides and top, leaving 12-inch opening for turning. Turn inside out and push lining to inside. Fold the edges that were left open for turning in ¼ inch and pin. Fold lining in ¼ inch to meet it. Topstitch in place close to corduroy edge, or close to edge of calico, ¾ inch down.

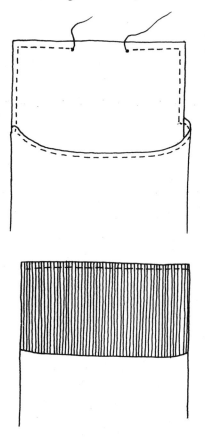

(optional if you use a 63″ backing calico rather than 62″)

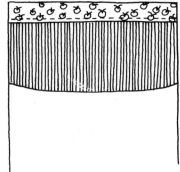

6. Turn entire sleeping bag inside out. With embroidery floss or yarn tack in approximately twelve places through lining and batting. A curved needle is actually necessary and can be purchased at most large fabric stores. (Full tacking instructions are on page 7.) Do not try to tack through patchwork top. It should already be well held by previous quilting.

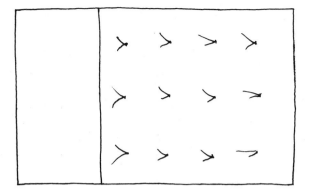

LAMB PAJAMA BAG

This design requires a bit of pattern piecing to make the large basic lamb shape. Although careful attention must be paid to what to cut and how, it is not nearly as complicated as it looks once you begin step by step. The end result will be a most loved and cuddled bedtime friend.

It is also the perfect size to hold a hot-water bottle.

Materials

Body, 20″ × 25″ sherpa fur, white or black
Legs, 5″ × 24½″ green velour, 5″ × 35¼″ black velour
Ear, 4½″ × 6¼″ pink bridal satin
Face, 1″ × 1″ white felt, 1″ × 2″ blue felt
Lining, 16″ × 34″ muslin

Ribbon, 45″ × 1″ plaid ribbon
Fabric fuser, 8″ × 18″
Velcro, 1½″

Patterns (see page 189)

To piece paper patterns see pattern hints page 4.

LAYOUT FOR LAMB FUR

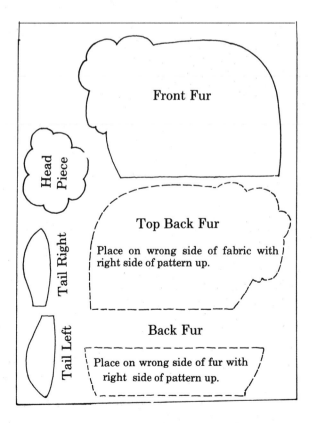

1. Piece A is going to be used to cut several pieces. To begin with you will have to make the pattern in full (note illustration). On a 17-inch by 16-inch sheet of tracing paper or thin paper, trace all four sections of piece A and match A3 sides, A2 sides, and A1 sides. To these four connected pieces, draw and add an 11¾-inch by 3⅞-inch piece to the bottom.

3. To make piece D draw a 4½-inch by 11¾-inch rectangle.

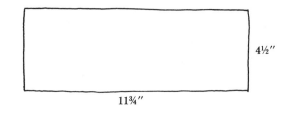

4½″

11¾″

4. Cut out one muslin front from entire piece A.

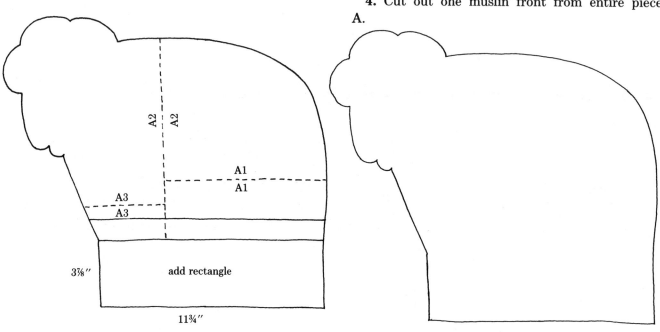

A2 A2

A1
A1

A3
A3

3⅞″   add rectangle

11¾″

2. To make piece B, trace both sections of piece B (1B and 2B) together. Trace all other shapes for patterns and follow carefully steps #3 through 11 for cutting pieces from the patterns you have made.

5. On full size pattern A, cut to *first* line from bottom for front fur piece. *Pin to right side of fur.* Cut out one. Mark face and ribbon placement with thread.

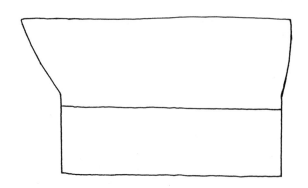

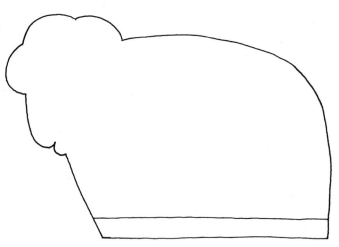

6. From pattern A in *step #5*, cut to *second* line from bottom for back fur and back top muslin (lamb-shaped piece). *Place pattern side up on wrong side of fur.* Pin and cut. Mark ribbon placement. Tape these pieces back together to make future lamb pajama bags.

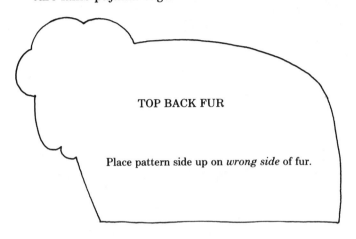

TOP BACK FUR

Place pattern side up on *wrong side* of fur.

7. Cut one piece of muslin from entire piece B, lower back.

8. Cut full piece B on line indicated on pattern and cut one piece of fur from remaining top pattern, again placing on *wrong side of fur.* This is called the lower back piece. Tape pieces together for future use.

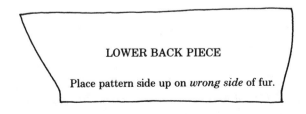

LOWER BACK PIECE

Place pattern side up on *wrong side* of fur.

9. For ears, fold pink satin and black velour in half when cutting so you will have a right and a left piece. Cut two black and two pink.

10. Pin tail piece to right side of one thickness of fur. Cut. Flip pattern piece over. Pin to right side of fur, giving you a right and left piece. (See lamb fur layout on page 107.)

11. Place pattern for face on *right* side of black velour. Pin and cut. Mark dots with white thread.

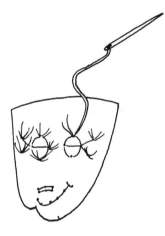

Assembly

1. To appliqué legs to green velour background (piece D), place a piece of fabric fuser behind each black leg. Put in place on green velour (see placement guide below). With a piece of fabric over legs, press for 5 to 10 seconds with a warm iron. If legs lift, press again for several more seconds. Fabric fuser usually does not fuse and hold velour very well, but it should do so enough that you can zigzag around legs to appliqué. You do not have to zigzag top. See zigzag hints page 7.

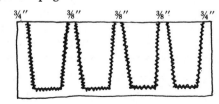

2. Mark placement of facial features through dots on pattern piece with white thread. Cut 2 blue felt ovals and 1 white felt oval. Cut white felt oval in half. Fuse the white felt, top of eye, onto blue felt.

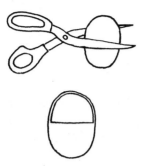

Use fabric fuser in same manner to apply eyes to face in proper place. This may only hold eyes in place while you zigzag. (If you don't want to use fabric fuser, you can baste eyes in place.) Use white thread to zigzag slowly around eyes, across slit and out to eyelashes.

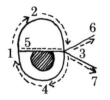

Zigzag nose and mouth through dots (double zigzag nose). If you prefer not to zigzag by machine, you can use a small chain stitch with white embroidery floss and achieve a very nice effect.

With black thread, wide zigzag or satin stitch across center of black pupil. You can use a touch of glue or fabric fuser to hold it in place. Give the lamb his or her own character with the direction of pupils—silly and almost cross-eyed, pretty, or

sleepy. Fabric fuse face to fur in same manner as legs. Zigzag all around.

3. With right sides together, sew pink satin to black velour ear. Clip curves and trim tip. Turn inside out.

4. Change thread to same color as lamb fur. Put small amount of stuffing (as much as you can fit), under fur head piece C and pin very well onto front main body piece. It should come over top of face and also leave at least a ⅜-inch seam allowance on the outside. Fold outside ear in half so pink shows, or as desired, and put ears in place under head piece as illustrated. Push under head piece at least ⅜ inch. Pin securely. With a machine straight stitch, topstitch around curves on head piece very close to edge. Stitching won't show through fur.

5. Cut two pieces of ribbon to 11½ inches in length. Pin ribbon where indicated on front and back of lamb. Ribbon pieces are going to match up at these points, so be accurate as to beginning and end. Pin in place. Topstitch close to edge, down both sides.

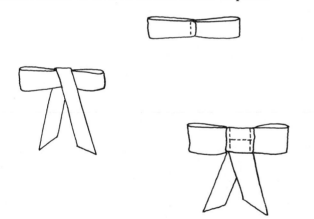

To make bow, cut a piece of ribbon 9 inches long. Fold ends in. Put remaining piece over ends in upside down "V" over first piece. Push top (longer side) up underneath in back to form bow. Pin. Machine stitch center of bow to ribbon on fur in place.

6. With right sides together and a 3/16-inch seam, sew tail around, leaving open where indicated on end. Clip curves and tip. Turn inside out. Sew up hole on side of tail.

7. With right sides together, sew leg piece to body front. Sew leg piece to lower body back. With right

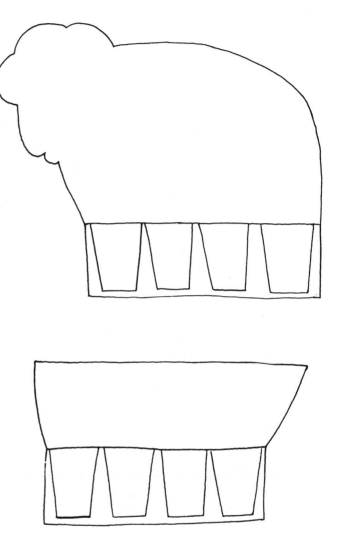

sides together, sew lower body back muslin to lower body back fur/leg piece on top.

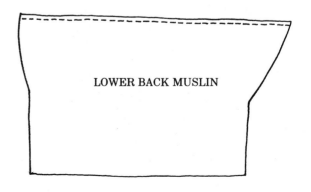

LOWER BACK MUSLIN

111

With right sides together, sew muslin to top back fur in same manner.

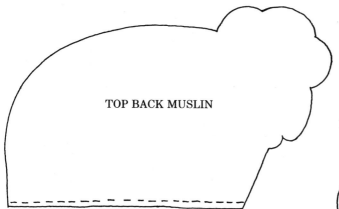

Fold muslin over to inside. Press seams and pin. Topstitch ⅛ inch from edge on both pieces.

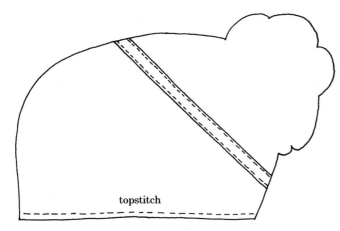

topstitch

8. Pin outside ear securely to stuffed fur head piece so it won't be caught in sewing.

Put muslin on wrong side of body front. Pin in place. Put right side of back top down to right side of front (fur). Match ribbon on front and back. Pin right side of bottom back to right side of front, overlapping back top. Put tail inside at direction shown so it will be sewn in seam. Extend it beyond seam ⅜ inch. Pin securely. If machine won't sew through tail thickness, do this small section by hand.

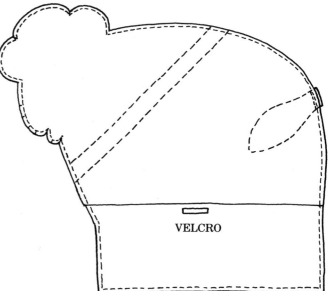

VELCRO

Sew all around with a ¼-inch seam. Reinforce over tail and to face dot. Clip curves and to dot under chin. Trim excess fur at curves. Turn inside out. Sew a Velcro closure ¼ inch down and 5 inches in from each edge. Sew bell in place.

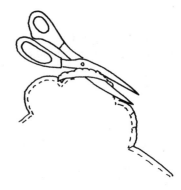

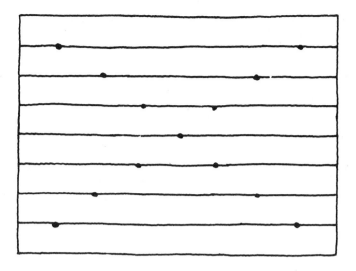

CHILD'S RAINBOW COVERLET

This coverlet can be made of velour, corduroy, flannel, or cotton. The technique is simple and quick, and the results can be stunning. The strips are sewn to the batting as you go, so very little quilting or tacking is later required.

Materials (finished size: 44″ × 32″)

44″ × 4½″ strips in eight colors: pink, red, orange, green, dark green, light blue, dark blue, and purple

Batting, 45″ × 33″

Backing, 45″ × 33″, flannel, color of your choice

Patterns

1. Make a heavy paper or cardboard pattern for fabric that is stretchy like velour. If you are using corduroy or cotton, you can draw the dimensions on the back side of the fabric with pencil and ruler. Cut 4½-inch strips the width (44 inches) of the fabric.

2. Cut batting 45 inches by 33 inches.

Assembly (for rainbow coverlet or rainbow tote bag)

1. Place cut batting on floor or table. Put first strip (pink) on one side with right side up. Put second strip (red) on top of first with wrong side up (strips have right sides together). Line up to edge of batting. Pin on both sides of strips. Sew down side away from edge with a ¼-inch seam.

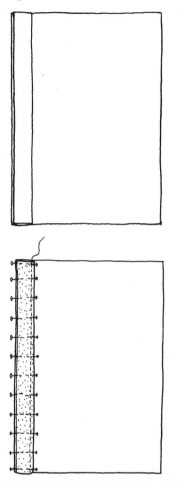

2. Flip second strip over so right side is up. Pin third strip, wrong side up, on top of second strip. Again, sew far edge.

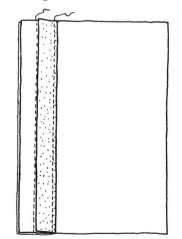

3. Continue with this method until all eight strips are sewn. Pin outside edges of first and eighth strip to hold in place. It is not necessary to sew these outside edges yet.

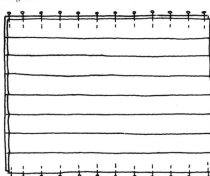

4. With right sides together, place stripped piece on top of flannel. Pin all three layers together. Trim backing to exact size of stripped piece. Sew all around, leaving 8 inches open on side of eighth strip for turning. Clip corners. Turn inside out. Stitch up hole with blind stitches.

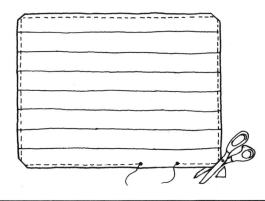

Tack at eleven or more points to hold backing to batting. (See how to tack on page 7.)

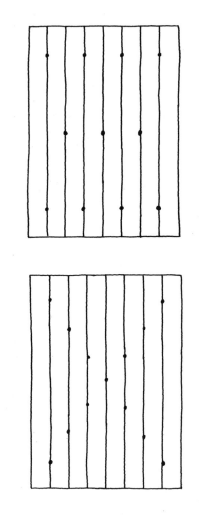

Hildy Hedgehog and Baby

Child's Rainbow Coverlet

Little Elephants

Baby Bears

Bird Crib String

Bird Mobile and Cloud

Dog Hand Puppets

Kara Kangaroo and Baby

Rupert Rabbit Puppet

Stacy Stegasaurus

Fluffy Ducks

Finger Puppets

Daddy Kitty and Junior

Bean Bags and Carry Bag

Mice with Tote and Cheese

Child's Knapsack

Heart Patch Tote

Rainbow Tote

Train and Heart Smocks

Applique Bibs

Country Rag Dolls

Wool Coverlet

Lamb Pajama Bag

Kaleidoscope Quilt

Draft-Stopper Cat

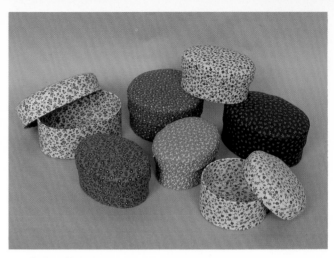

Calico Boxes

Patchwork Potholders

Walnut Mice

Rainbow Balls

Calico-Covered Photograph Frames

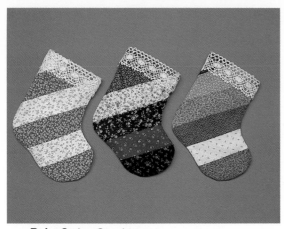

Baby Stripe Stockings

Collector Doll

Angel Ornaments

Country Patchwork Stockings

Braided Wreath

Little Lambs

Heart Quilt

Sleeping Bag

Kitty Applique Blanket

Train Applique Blanket

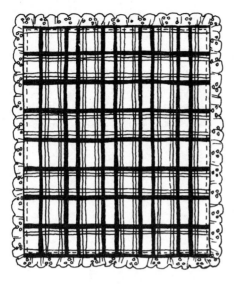

PLAID WOOL COVERLET

If you have purchased the materials beforehand, you can have a finished coverlet in an hour or so. I look for one-yard wool remnants that usually measure 60 inches wide. This gives enough fabric for two blankets, and I often make them at the same time. If made of good wool, this antique-looking coverlet will last and be treasured for years.

Materials (finished size: 30″ × 36″)

1 yard of plaid wool or flannel (You will actually need a piece 30″ × 36″. Many wool plaids come 60″ wide, which is enough for two blankets.)

30″ × 36″ batting or same size as wool (I use a light- to medium-weight batting because the wool is already quite warm)

30″ × 36″ muslin for backing

4 yards of white 1″ ruffled eyelet, already gathered (If not already gathered, use 8 yards scalloped eyelet lace. Gather to 4 yards.)

Assembly

1. Cut a piece of wool or flannel, batting, and muslin to 30 inches by 36 inches. Often you can fol-

low the lines in the plaid fabric as a guide. Pin lace all around to right side of wool or flannel. Stitch all around on top of lace binding stitches at $\frac{3}{16}$ inch.

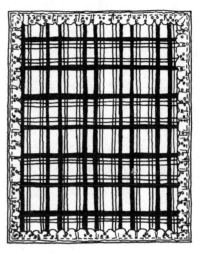

2. Put muslin on top of right side of wool. Put batting on top of muslin. Pin all three layers together. Your bobbin thread should match the muslin; the top thread should match the wool. Sew with the wool side up. Stitch all around with a ¼-inch seam, leaving 6 inches open for turning. Clip corners.

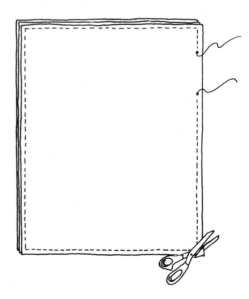

Turn inside out. Fold seam left open for turning in ¼ inch and pin. On right side, pin all three layers together close to lace edge. Topstitch ³⁄₁₆ inch from edge all around. This will close turning hole.

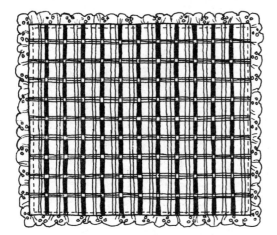

3. With embroidery floss that matches the plaid, tack at corners of design every 6 to 12 inches. Start on muslin side of coverlet and come up through to wool side, leaving 1½ inches of floss on muslin side. Go back through coverlet to muslin side. Cut at 1½ inches. Tie floss in a square knot on back side. Your initials or baby's name and date can be embroidered in the corner.

Daddy Kitty

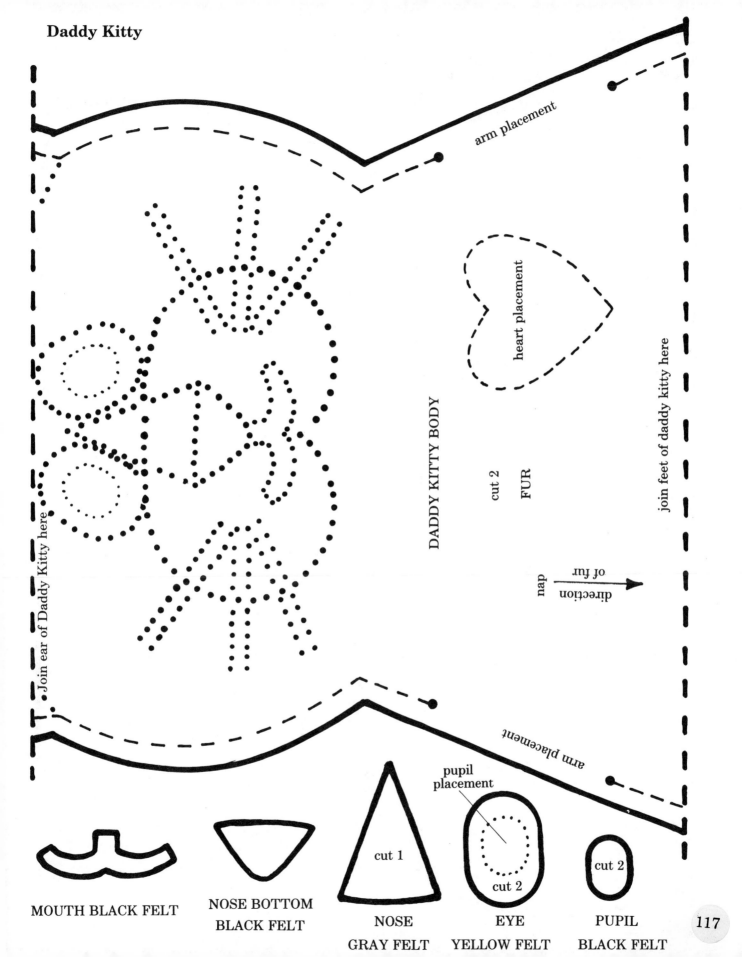

arm placement

Join ear of Daddy Kitty here

DADDY KITTY BODY

cut 2

FUR

heart placement

nap → direction of fur

join feet of daddy kitty here

arm placement

pupil placement

cut 1

cut 2

cut 2

MOUTH BLACK FELT

NOSE BOTTOM
BLACK FELT

NOSE
GRAY FELT

EYE
YELLOW FELT

PUPIL
BLACK FELT

117

Daddy Kitty

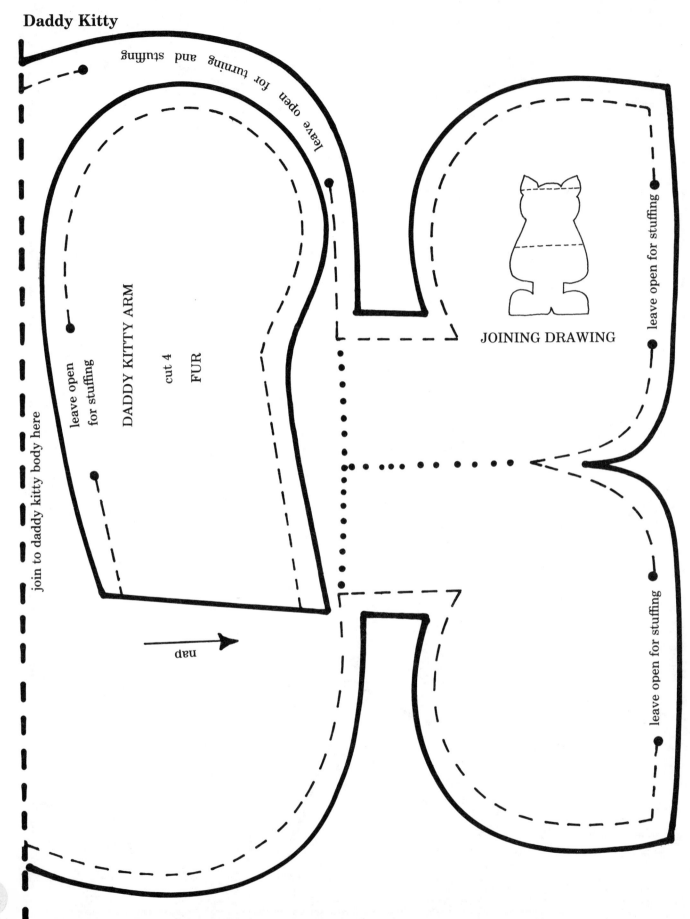

leave open for turning and stuffing

DADDY KITTY ARM

cut 4

FUR

leave open for stuffing

join to daddy kitty body here

nap

JOINING DRAWING

leave open for stuffing

leave open for stuffing

Daddy Kitty

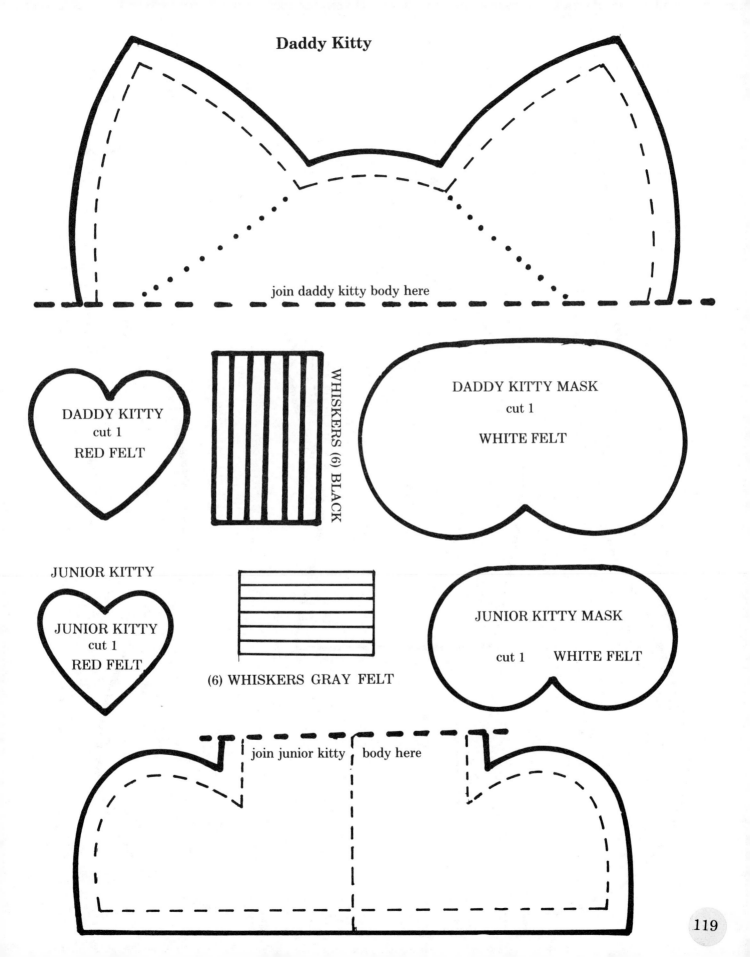

join daddy kitty body here

DADDY KITTY
cut 1
RED FELT

WHISKERS (6) BLACK

DADDY KITTY MASK
cut 1
WHITE FELT

JUNIOR KITTY

JUNIOR KITTY
cut 1
RED FELT

(6) WHISKERS GRAY FELT

JUNIOR KITTY MASK

cut 1   WHITE FELT

join junior kitty ┊ body here

119

Junior Kitty

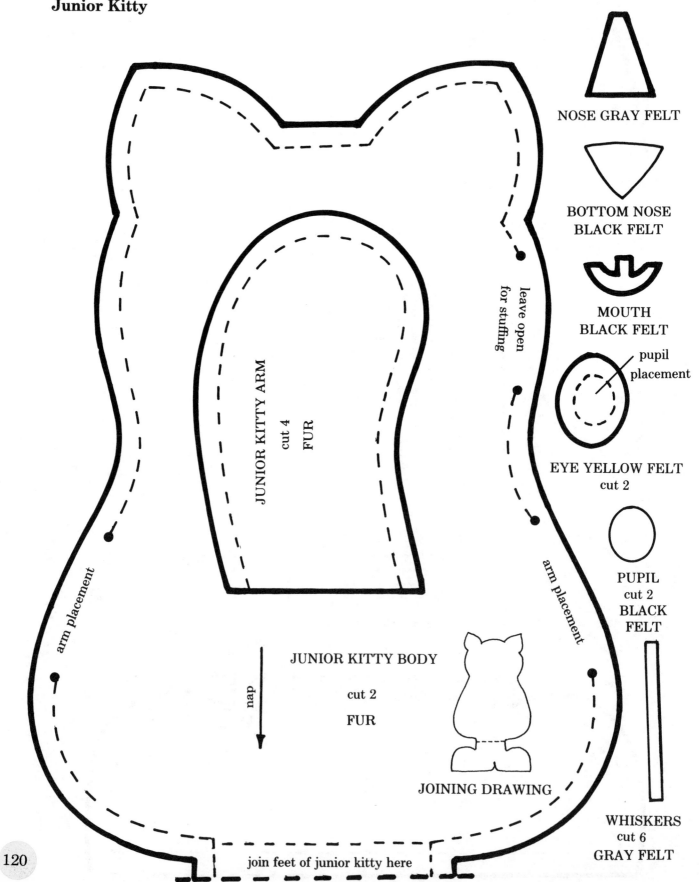

NOSE GRAY FELT

BOTTOM NOSE
BLACK FELT

MOUTH
BLACK FELT

pupil
placement

EYE YELLOW FELT
cut 2

PUPIL
cut 2
BLACK
FELT

WHISKERS
cut 6
GRAY FELT

leave open
for stuffing

JUNIOR KITTY ARM

cut 4

FUR

arm placement

arm placement

nap

JUNIOR KITTY BODY

cut 2

FUR

JOINING DRAWING

join feet of junior kitty here

120

BABY BEARS

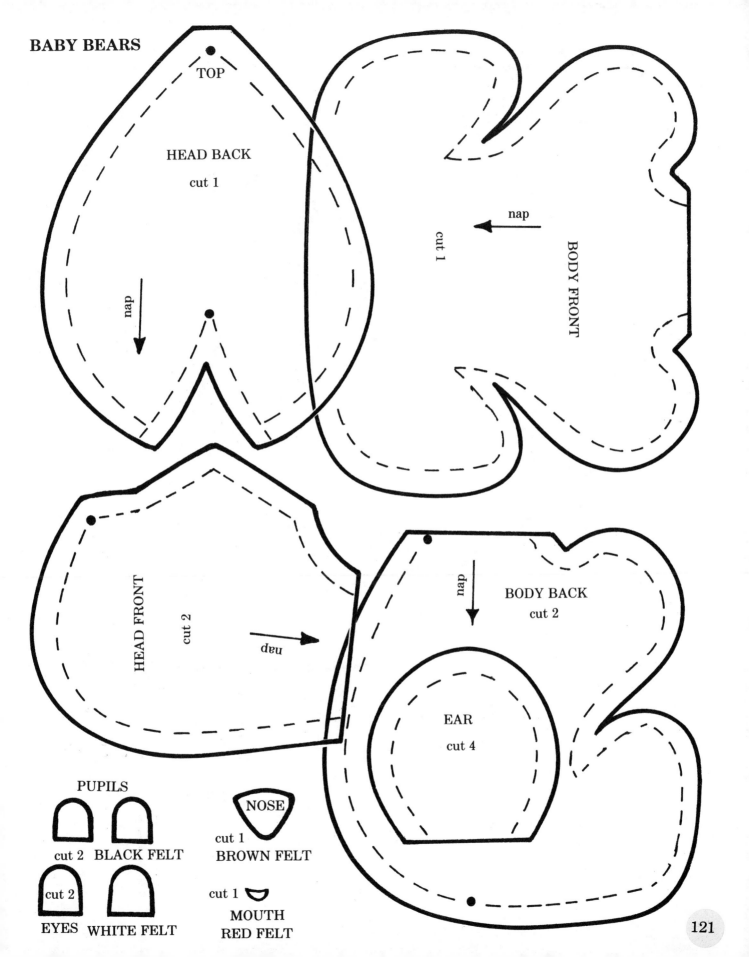

TOP

HEAD BACK
cut 1

nap

cut 1

BODY FRONT

nap

HEAD FRONT
cut 2

nap

BODY BACK
cut 2

nap

EAR
cut 4

PUPILS

cut 2 BLACK FELT

cut 2
EYES WHITE FELT

NOSE
cut 1
BROWN FELT

cut 1
MOUTH
RED FELT

121

DRAFT STOPPER CATS

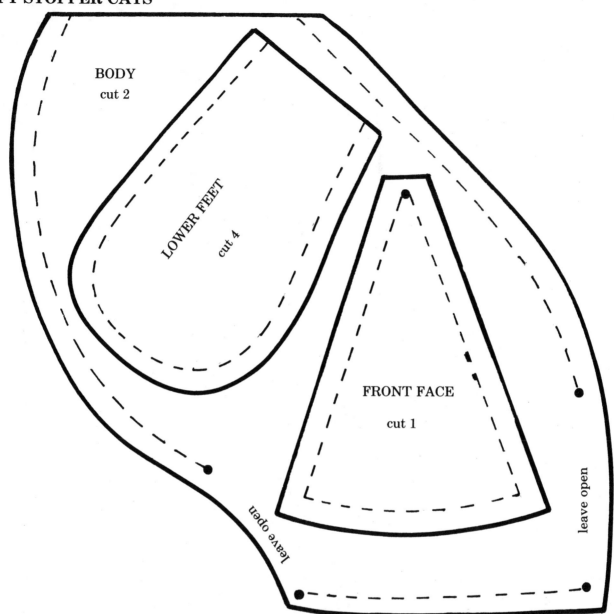

BODY
cut 2

LOWER FEET
cut 4

FRONT FACE
cut 1

leave open

leave open

To cut whiskers, pin entire box to black felt.

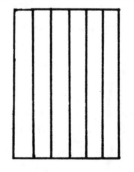

122

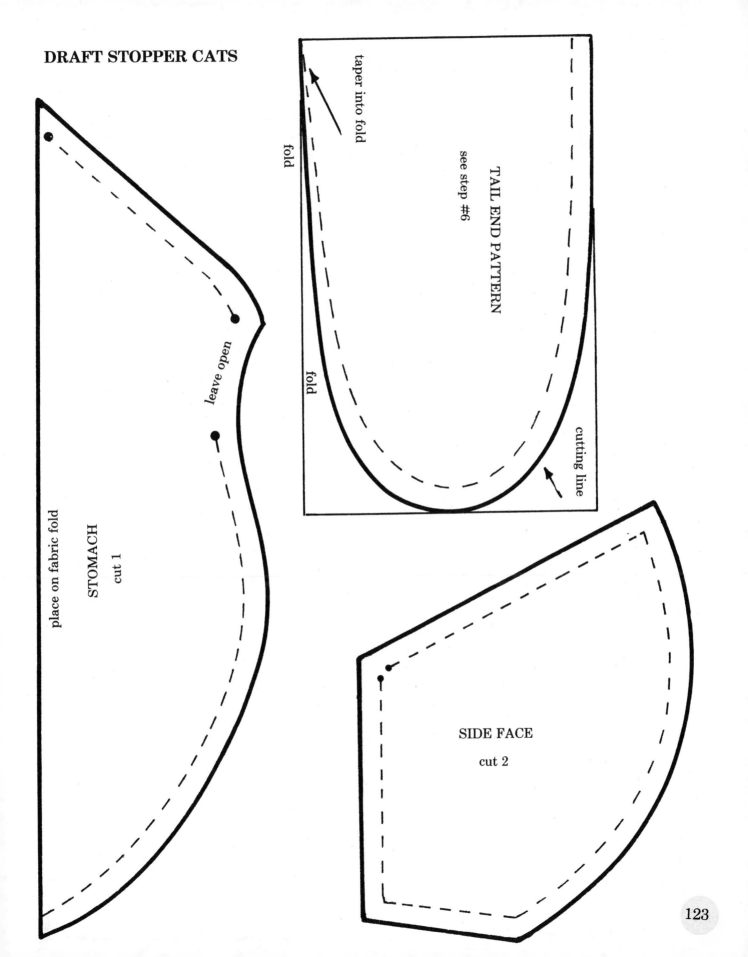

DRAFT STOPPER CATS

STOMACH

place on fabric fold

cut 1

leave open

TAIL END PATTERN

see step #6

fold

taper into fold

fold

cutting line

SIDE FACE

cut 2

123

DRAFT STOPPER CATS

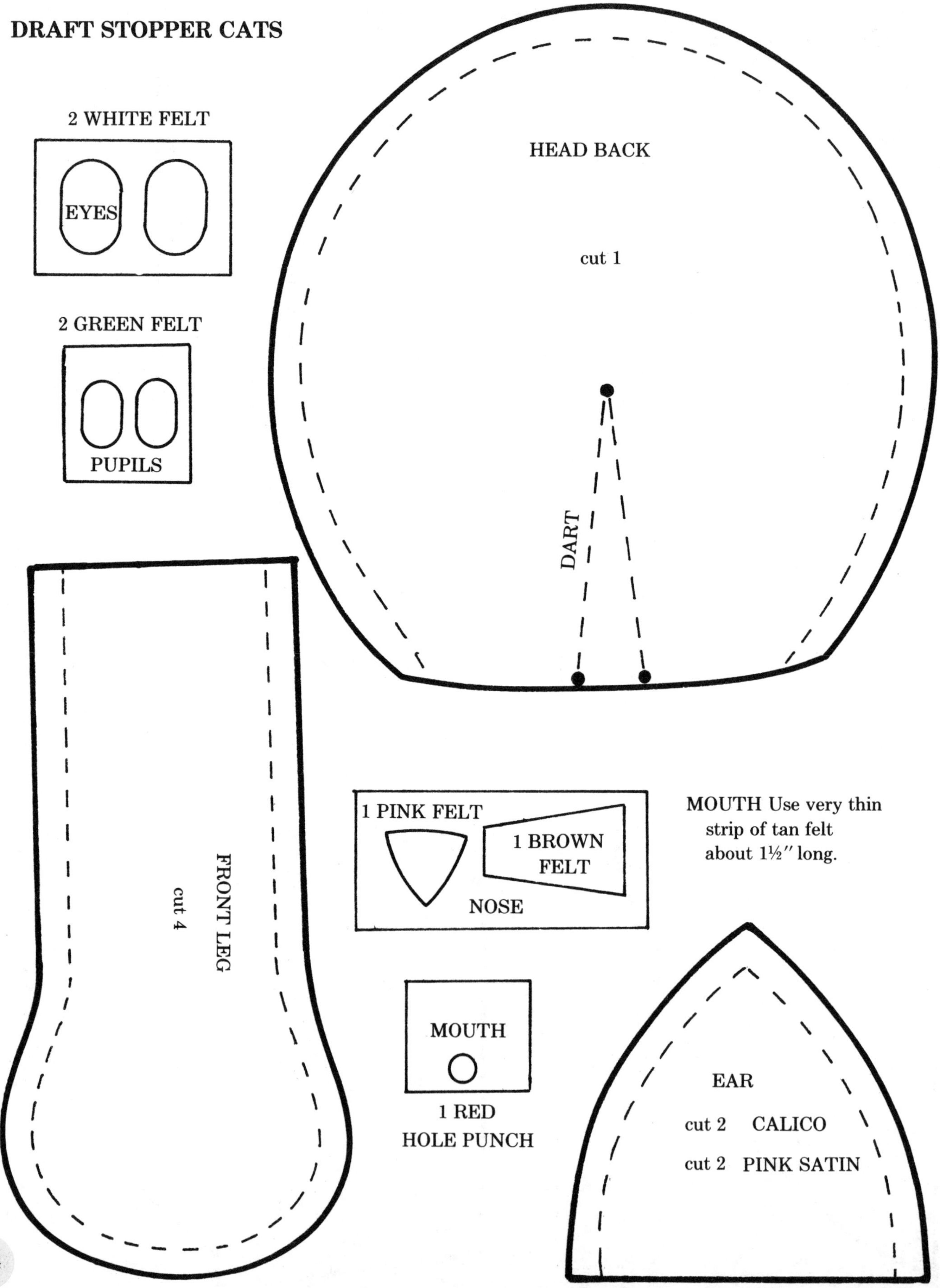

2 WHITE FELT

EYES

2 GREEN FELT

PUPILS

HEAD BACK

cut 1

DART

FRONT LEG

cut 4

1 PINK FELT

1 BROWN FELT

NOSE

MOUTH Use very thin strip of tan felt about 1½″ long.

MOUTH

1 RED
HOLE PUNCH

EAR

cut 2   CALICO

cut 2   PINK SATIN

FLUFFY DUCKS   **Elephant Ear**

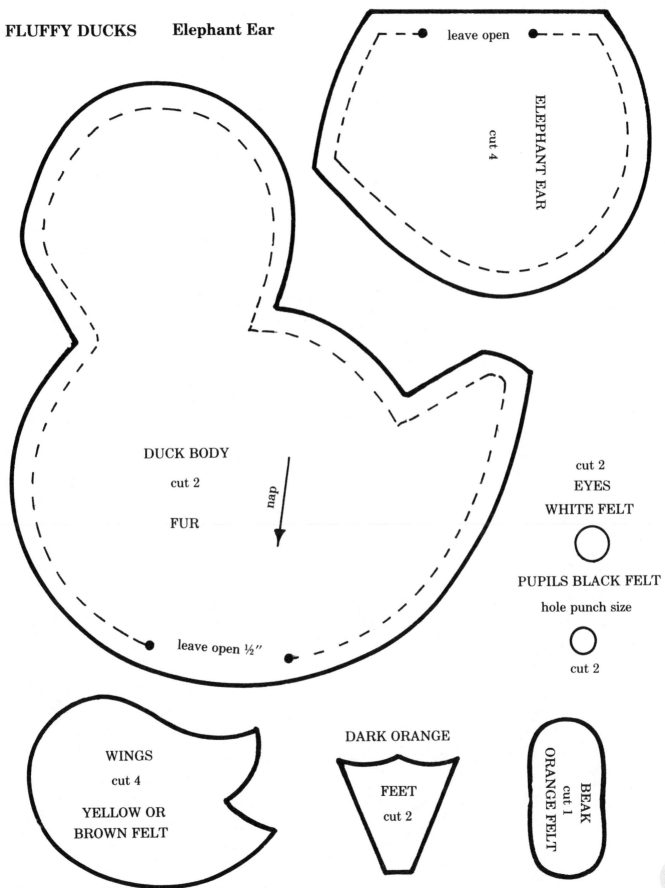

leave open

ELEPHANT EAR

cut 4

DUCK BODY

cut 2

FUR

nap

leave open ½"

cut 2
EYES
WHITE FELT

PUPILS BLACK FELT

hole punch size

cut 2

WINGS

cut 4

YELLOW OR
BROWN FELT

DARK ORANGE

FEET

cut 2

BEAK
cut 1
ORANGE FELT

125

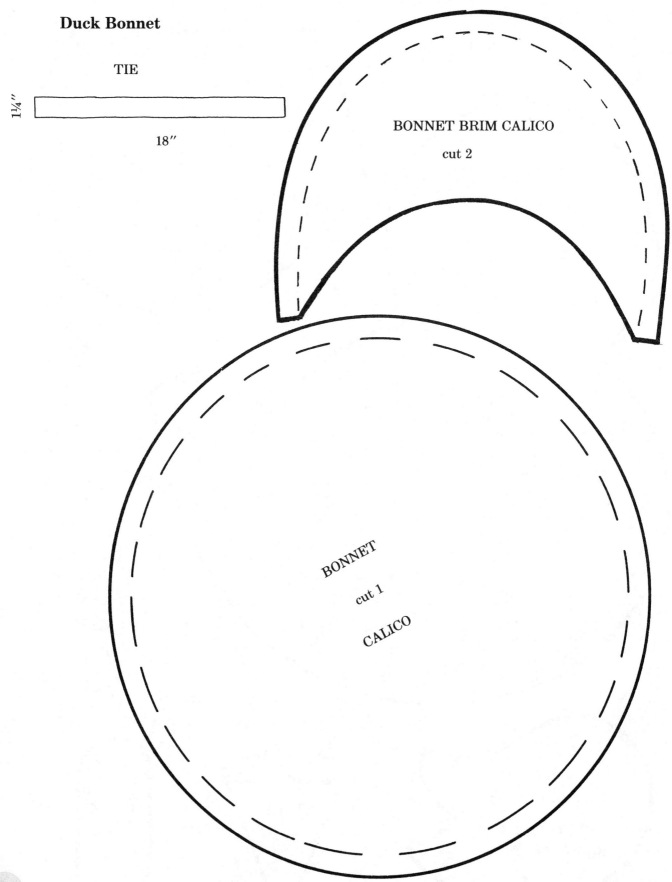

Duck Bonnet

TIE

1¼″

18″

BONNET BRIM CALICO

cut 2

BONNET

cut 1

CALICO

126

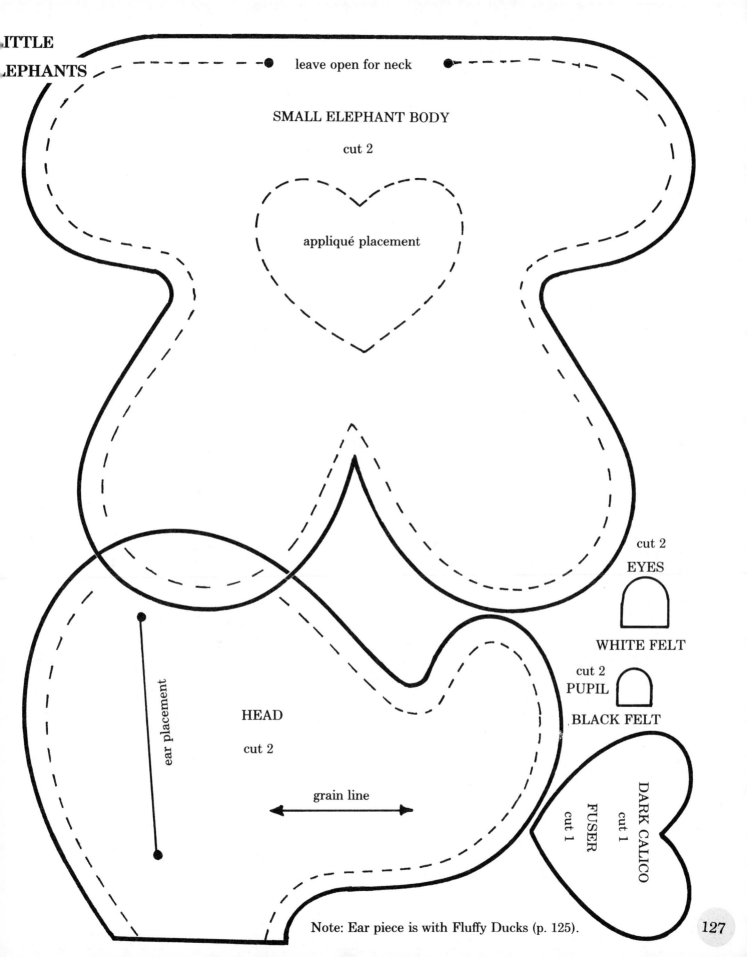

LITTLE ELEPHANTS

leave open for neck

SMALL ELEPHANT BODY

cut 2

appliqué placement

cut 2
EYES

WHITE FELT

cut 2
PUPIL

BLACK FELT

ear placement

HEAD

cut 2

grain line

FUSER
cut 1

DARK CALICO
cut 1

Note: Ear piece is with Fluffy Ducks (p. 125).

127

HILDY HEDGEHOG AND BABY

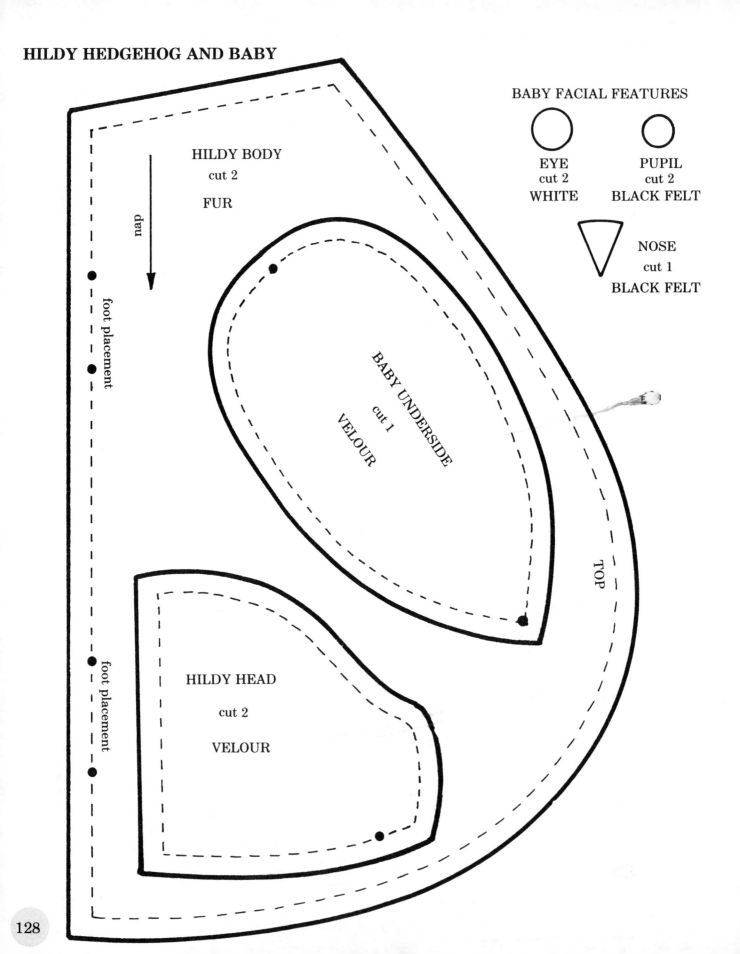

HILDY BODY

cut 2

FUR

nap

foot placement

foot placement

BABY FACIAL FEATURES

EYE
cut 2
WHITE

PUPIL
cut 2
BLACK FELT

NOSE
cut 1
BLACK FELT

BABY UNDERSIDE

cut 1

VELOUR

TOP

HILDY HEAD

cut 2

VELOUR

128

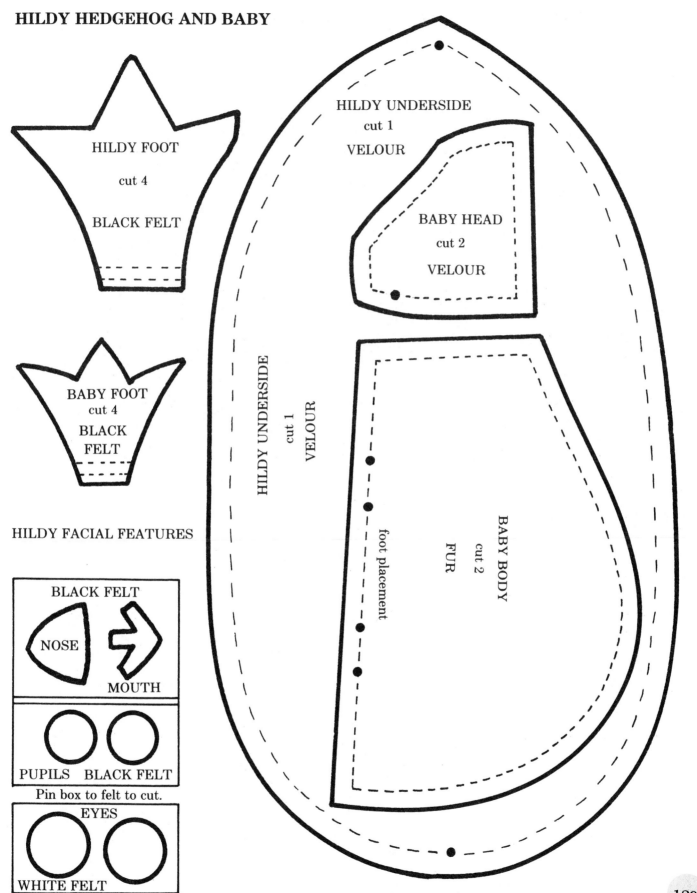

HILDY HEDGEHOG AND BABY

HILDY FOOT

cut 4

BLACK FELT

BABY FOOT
cut 4
BLACK
FELT

HILDY FACIAL FEATURES

BLACK FELT

NOSE

MOUTH

PUPILS   BLACK FELT

Pin box to felt to cut.

EYES

WHITE FELT

HILDY UNDERSIDE

cut 1

VELOUR

HILDY UNDERSIDE   cut 1   VELOUR

BABY HEAD
cut 2
VELOUR

foot placement

BABY BODY
cut 2
FUR

129

KARA KANGAROO AND BABY

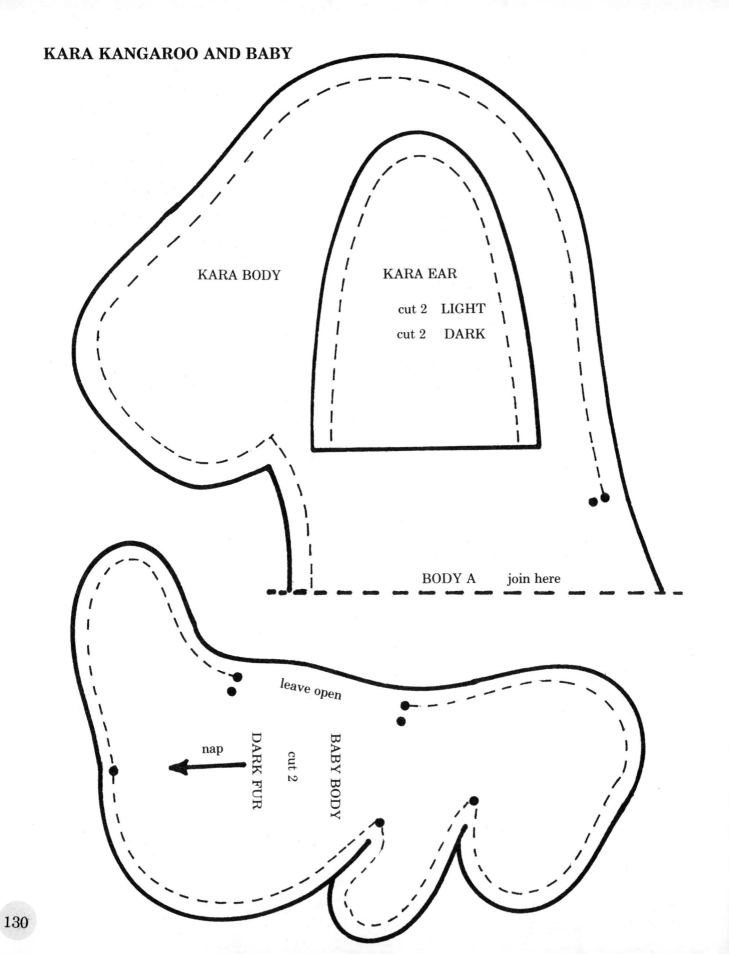

KARA BODY

KARA EAR

cut 2   LIGHT

cut 2   DARK

BODY A   join here

leave open

nap

DARK FUR

cut 2

BABY BODY

130

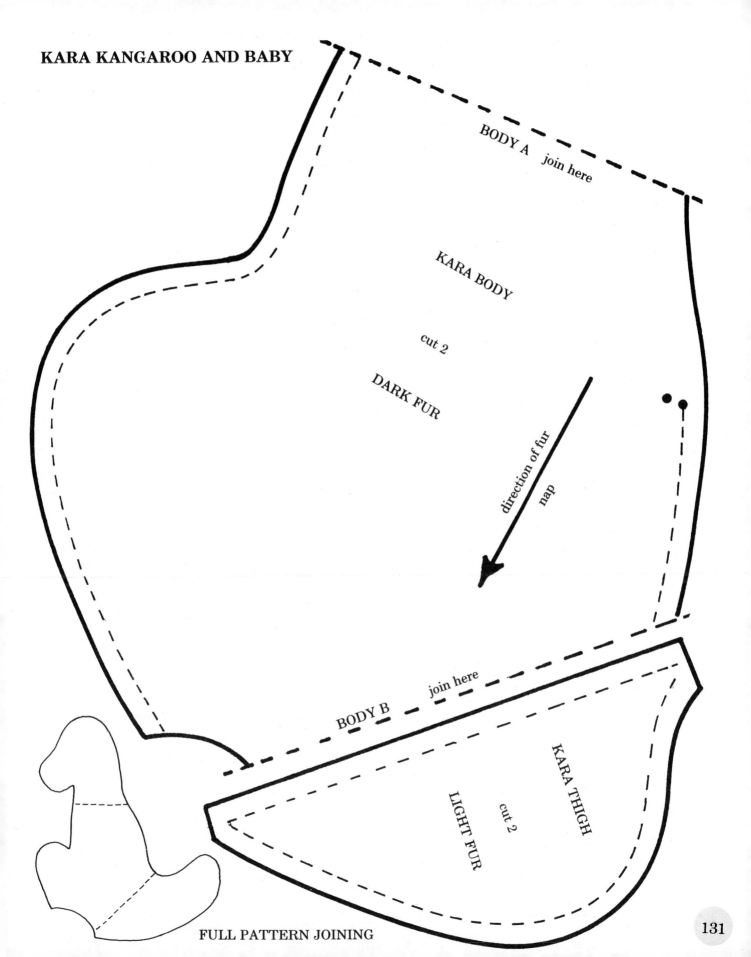

KARA KANGAROO AND BABY

BODY A   *join here*

KARA BODY

cut 2

DARK FUR

direction of fur   *nap*

BODY B   — *join here*

KARA THIGH

cut 2

LIGHT FUR

FULL PATTERN JOINING

131

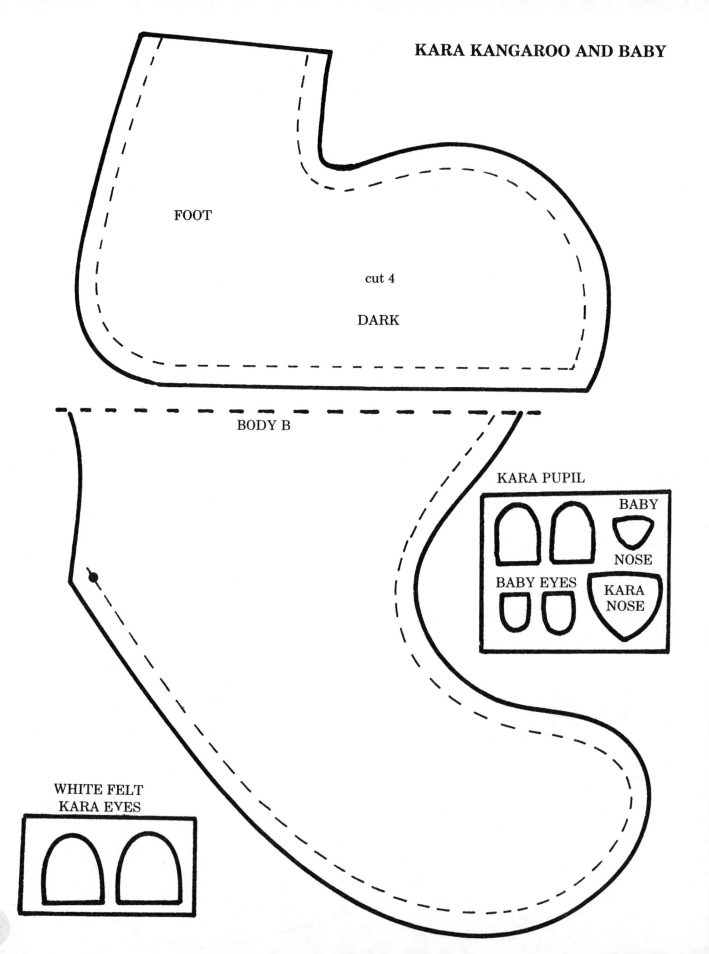

KARA KANGAROO AND BABY

FOOT

cut 4

DARK

BODY B

KARA PUPIL

BABY
NOSE

BABY EYES

KARA
NOSE

WHITE FELT
KARA EYES

132

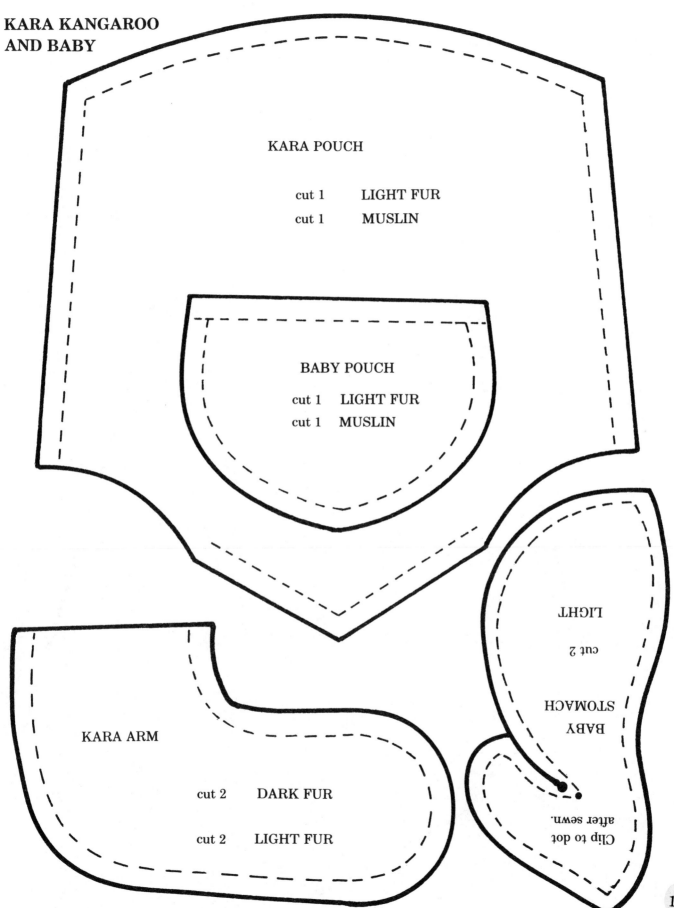

KARA KANGAROO AND BABY

KARA POUCH

cut 1   LIGHT FUR

cut 1   MUSLIN

BABY POUCH

cut 1   LIGHT FUR

cut 1   MUSLIN

KARA ARM

cut 2   DARK FUR

cut 2   LIGHT FUR

LIGHT

cut 2

BABY STOMACH

Clip to dot after sewn.

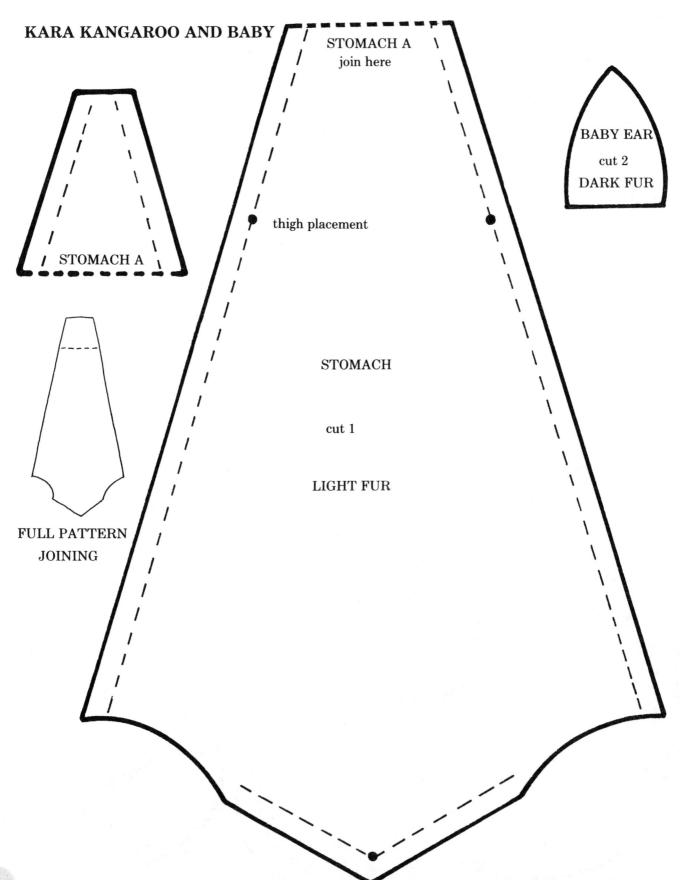

KARA KANGAROO AND BABY

STOMACH A
join here

STOMACH A

BABY EAR
cut 2
DARK FUR

thigh placement

STOMACH

cut 1

LIGHT FUR

FULL PATTERN
JOINING

MICE WITH TOTE AND CHEESE

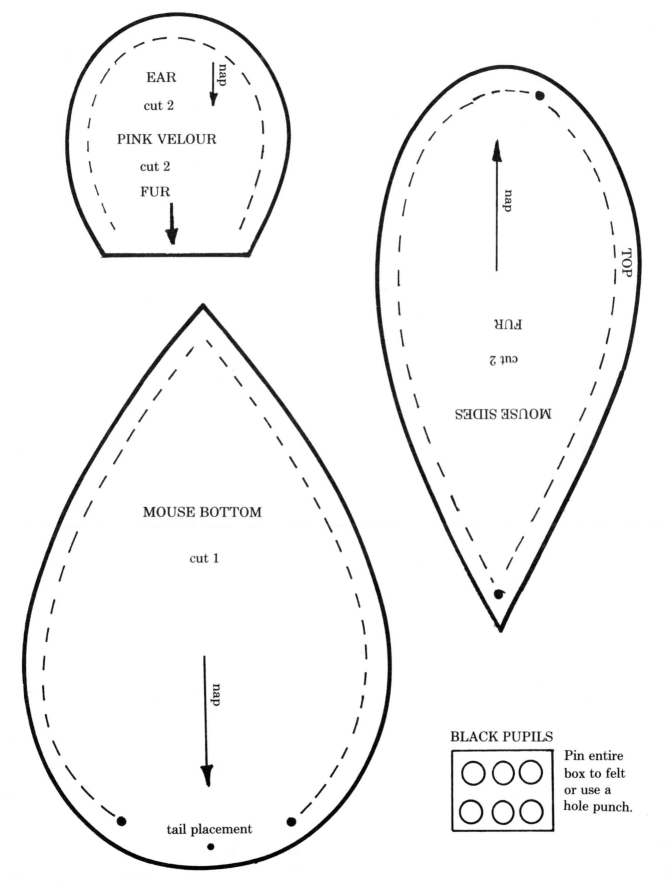

EAR

cut 2

PINK VELOUR

cut 2

FUR

nap

TOP

nap

FUR

cut 2

MOUSE SIDES

MOUSE BOTTOM

cut 1

nap

tail placement

BLACK PUPILS

Pin entire
box to felt
or use a
hole punch.

135

MICE WITH TOTE AND CHEESE

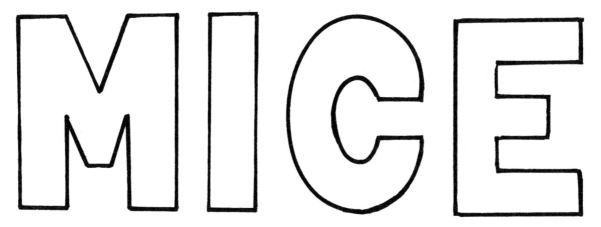

Cut one of each letter from calico and fabric fuser.

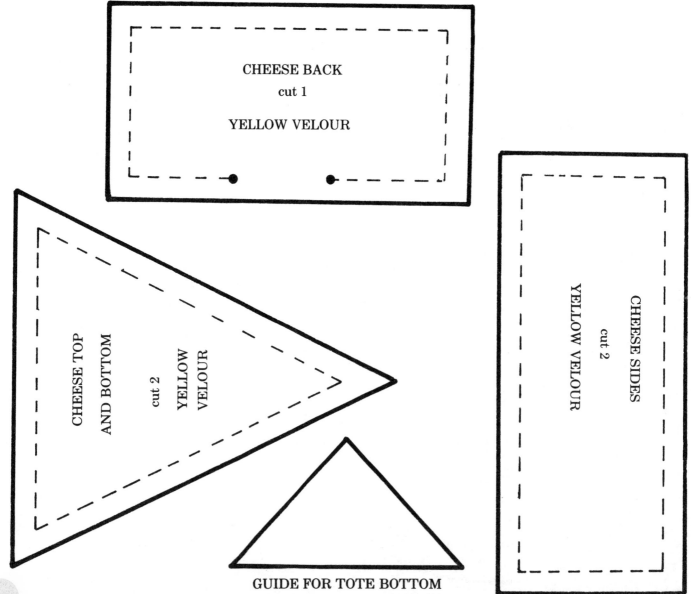

CHEESE BACK
cut 1
YELLOW VELOUR

CHEESE TOP
AND BOTTOM
cut 2
YELLOW VELOUR

CHEESE SIDES
cut 2
YELLOW VELOUR

GUIDE FOR TOTE BOTTOM

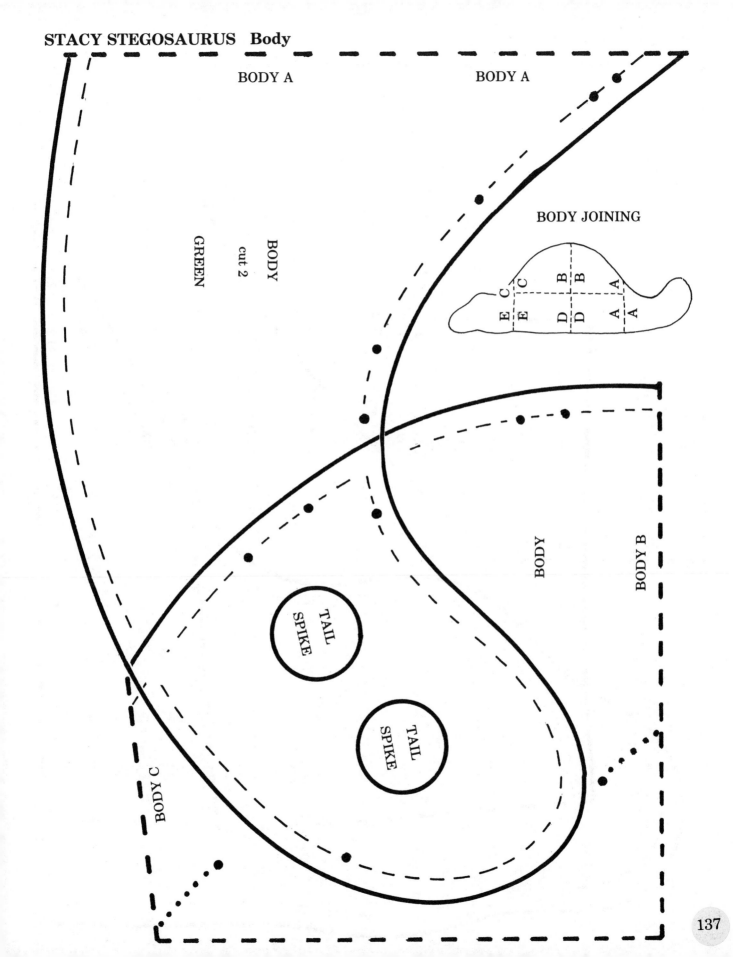

STACY STEGOSAURUS Body

BODY A

BODY A

BODY JOINING

GREEN

BODY

cut 2

BODY

BODY B

TAIL
SPIKE

TAIL
SPIKE

BODY C

137

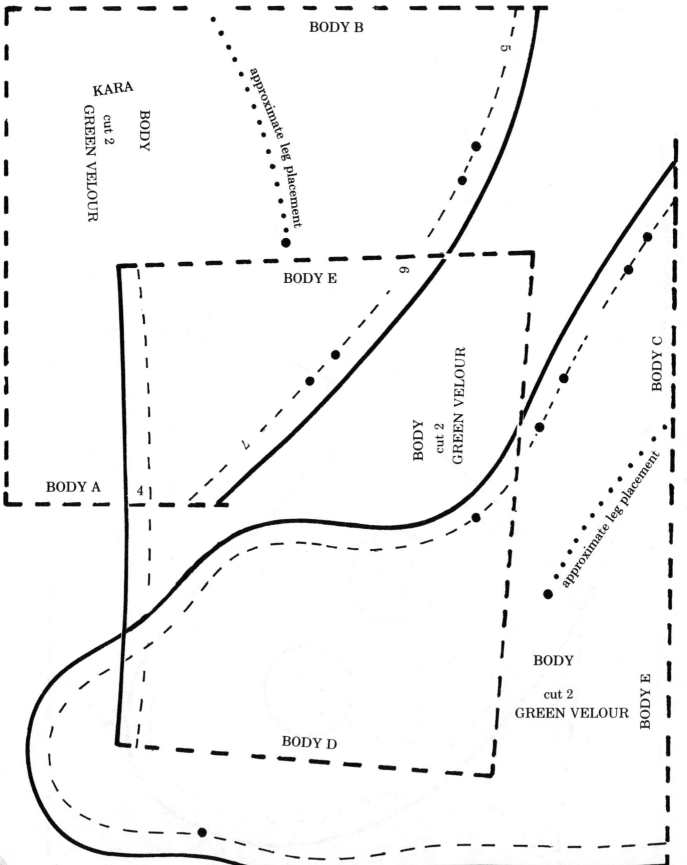

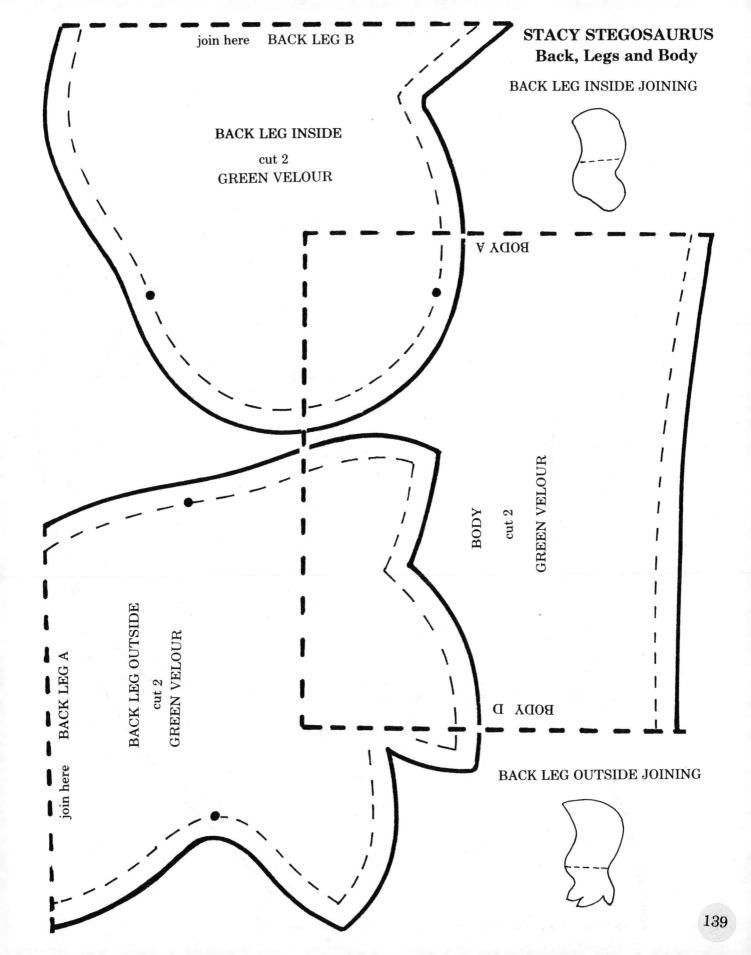

join here   BACK LEG B

STACY STEGOSAURUS
Back, Legs and Body

BACK LEG INSIDE JOINING

BACK LEG INSIDE

cut 2
GREEN VELOUR

BODY A

GREEN VELOUR

BODY

cut 2

GREEN VELOUR

BACK LEG A

BACK LEG OUTSIDE
cut 2
GREEN VELOUR

BODY D

join here

BACK LEG OUTSIDE JOINING

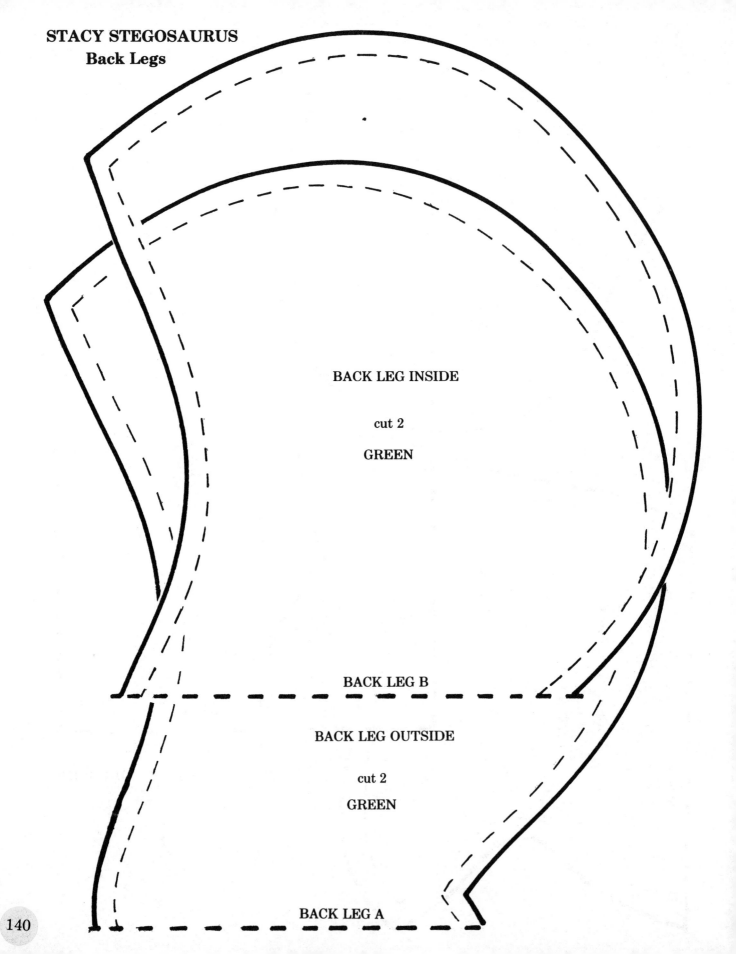

STACY STEGOSAURUS
Back Legs

BACK LEG INSIDE

cut 2

GREEN

BACK LEG B

BACK LEG OUTSIDE

cut 2

GREEN

BACK LEG A

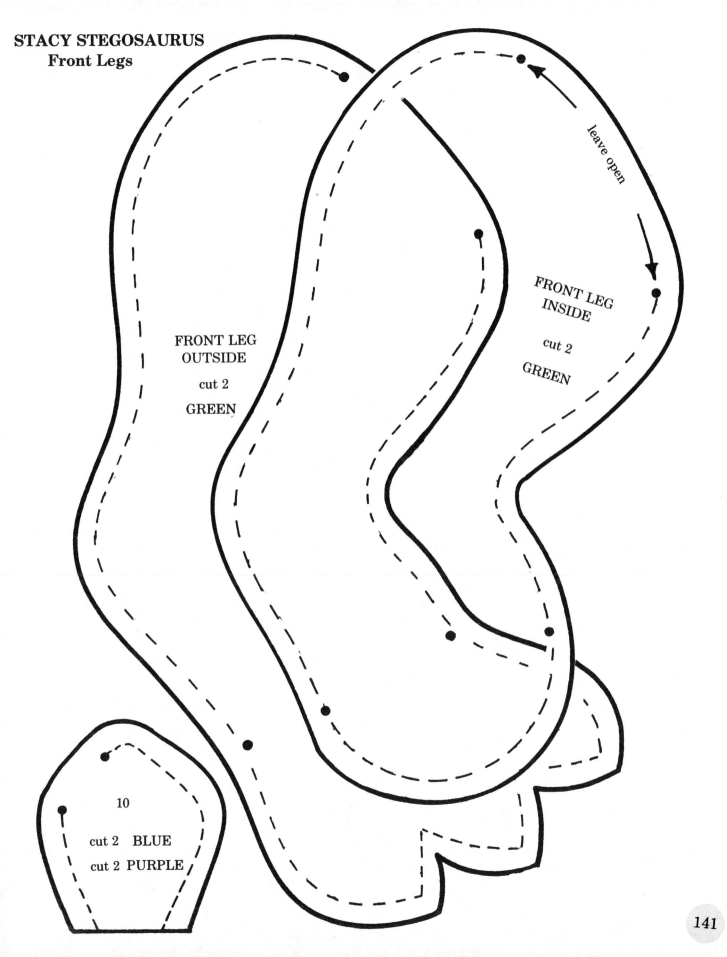

STACY STEGOSAURUS
Front Legs

leave open

FRONT LEG
INSIDE

cut 2

GREEN

FRONT LEG
OUTSIDE

cut 2

GREEN

10

cut 2   BLUE

cut 2   PURPLE

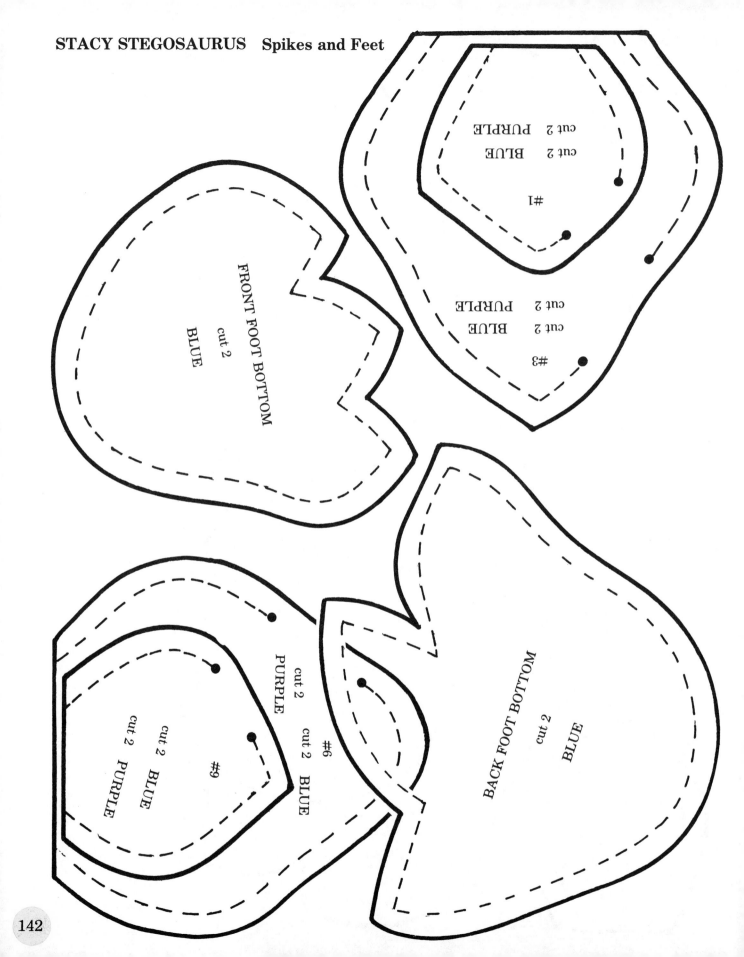

STACY STEGOSAURUS   **Spikes and Feet**

PURPLE
cut 2
BLUE
cut 2
#1

PURPLE
cut 2
BLUE
cut 2
#3

FRONT FOOT BOTTOM
cut 2
BLUE

PURPLE
cut 2
#9
BLUE
cut 2
#6
BLUE
cut 2
PURPLE

BACK FOOT BOTTOM
cut 2
BLUE

142

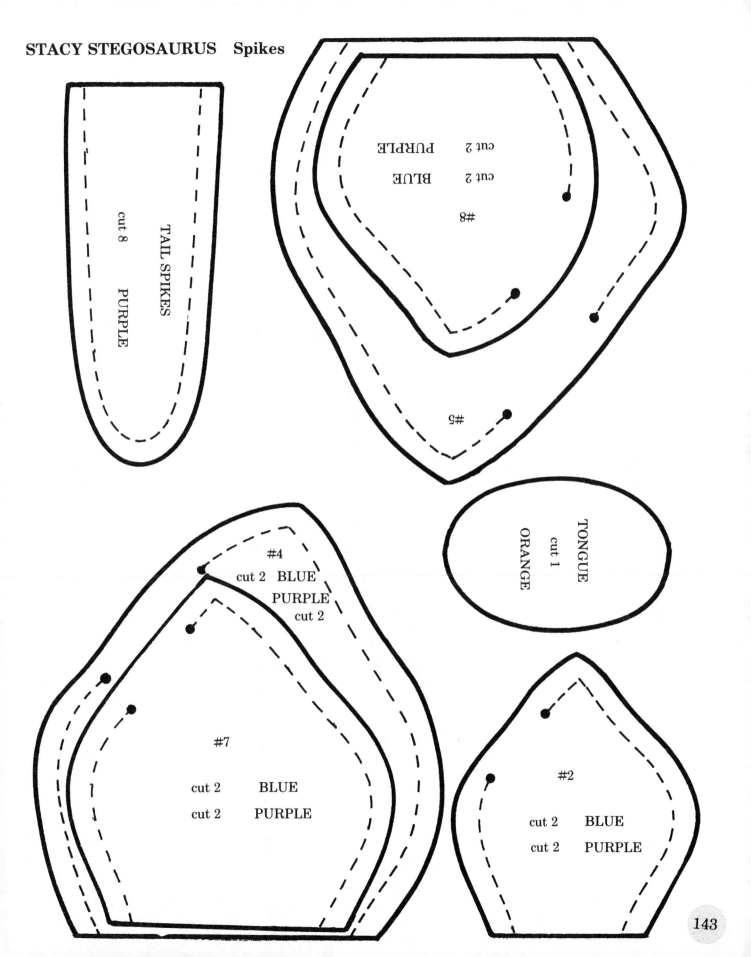

STACY STEGOSAURUS   Spikes

TAIL SPIKES

cut 8

PURPLE

#8

cut 2   BLUE

cut 2   PURPLE

#5

TONGUE
cut 1
ORANGE

#4
cut 2   BLUE
PURPLE
cut 2

#7

cut 2   BLUE
cut 2   PURPLE

#2

cut 2   BLUE
cut 2   PURPLE

STACY STEGOSAURUS, BOTTOM

FULL-SIZE PATTERN
JOINING BOTTOM

BOTTOM A   join here

BOTTOM A   join here

leave open

BOTTOM
cut 1
GREEN

BOTTOM
cut 1
GREEN

join here   BOTTOM B

join here   BOTTOM B

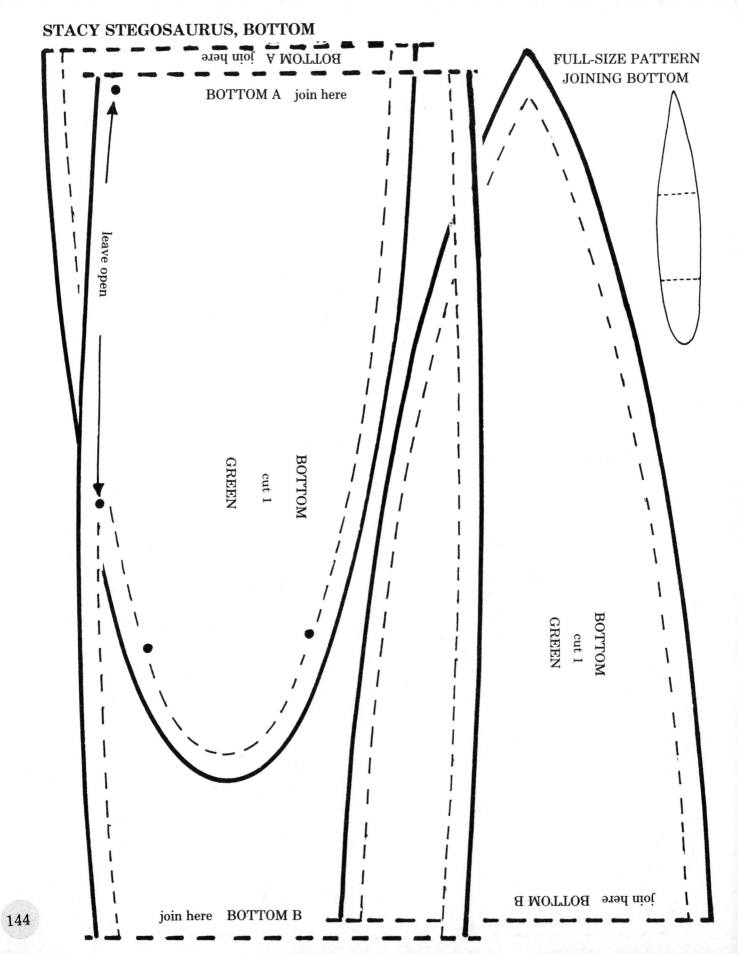

BIRD MOBILE OR CRIB STRING

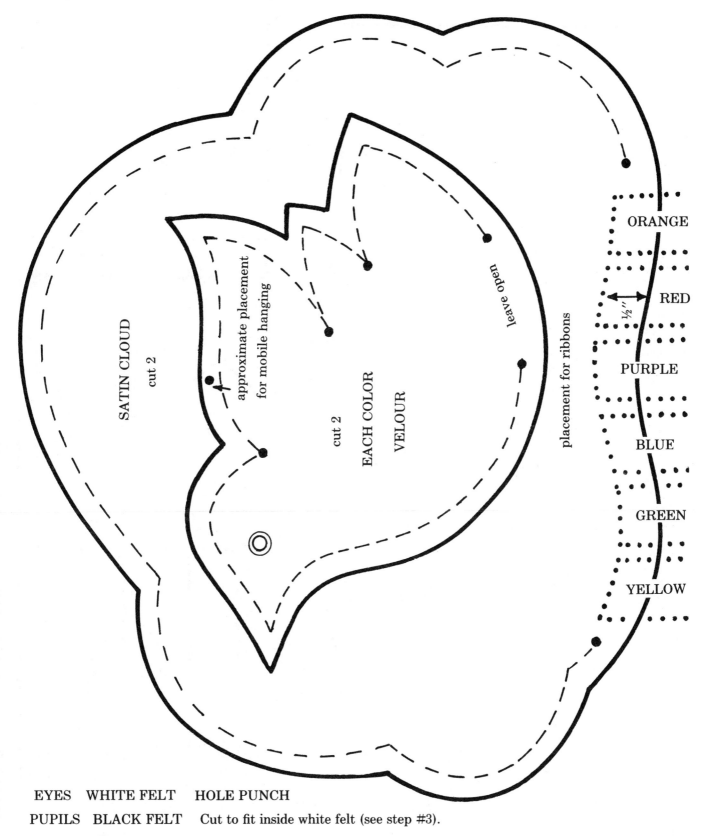

SATIN CLOUD

cut 2

approximate placement
for mobile hanging

cut 2

EACH COLOR

VELOUR

leave open

placement for ribbons

ORANGE

½"

RED

PURPLE

BLUE

GREEN

YELLOW

EYES   WHITE FELT   HOLE PUNCH

PUPILS   BLACK FELT   Cut to fit inside white felt (see step #3).

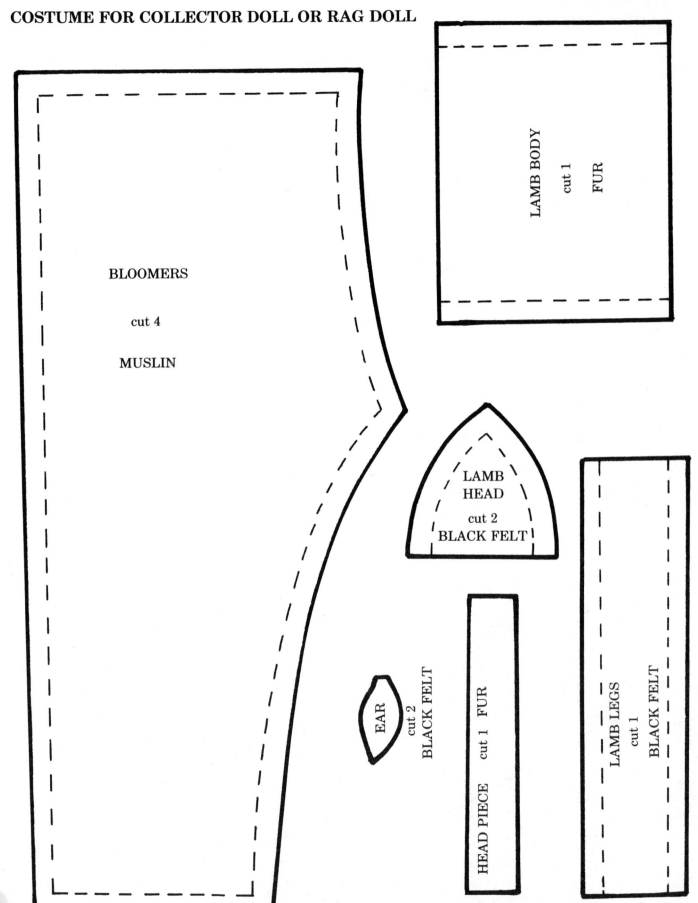

LAMB BODY

cut 1

FUR

BLOOMERS

cut 4

MUSLIN

LAMB
HEAD

cut 2
BLACK FELT

EAR

cut 2
BLACK FELT

HEAD PIECE   cut 1 FUR

LAMB LEGS

cut 1
BLACK FELT

COSTUME FOR COLLECTOR DOLL OR RAG DOLL

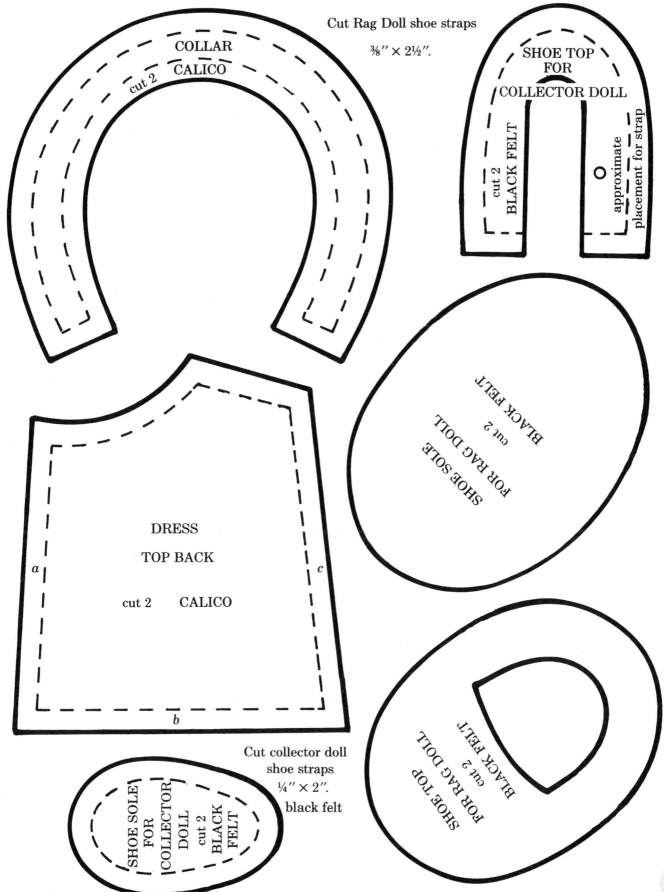

Cut Rag Doll shoe straps
⅜″ × 2½″.

COLLAR
CALICO
cut 2

SHOE TOP
FOR
COLLECTOR DOLL

cut 2
BLACK FELT

approximate placement for strap

DRESS
TOP BACK
cut 2   CALICO

a

c

b

SHOE SOLE
FOR RAG DOLL
cut 2
BLACK FELT

SHOE TOP
FOR RAG DOLL
cut 2
BLACK FELT

Cut collector doll
shoe straps
¼″ × 2″.
black felt

SHOE SOLE
FOR
COLLECTOR
DOLL
cut 2
BLACK
FELT

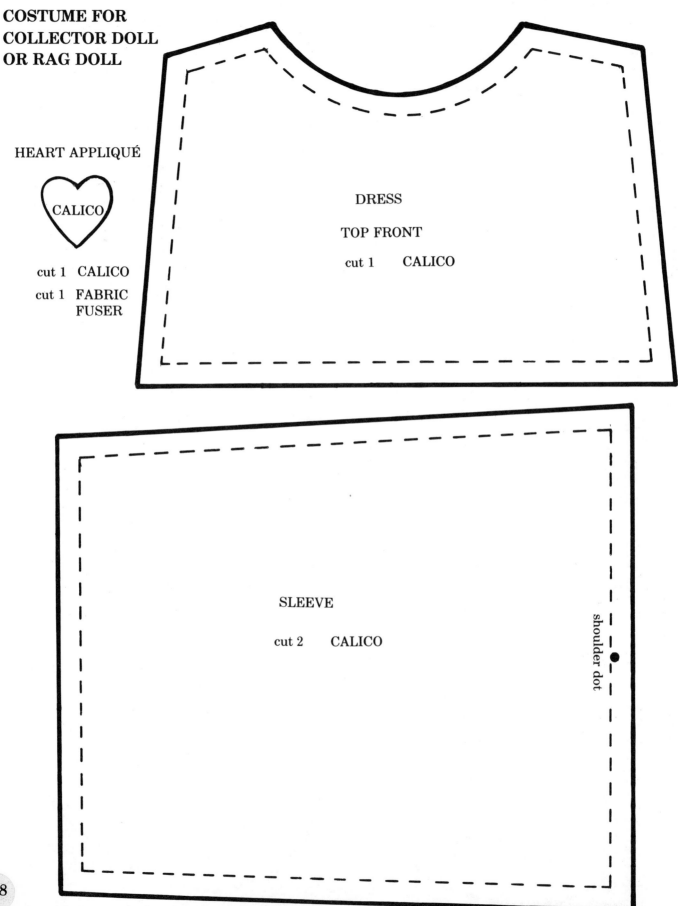

COSTUME FOR COLLECTOR DOLL OR RAG DOLL

HEART APPLIQUÉ

CALICO

cut 1   CALICO
cut 1   FABRIC FUSER

DRESS

TOP FRONT

cut 1   CALICO

SLEEVE

cut 2   CALICO

shoulder dot

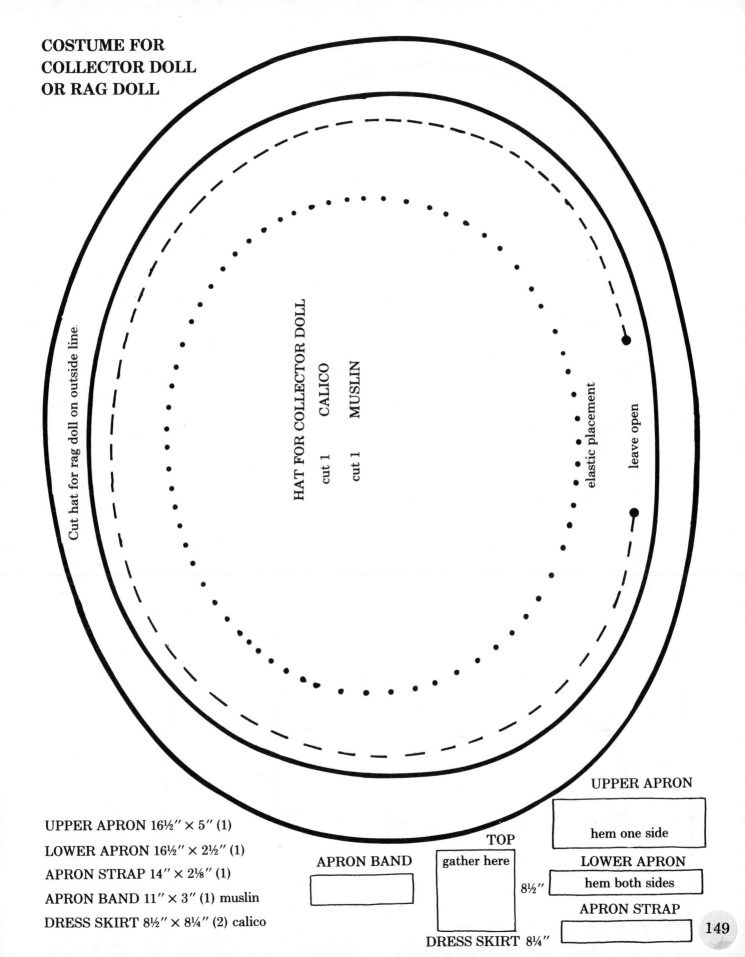

**COSTUME FOR
COLLECTOR DOLL
OR RAG DOLL**

Cut hat for rag doll on outside line.

HAT FOR COLLECTOR DOLL

cut 1   CALICO

cut 1   MUSLIN

elastic placement

leave open

UPPER APRON 16½″ × 5″ (1)

LOWER APRON 16½″ × 2½″ (1)

APRON STRAP 14″ × 2⅛″ (1)

APRON BAND 11″ × 3″ (1) muslin

DRESS SKIRT 8½″ × 8¼″ (2) calico

APRON BAND

TOP

gather here

8½″

DRESS SKIRT 8¼″

UPPER APRON

hem one side

LOWER APRON

hem both sides

APRON STRAP

149

CLOTH RAG DOLL

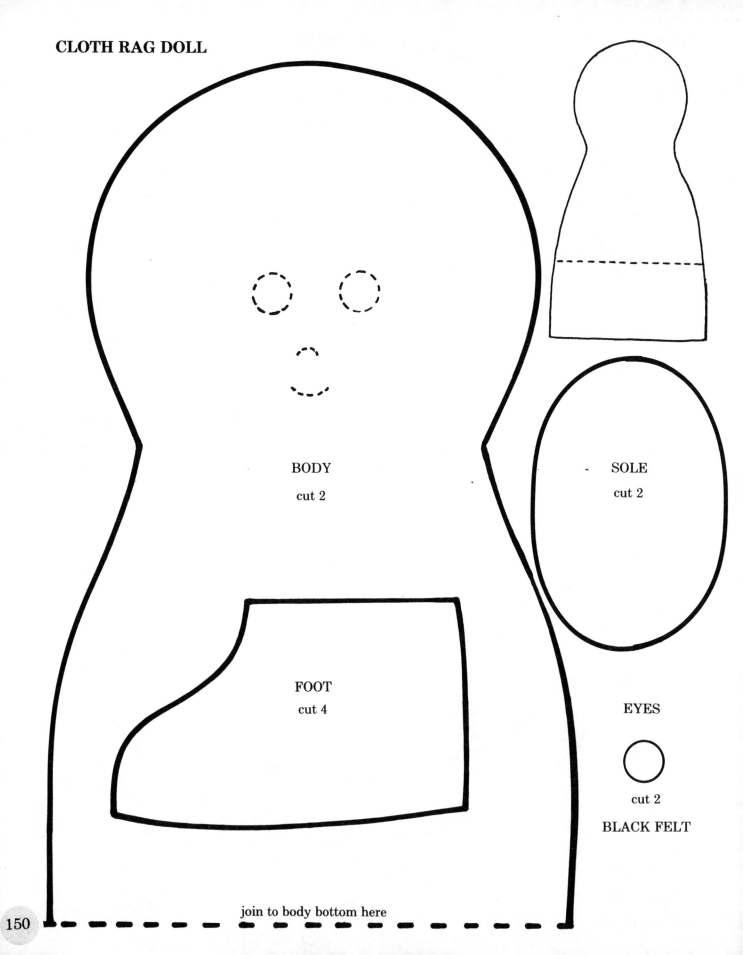

BODY

cut 2

SOLE

cut 2

FOOT

cut 4

EYES

cut 2

BLACK FELT

join to body bottom here

CLOTH RAG DOLL

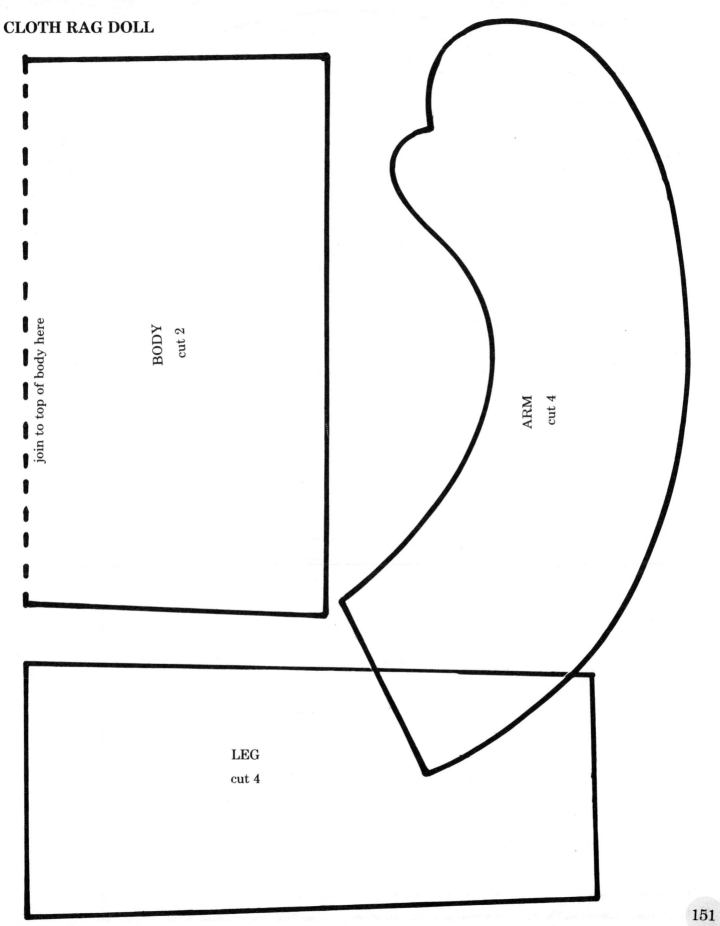

join to top of body here

BODY

cut 2

ARM

cut 4

LEG

cut 4

151

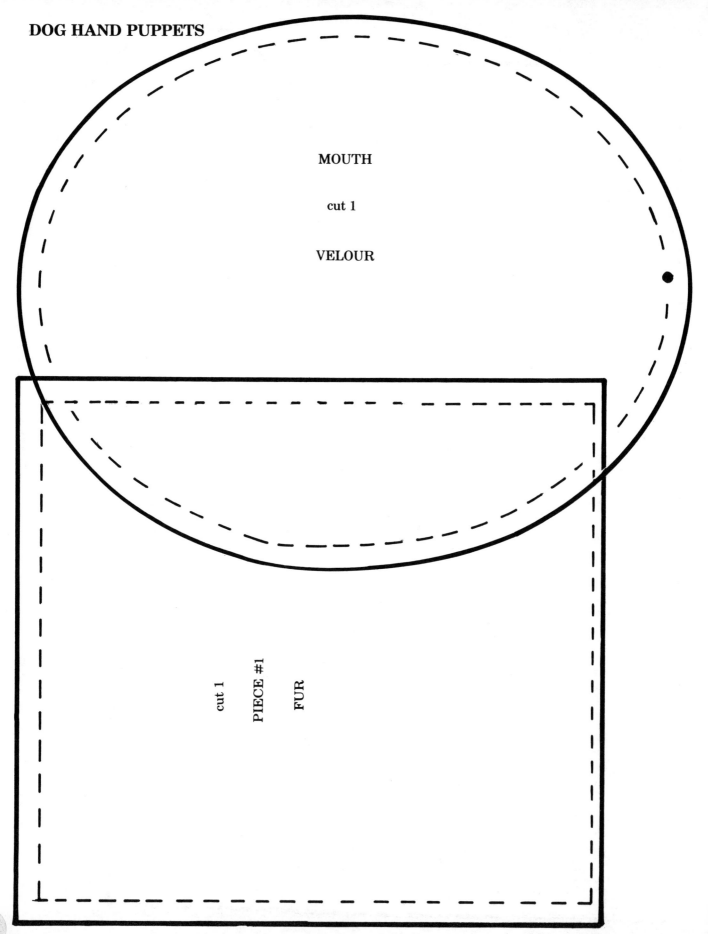

MOUTH

cut 1

VELOUR

cut 1

PIECE #1

FUR

DOG HAND PUPPETS

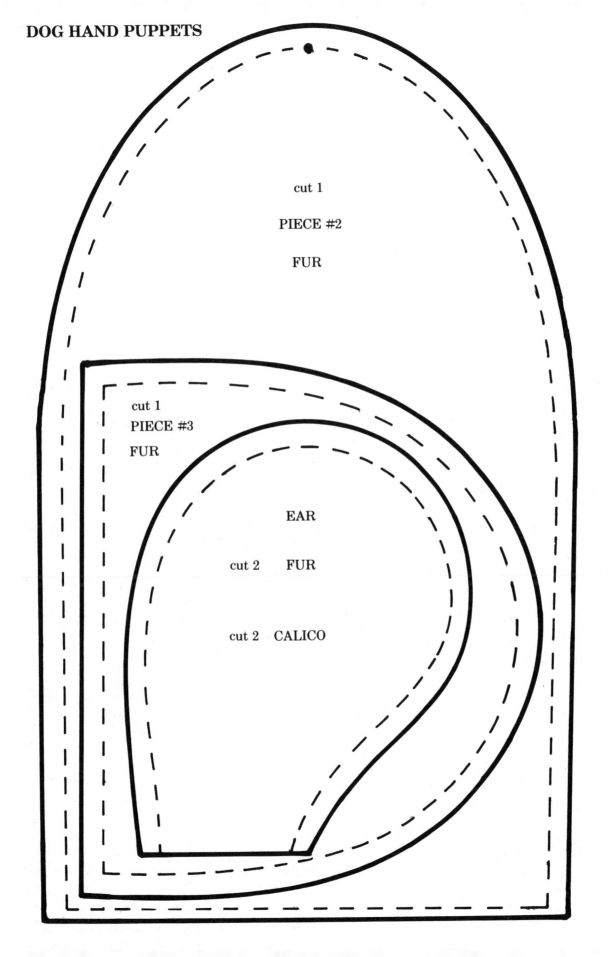

cut 1

PIECE #2

FUR

cut 1
PIECE #3
FUR

EAR

cut 2   FUR

cut 2   CALICO

153

FINGER PUPPETS

BASIC BODY PATTERN

Piggy

OUTER EYE
(2) WHITE

EAR
(2)

DARK PINK

PUNCH EYE

BLACK (2)

LIGHT PINK

NOSE
DARK PINK
(1)

(1) TAIL

MOUTH

(1) DARK ORANGE

BODY

LIGHT PINK

Kitty

BODY GRAY

EAR
(2) GRAY

TAIL (1)
GRAY

NOSE (1)

MOUTH

DARK BROWN

(1) RED

WHISKERS (6) BLACK

Duck

HEAD
FEATHER
LIGHT
ORANGE

(1)

(1)

HEAD
FEATHER

LIGHT
ORANGE

(1)

(1)

Attach top
to bottom
just on dotted
line so beak
can open.

WING (2)

BEAK
BOTTOM

BEAK
TOP
DARK
ORANGE

OUTER EYE
WHITE

PUNCH
EYE

(2)

(2) BLACK

LIGHT
ORANGE

BODY
YELLOW

Parrot

OUTER EYE

(1)

BEAK
(1)

YELLOW

DARK ORANGE

(1)

BLACK EYE

WING (1)
LIGHT ORANGE

BODY
DARK GREEN

FINGER PUPPETS

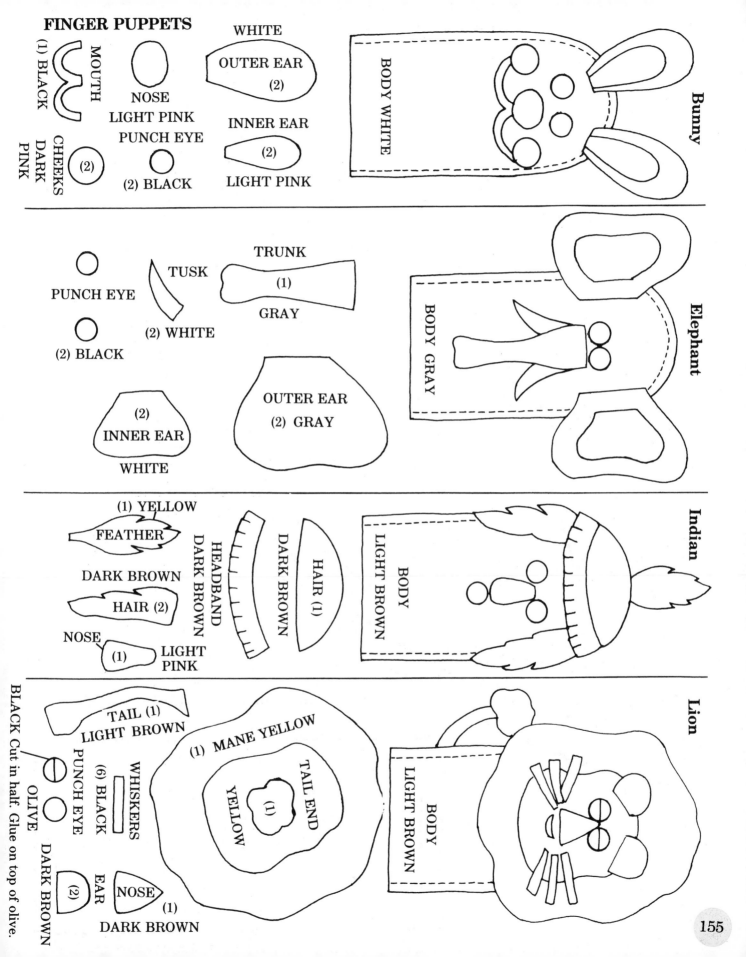

Bunny

MOUTH
(1) BLACK

CHEEKS
DARK
PINK
(2)

NOSE
LIGHT PINK

PUNCH EYE
(2) BLACK

WHITE
OUTER EAR
(2)

INNER EAR
(2)
LIGHT PINK

BODY WHITE

Elephant

PUNCH EYE

(2) BLACK

TUSK
(2) WHITE

TRUNK
(1)
GRAY

OUTER EAR
(2) GRAY

INNER EAR
(2)
WHITE

BODY GRAY

Indian

(1) YELLOW
FEATHER

DARK BROWN

HAIR (2)

NOSE
(1) LIGHT PINK

HEADBAND
DARK BROWN

DARK BROWN
HAIR (1)

BODY
LIGHT BROWN

Lion

TAIL (1)
LIGHT BROWN

PUNCH EYE
(6) BLACK

WHISKERS

OLIVE

DARK BROWN

EAR
(2)
DARK BROWN

NOSE
(1)

(1) MANE YELLOW

TAIL END
YELLOW
(1)

BODY
LIGHT BROWN

BLACK Cut in half. Glue on top of olive.

155

RAINBOW BALLS (SMALL, MEDIUM AND LARGE)

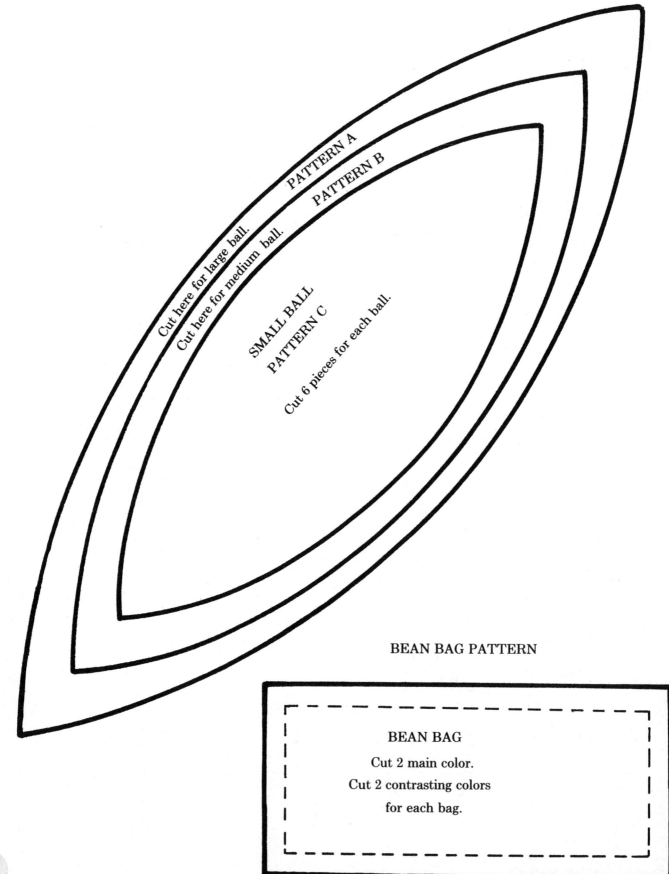

PATTERN A

PATTERN B

Cut here for large ball.

Cut here for medium ball.

SMALL BALL
PATTERN C

Cut 6 pieces for each ball.

BEAN BAG PATTERN

BEAN BAG

Cut 2 main color.

Cut 2 contrasting colors

for each bag.

RUPERT RABBIT PUPPET

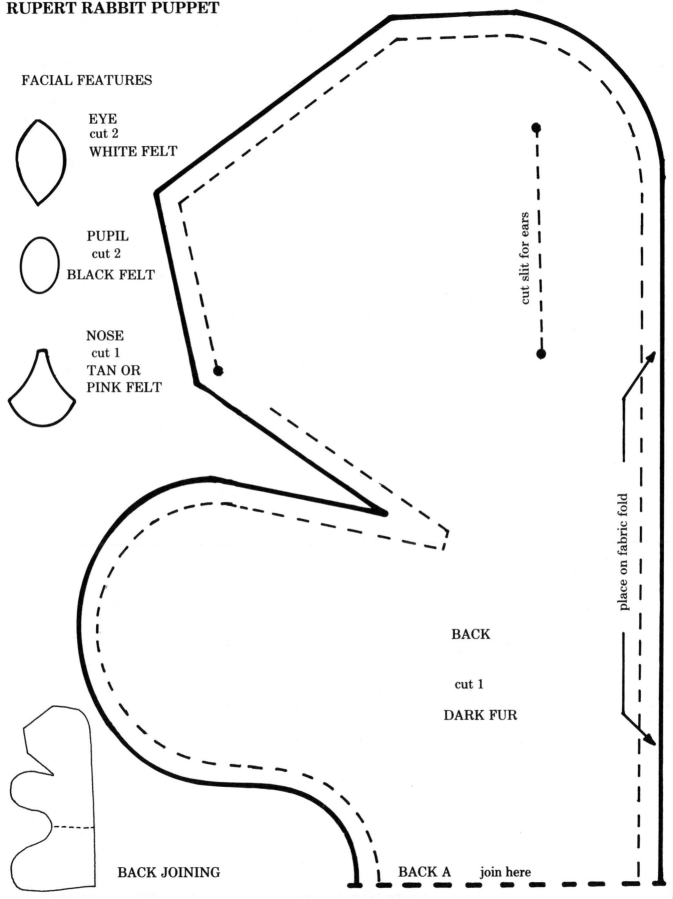

FACIAL FEATURES

EYE
cut 2
WHITE FELT

PUPIL
cut 2
BLACK FELT

NOSE
cut 1
TAN OR
PINK FELT

cut slit for ears

place on fabric fold

BACK

cut 1

DARK FUR

BACK JOINING

BACK A   join here

157

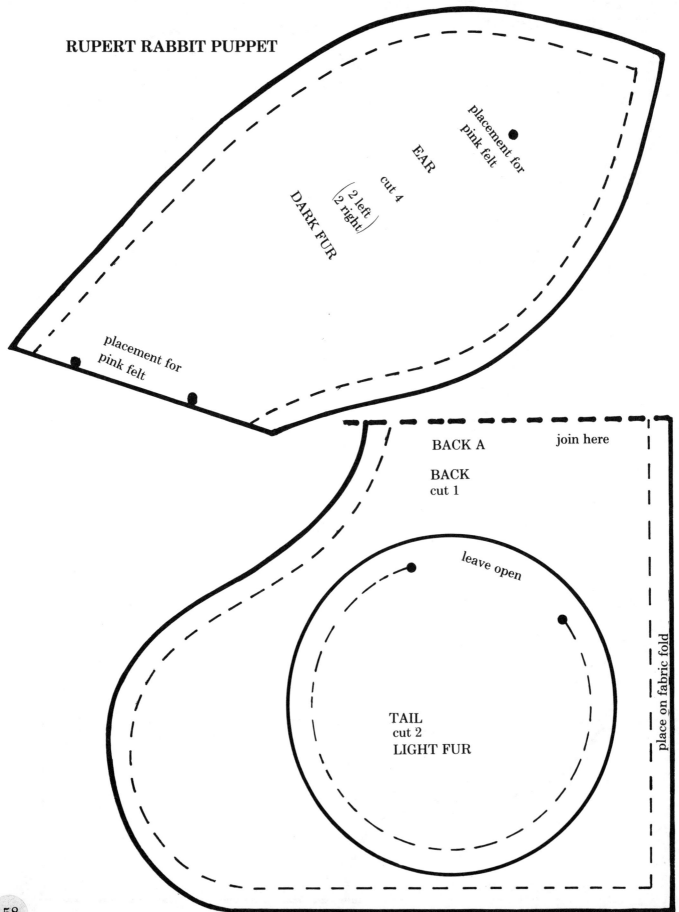

RUPERT RABBIT PUPPET

placement for
pink felt

EAR

cut 4

2 left
2 right

DARK FUR

placement for
pink felt

BACK A

join here

BACK
cut 1

leave open

TAIL
cut 2
LIGHT FUR

place on fabric fold

RUPERT RABBIT PUPPET

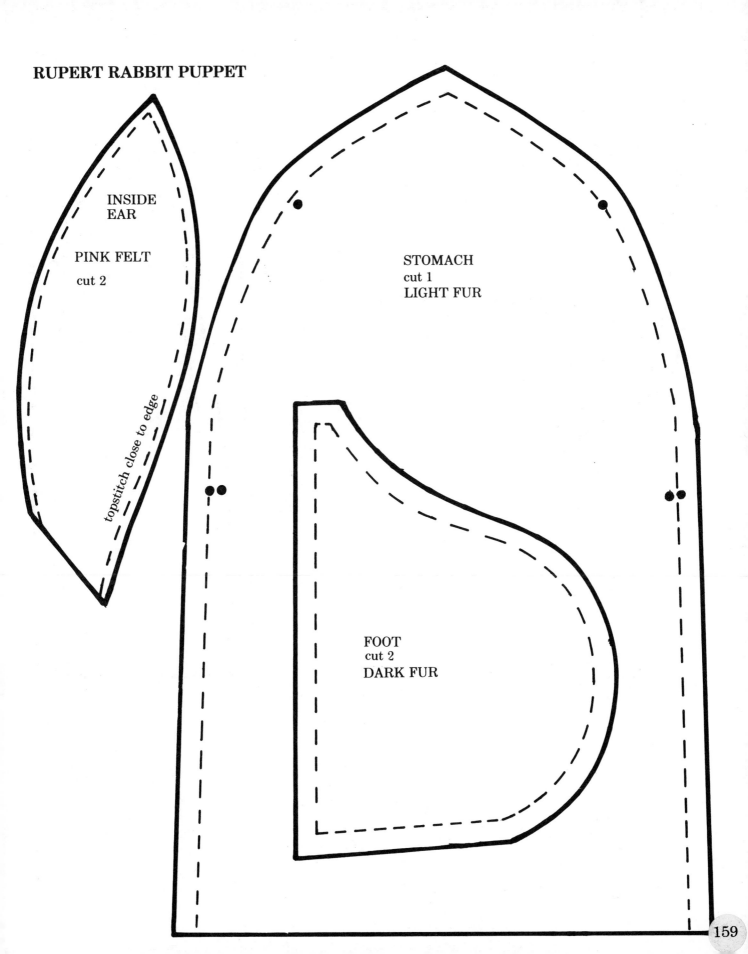

INSIDE
EAR

PINK FELT

cut 2

topstitch close to edge

STOMACH
cut 1
LIGHT FUR

FOOT
cut 2
DARK FUR

159

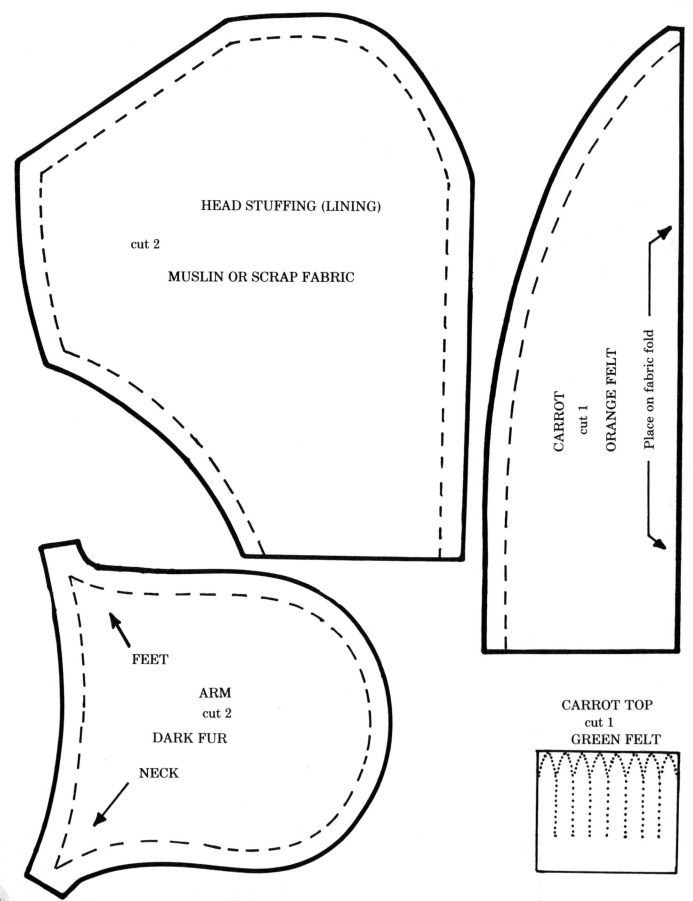

HEAD STUFFING (LINING)

cut 2

MUSLIN OR SCRAP FABRIC

CARROT

cut 1

ORANGE FELT

Place on fabric fold

FEET

ARM

cut 2

DARK FUR

NECK

CARROT TOP

cut 1

GREEN FELT

160

ANGEL ORNAMENTS

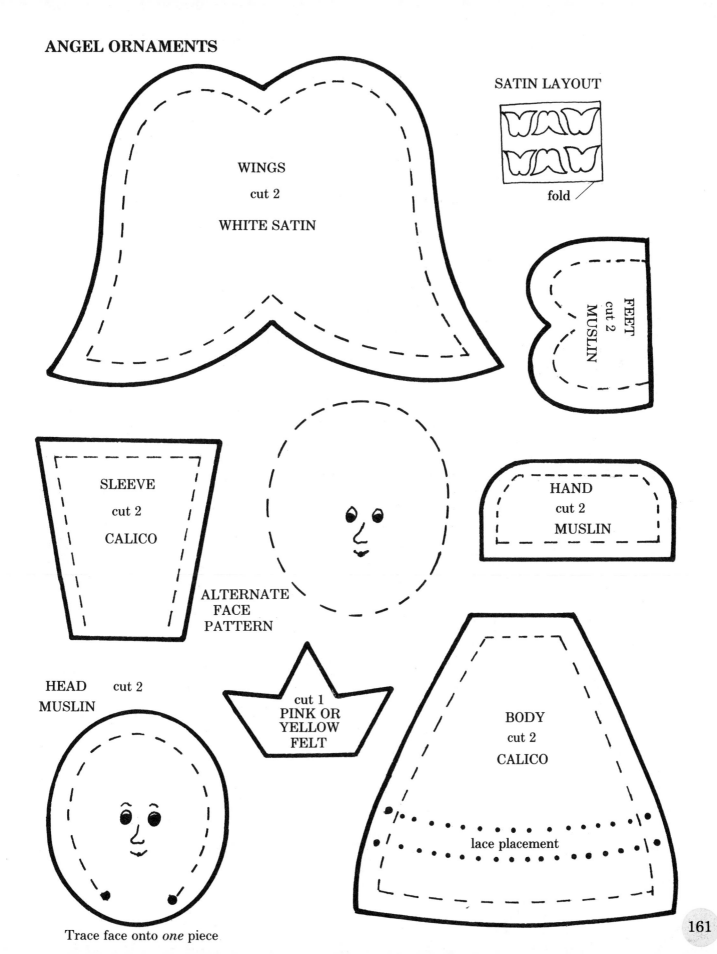

WINGS

cut 2

WHITE SATIN

SATIN LAYOUT

fold

FEET
cut 2
MUSLIN

SLEEVE

cut 2

CALICO

ALTERNATE
FACE
PATTERN

HAND
cut 2
MUSLIN

HEAD   cut 2

MUSLIN

cut 1
PINK OR
YELLOW
FELT

BODY
cut 2
CALICO

lace placement

Trace face onto *one* piece

161

BRAIDED WREATH

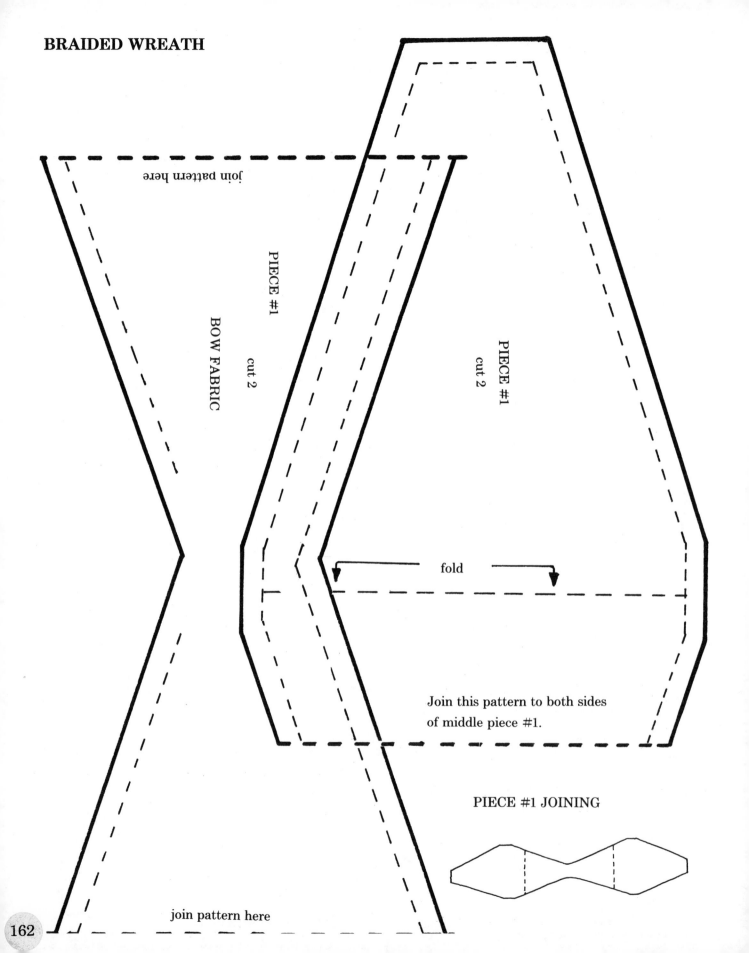

join pattern here

PIECE #1

BOW FABRIC

cut 2

PIECE #1

cut 2

fold

Join this pattern to both sides
of middle piece #1.

PIECE #1 JOINING

BRAIDED WREATH

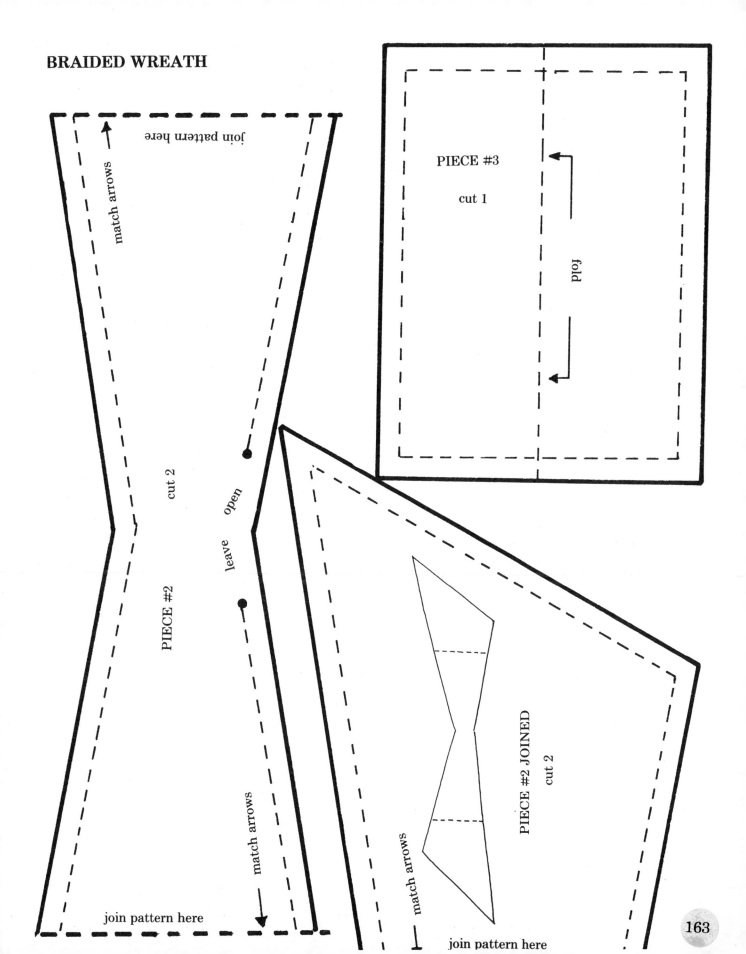

PIECE #3

cut 1

fold

join pattern here

match arrows

cut 2

PIECE #2

leave   open

match arrows

join pattern here

match arrows

PIECE #2 JOINED

cut 2

match arrows

join pattern here

163

Round Boxes (Large and Small)

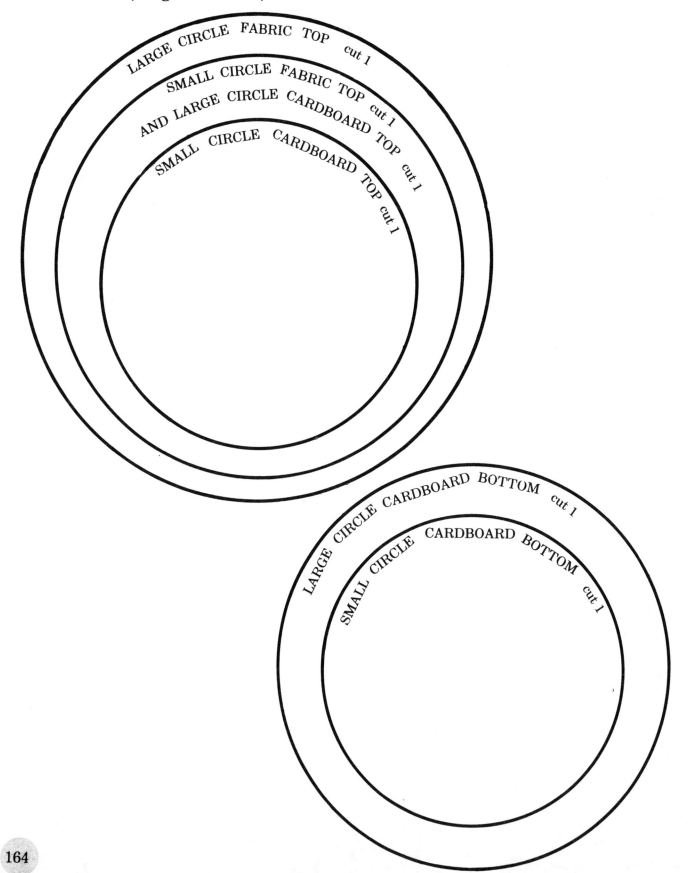

LARGE CIRCLE FABRIC TOP cut 1

SMALL CIRCLE FABRIC TOP cut 1

AND LARGE CIRCLE CARDBOARD TOP cut 1

SMALL CIRCLE CARDBOARD TOP cut 1

LARGE CIRCLE CARDBOARD BOTTOM cut 1

SMALL CIRCLE CARDBOARD BOTTOM cut 1

Oval Boxes (Large and Small)

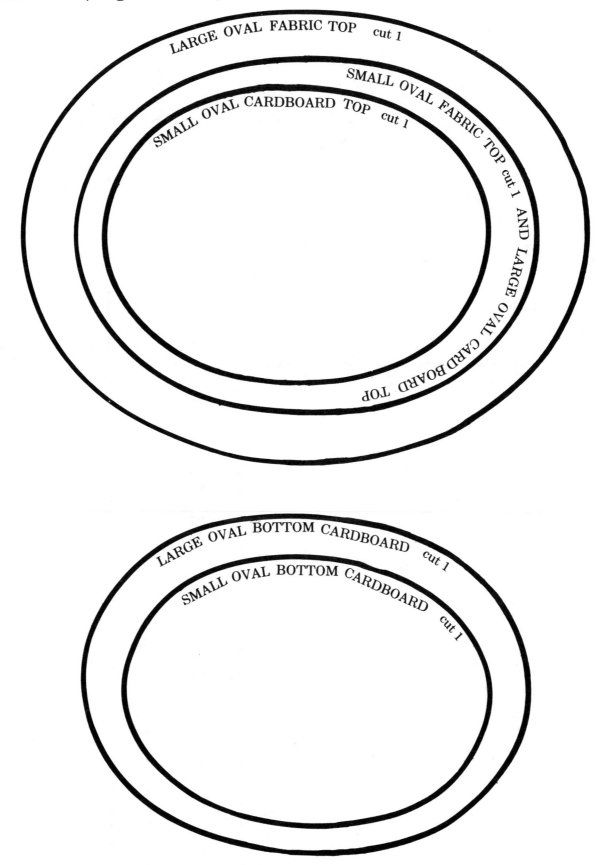

LARGE OVAL FABRIC TOP   cut 1

SMALL OVAL FABRIC TOP cut 1 AND LARGE OVAL CARDBOARD TOP

SMALL OVAL CARDBOARD TOP   cut 1

LARGE OVAL BOTTOM CARDBOARD   cut 1

SMALL OVAL BOTTOM CARDBOARD   cut 1

LAMB ORNAMENTS OR TOYS

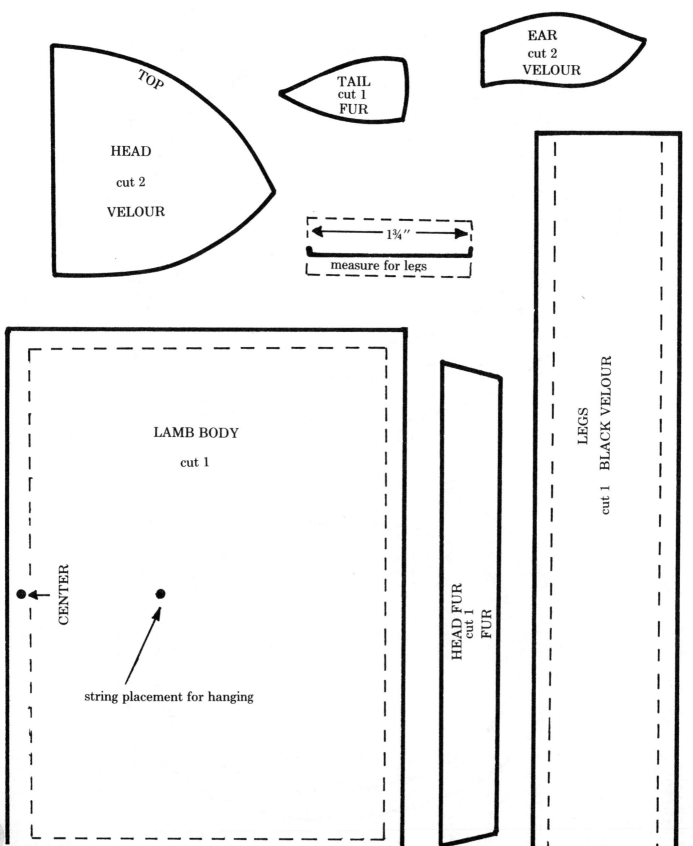

TOP

HEAD

cut 2

VELOUR

TAIL
cut 1
FUR

EAR
cut 2
VELOUR

←— 1¾″ —→

measure for legs

LAMB BODY

cut 1

CENTER

string placement for hanging

HEAD FUR
cut 1
FUR

LEGS

cut 1 BLACK VELOUR

PATCHWORK POTHOLDERS

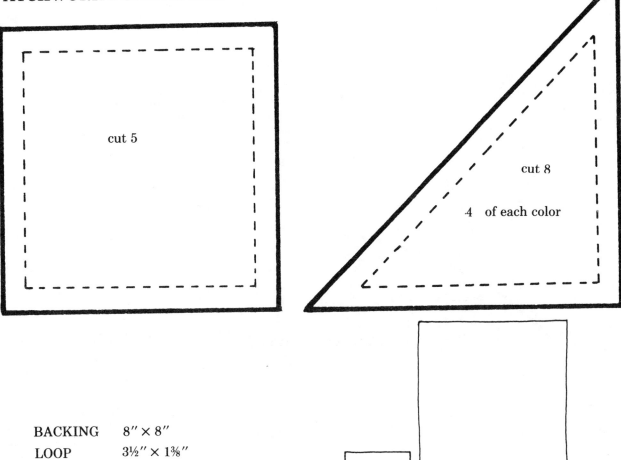

cut 5

cut 8

4 of each color

BACKING   8″ × 8″
LOOP   3½″ × 1⅜″

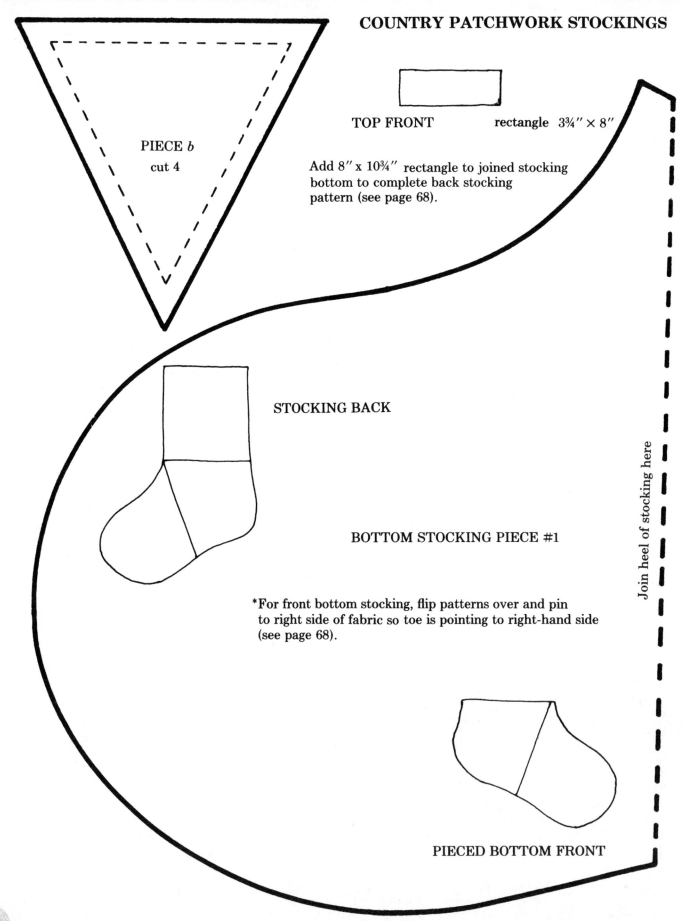

COUNTRY PATCHWORK STOCKINGS

PIECE *b*
cut 4

TOP FRONT   rectangle 3¾" × 8"

Add 8" x 10¾" rectangle to joined stocking bottom to complete back stocking pattern (see page 68).

STOCKING BACK

BOTTOM STOCKING PIECE #1

*For front bottom stocking, flip patterns over and pin to right side of fabric so toe is pointing to right-hand side (see page 68).

Join heel of stocking here

PIECED BOTTOM FRONT

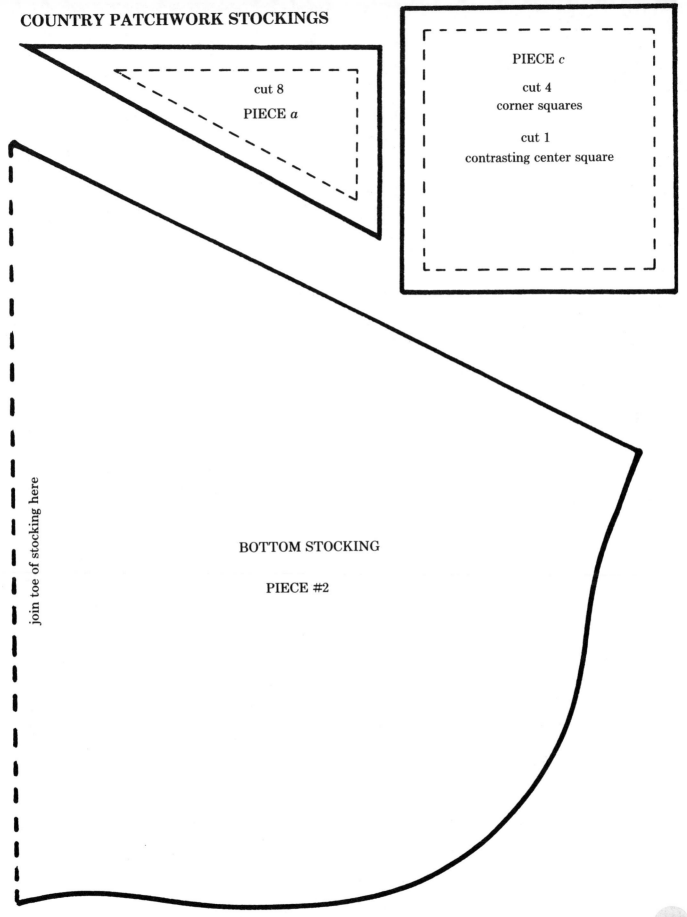

COUNTRY PATCHWORK STOCKINGS

cut 8
PIECE *a*

PIECE *c*

cut 4
corner squares

cut 1
contrasting center square

join toe of stocking here

BOTTOM STOCKING

PIECE #2

BABY STRIPED STOCKINGS

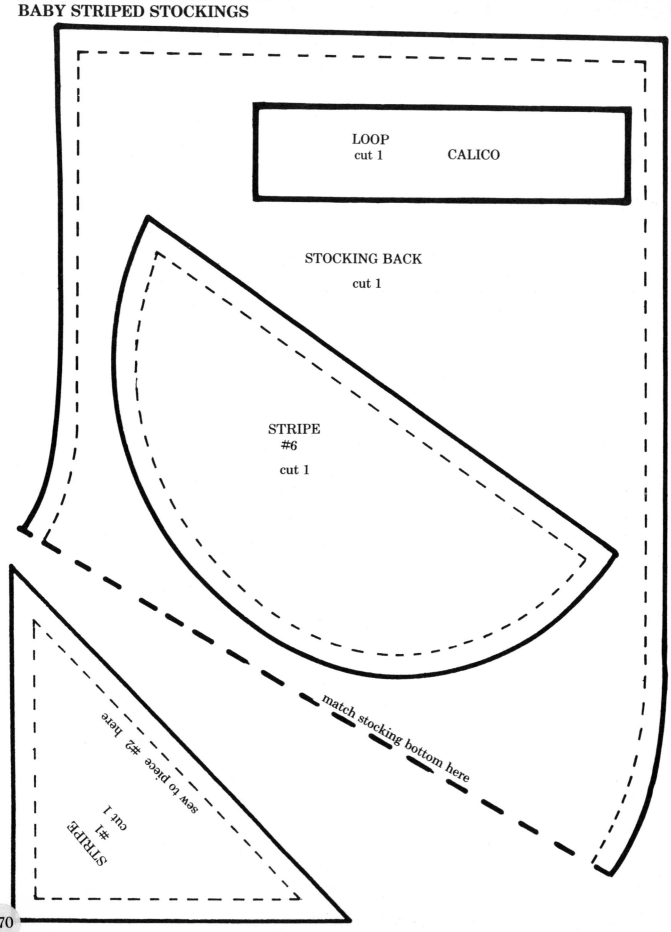

LOOP
cut 1   CALICO

STOCKING BACK

cut 1

STRIPE
#6

cut 1

match stocking bottom here

sew to piece #2 here

STRIPE
#1
cut 1

BABY STRIPED STOCKINGS

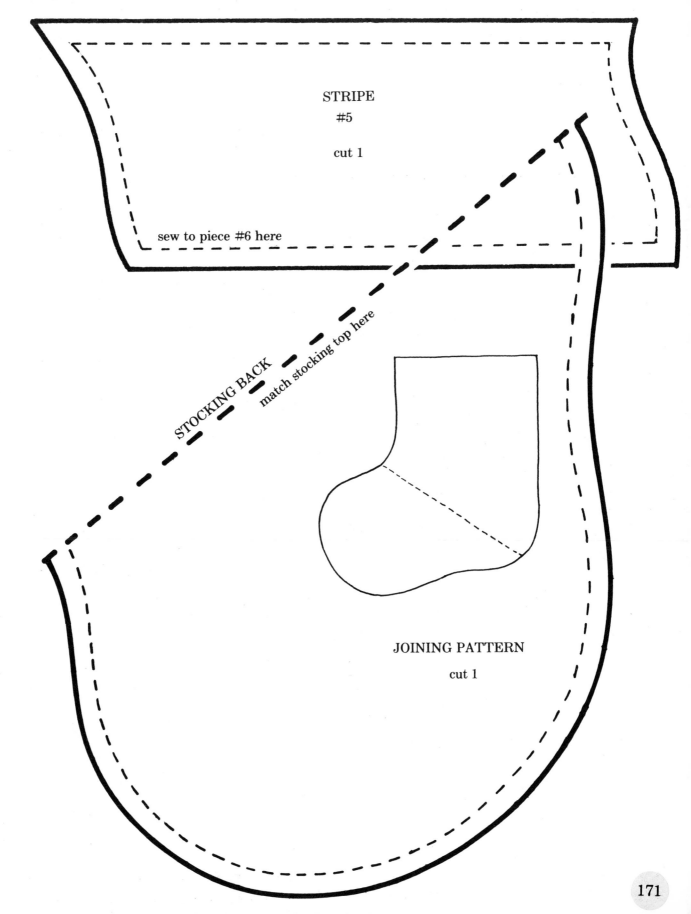

STRIPE
#5

cut 1

sew to piece #6 here

STOCKING BACK

match stocking top here

JOINING PATTERN

cut 1

BABY STRIPED STOCKINGS

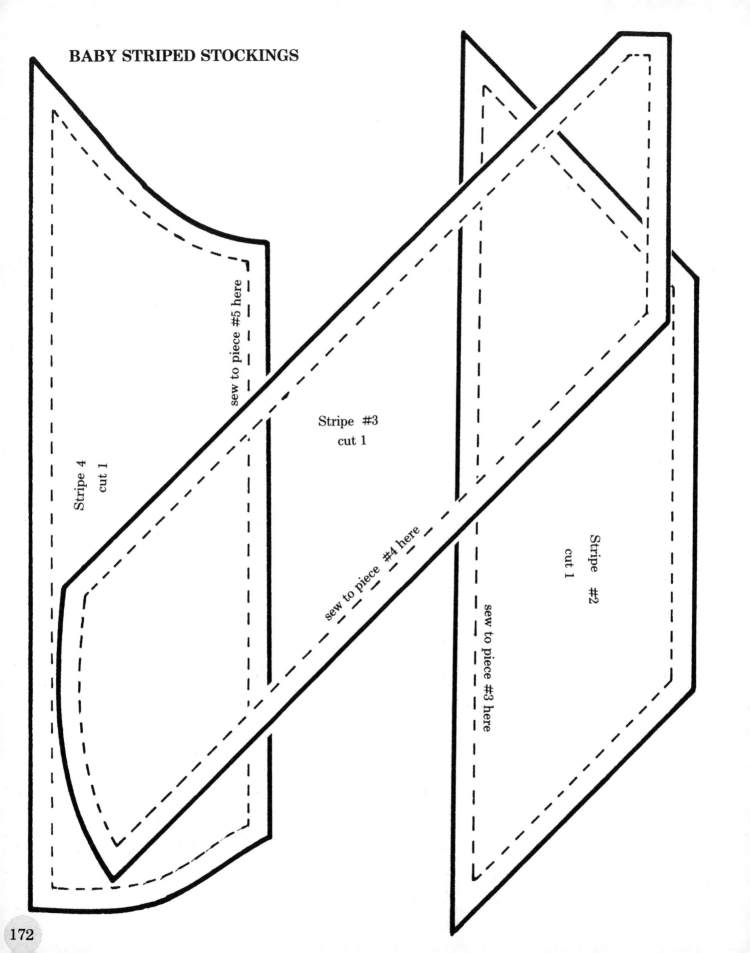

sew to piece #5 here

Stripe 4
cut 1

Stripe #3
cut 1

sew to piece #4 here

Stripe #2
cut 1

sew to piece #3 here

172

WALNUT MICE

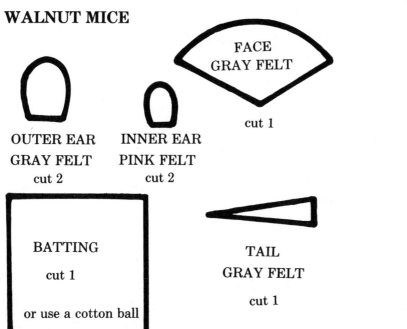

OUTER EAR
GRAY FELT
cut 2

INNER EAR
PINK FELT
cut 2

FACE
GRAY FELT
cut 1

BATTING

cut 1

or use a cotton ball

TAIL
GRAY FELT

cut 1

CALICO COVERLET

cut 1

BABY BIBS

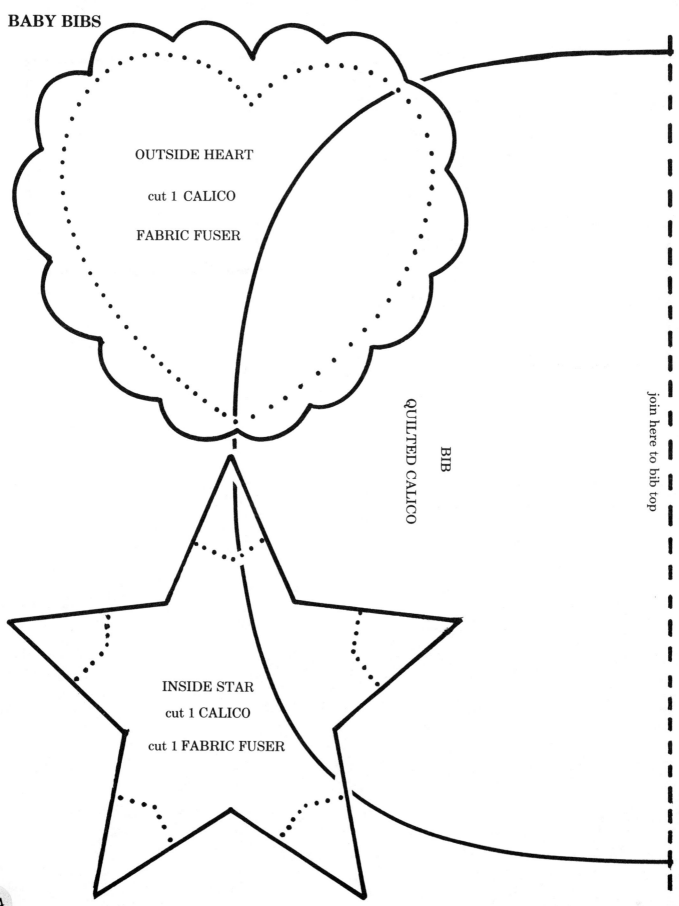

OUTSIDE HEART

cut 1 CALICO

FABRIC FUSER

BIB

QUILTED CALICO

join here to bib top

INSIDE STAR

cut 1 CALICO

cut 1 FABRIC FUSER

BABY BIBS

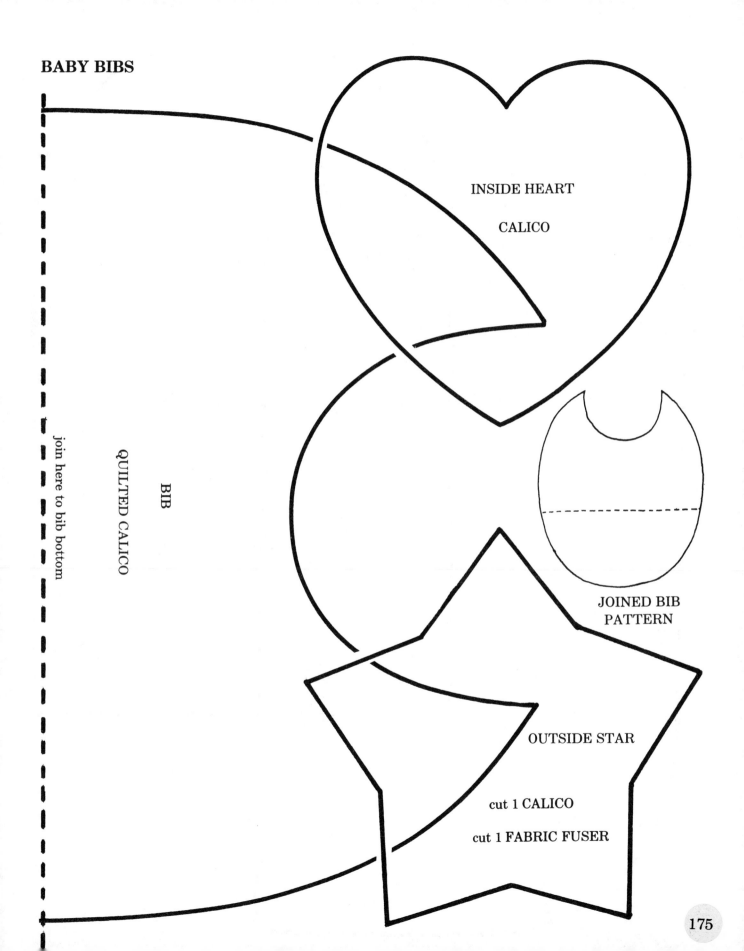

INSIDE HEART

CALICO

join here to bib bottom

QUILTED CALICO

BIB

JOINED BIB
PATTERN

OUTSIDE STAR

cut 1 CALICO

cut 1 FABRIC FUSER

CHILD'S KNAPSACK

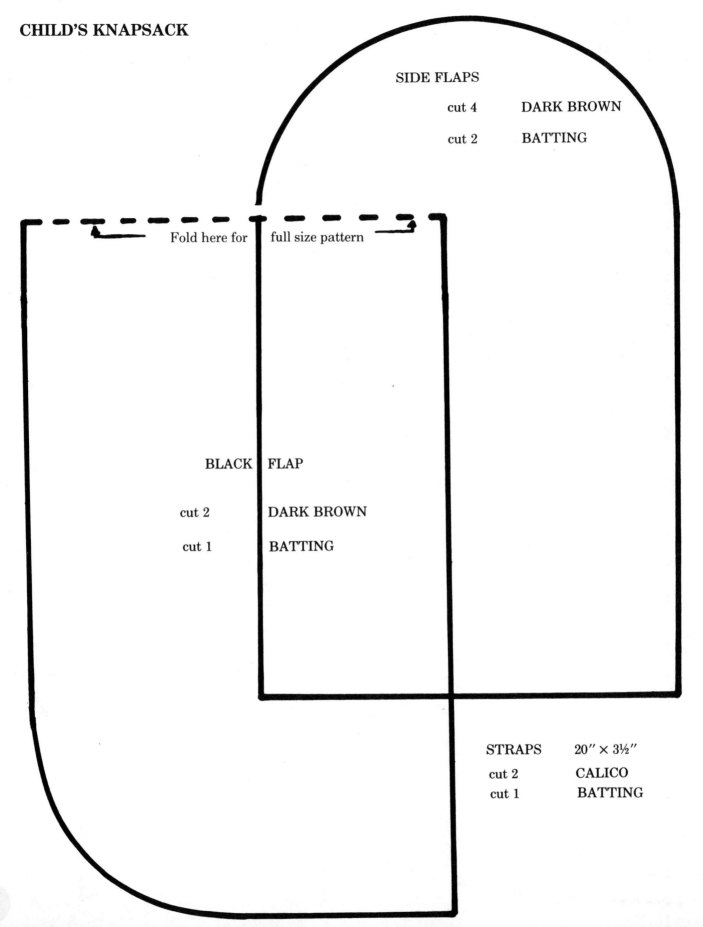

SIDE FLAPS

cut 4   DARK BROWN

cut 2   BATTING

Fold here for | full size pattern

BLACK | FLAP

cut 2   DARK BROWN

cut 1   BATTING

STRAPS   20″ × 3½″

cut 2   CALICO

cut 1   BATTING

TRAIN AND HEART SMOCKS

POCKET

3¾″ × 16¾″

see instructions

JOINING DRAWING

STRAPS (2) 18″ × 2½″

(2) 16″ × 2½″

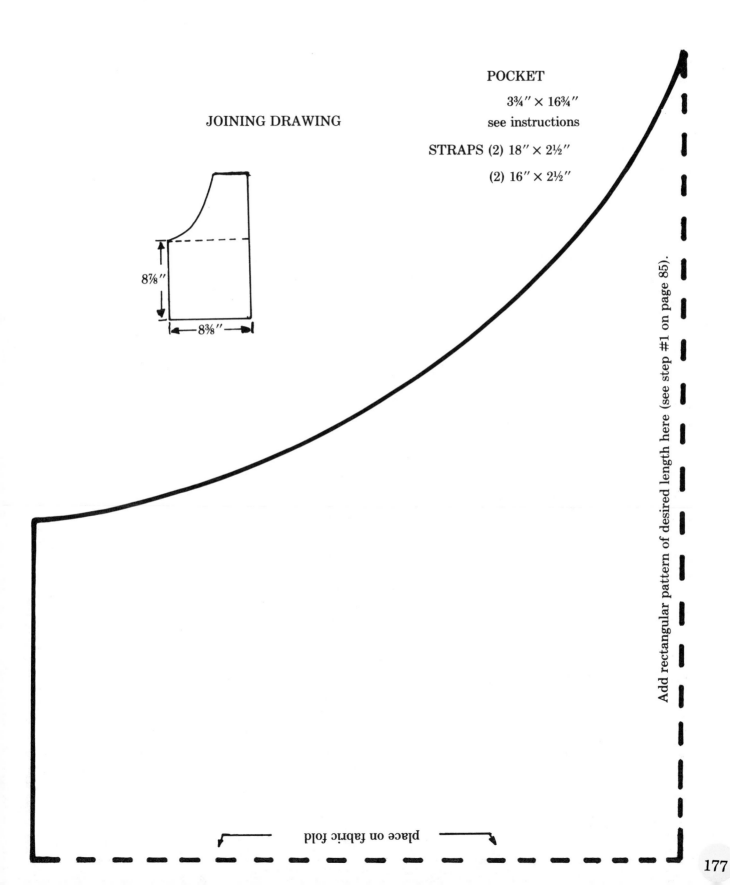

8⅞″

8⅜″

Add rectangular pattern of desired length here (see step #1 on page 85).

place on fabric fold

TRAIN FOR SMOCK APPLIQUÉ

YELLOW
#5

GRAY
#12

RUST
#11

WHITE
#1

MEDIUM BLUE
#3

GRAY
#9

#13
YELLOW

PURPLE
cut 2
#8

YELLOW
#10

LIGHT BLUE
#2

MEDIUM BLUE
#4

GREEN
#7

YELLOW
#6

Heart Appliqué

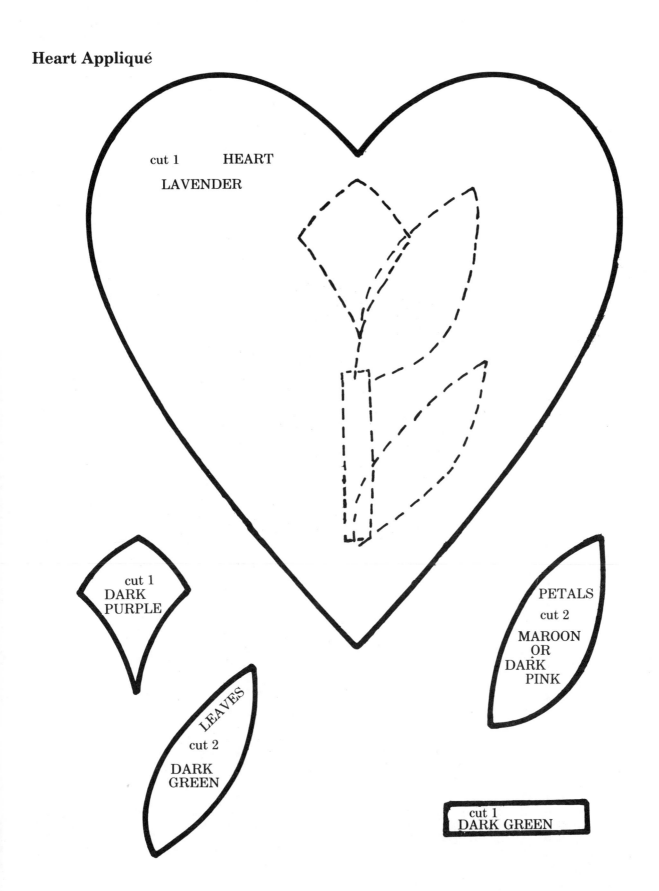

cut 1   HEART

LAVENDER

cut 1
DARK
PURPLE

PETALS

cut 2

MAROON
OR
DARK
PINK

LEAVES

cut 2

DARK
GREEN

cut 1
DARK GREEN

HEART PATCH TOTE

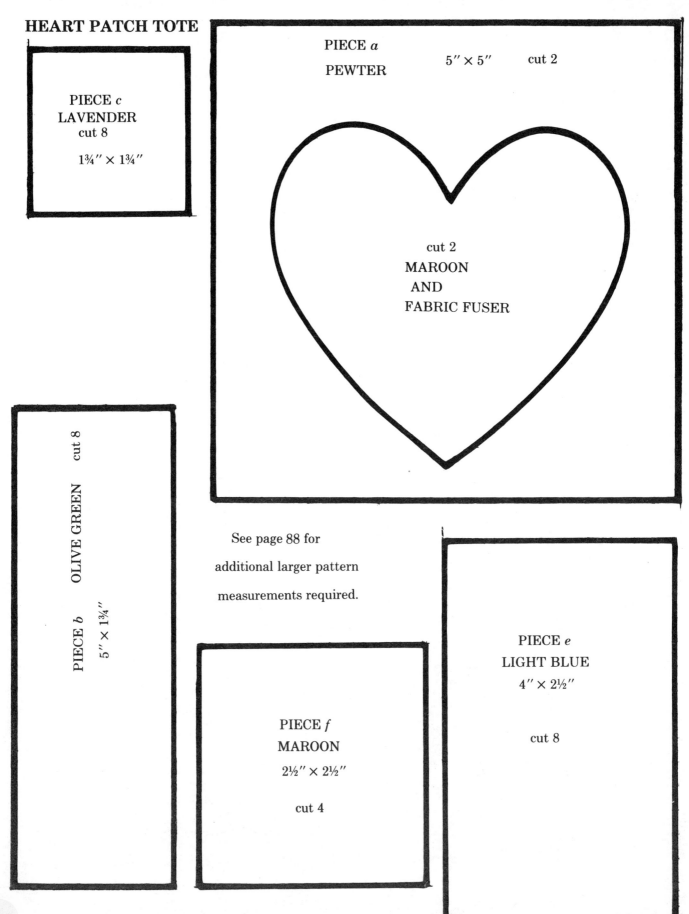

PIECE *c*
LAVENDER
cut 8

1¾″ × 1¾″

PIECE *a*

PEWTER 5″ × 5″ cut 2

cut 2
MAROON
AND
FABRIC FUSER

PIECE *b* OLIVE GREEN cut 8

5″ × 1¾″

See page 88 for

additional larger pattern

measurements required.

PIECE *e*
LIGHT BLUE
4″ × 2½″

cut 8

PIECE *f*
MAROON

2½″ × 2½″

cut 4

180

HEART QUILT AND SLEEPING BAG APPLIQUÉ

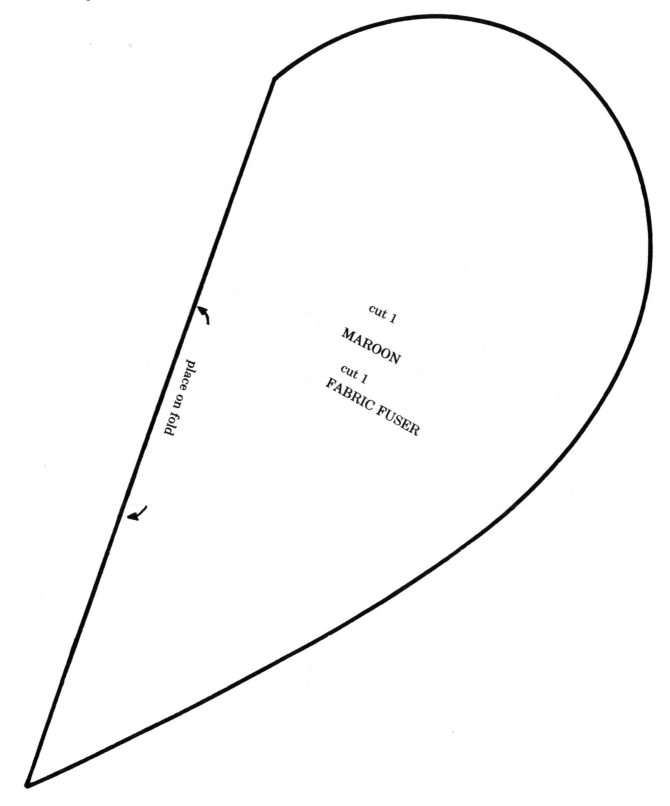

cut 1

MAROON

cut 1
FABRIC FUSER

place on fold

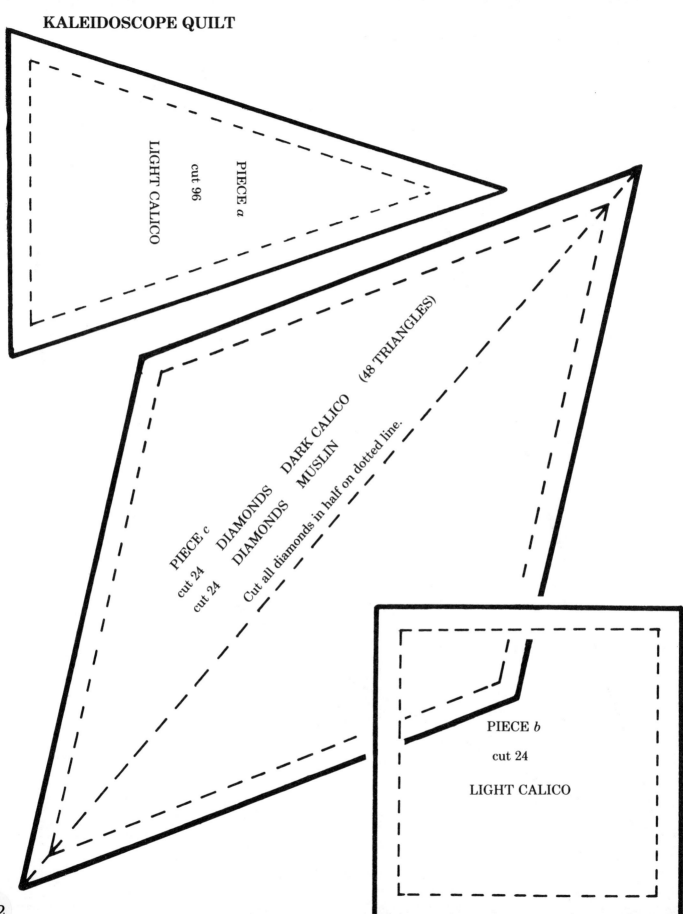

LIGHT CALICO

PIECE *a*

cut 96

PIECE *c*   DIAMONDS   DARK CALICO   (48 TRIANGLES)

cut 24   DIAMONDS   MUSLIN

cut 24   Cut all diamonds in half on dotted line.

PIECE *b*

cut 24

LIGHT CALICO

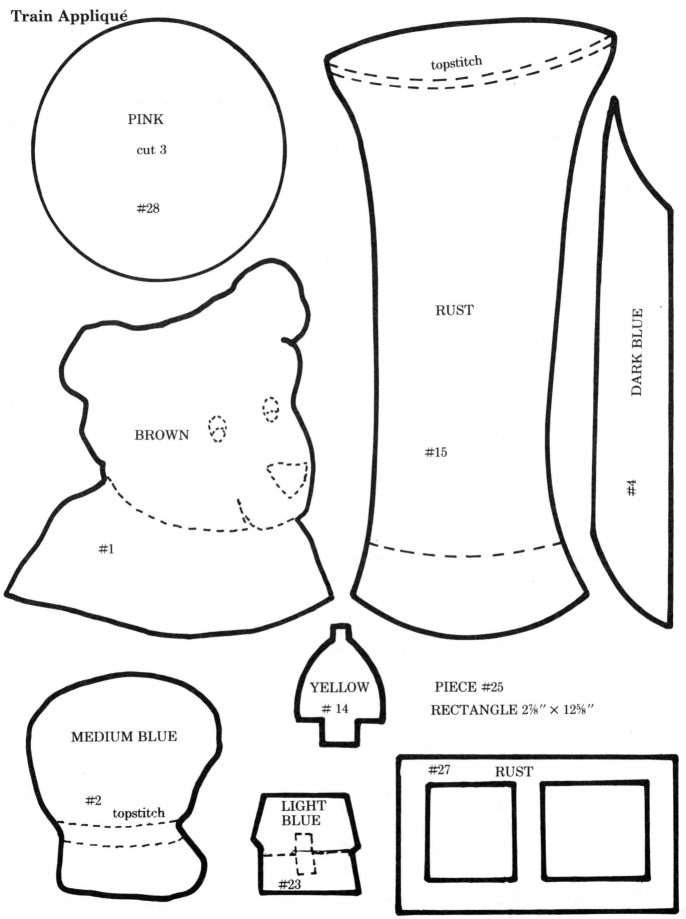

Train Appliqué

PINK

cut 3

#28

topstitch

RUST

#15

DARK BLUE

#4

BROWN

#1

YELLOW

14

PIECE #25

RECTANGLE 2⅞″ × 12⅝″

MEDIUM BLUE

#2   topstitch

LIGHT
BLUE

#23

#27   RUST

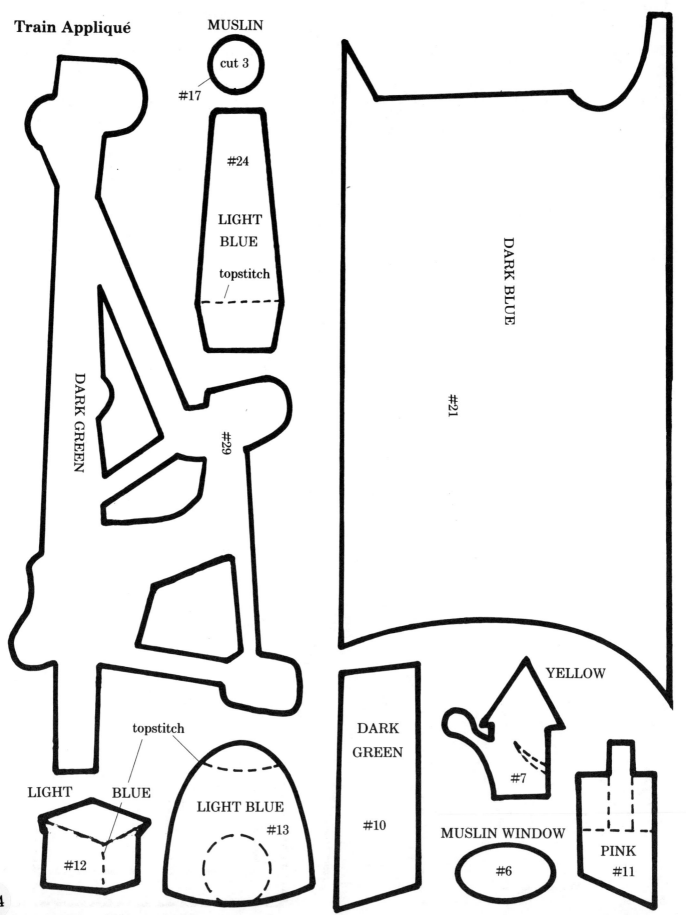

Train Appliqué

MUSLIN

cut 3

#17

#24

LIGHT
BLUE

topstitch

DARK GREEN

#29

DARK BLUE

#21

topstitch

LIGHT   BLUE

#12

LIGHT BLUE

#13

DARK
GREEN

#10

YELLOW

#7

MUSLIN WINDOW

#6

PINK
#11

184

Train Appliqué

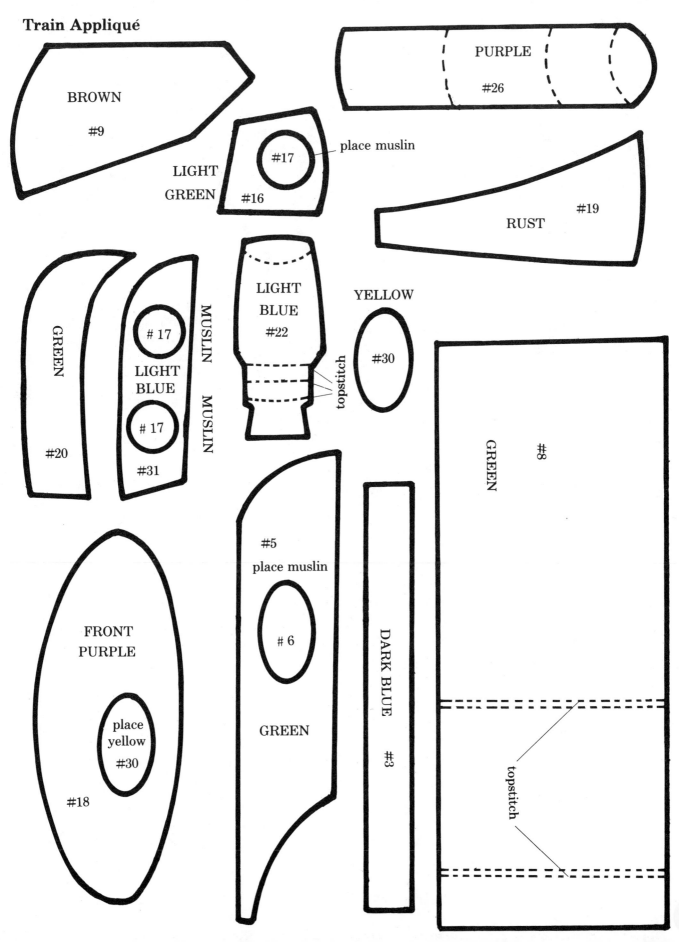

BROWN
#9

PURPLE
#26

LIGHT
GREEN
#16

#17
place muslin

RUST
#19

GREEN
#20

LIGHT
BLUE
#31

17

17

MUSLIN

MUSLIN

LIGHT
BLUE
#22

topstitch

YELLOW
#30

GREEN
#8

FRONT
PURPLE

place
yellow
#30

#18

#5
place muslin

6

GREEN

DARK BLUE
#3

topstitch

185

KITTY APPLIQUÉ

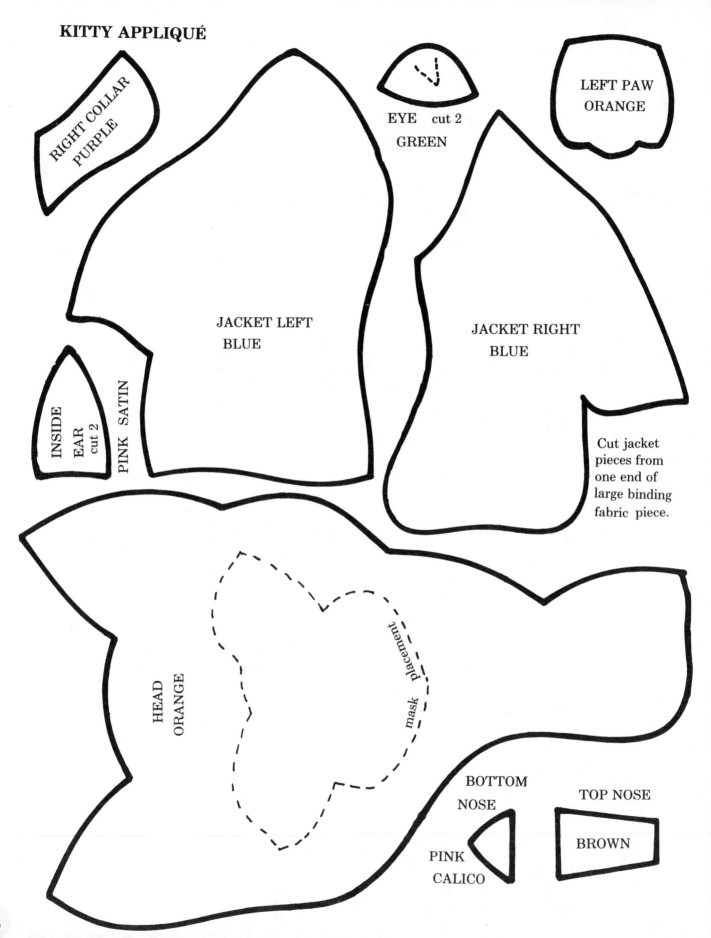

RIGHT COLLAR
PURPLE

EYE   cut 2
GREEN

LEFT PAW
ORANGE

JACKET LEFT
BLUE

JACKET RIGHT
BLUE

INSIDE
EAR
cut 2   PINK SATIN

Cut jacket
pieces from
one end of
large binding
fabric piece.

HEAD
ORANGE

mask   placement

BOTTOM
NOSE

TOP NOSE

BROWN

PINK
CALICO

KITTY APPLIQUÉ

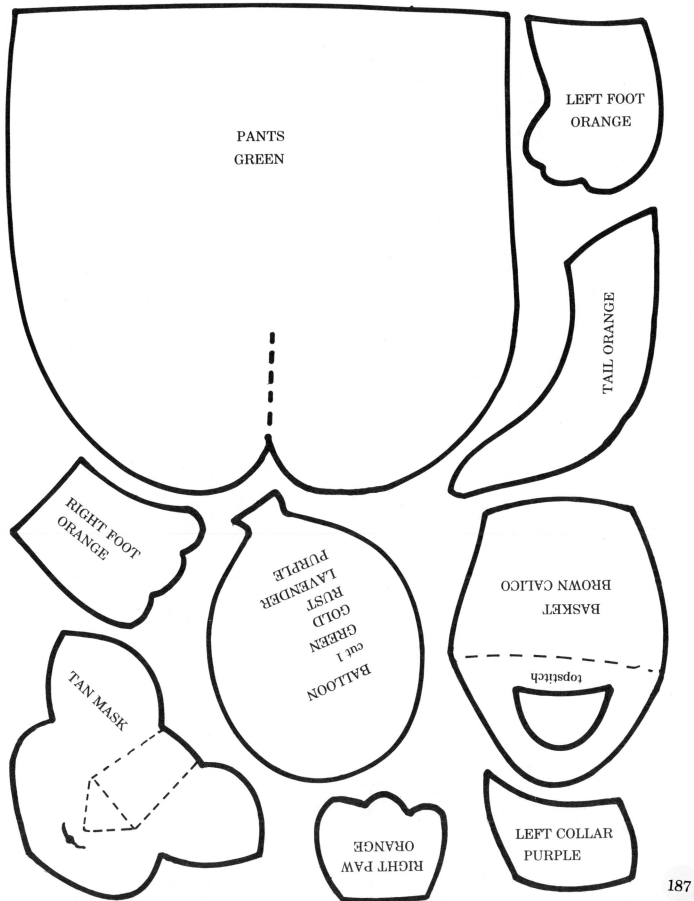

PANTS
GREEN

LEFT FOOT
ORANGE

TAIL ORANGE

RIGHT FOOT
ORANGE

BALLOON
cut 1
GREEN
GOLD
RUST
LAVENDER
PURPLE

BASKET
BROWN CALICO

topstitch

TAN MASK

LEFT COLLAR
PURPLE

RIGHT PAW
ORANGE

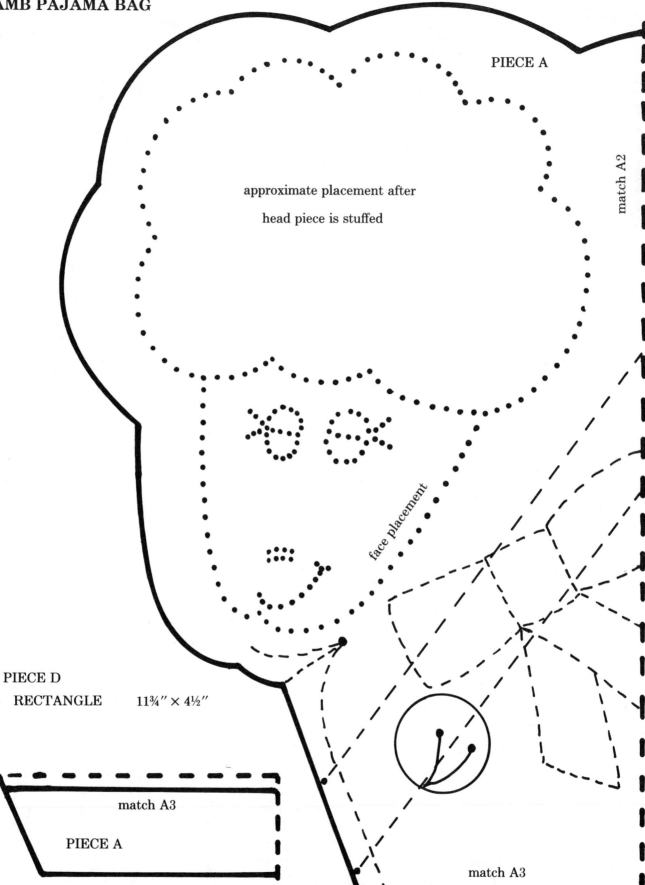

PIECE A

match A2

approximate placement after

head piece is stuffed

face placement

PIECE D

RECTANGLE   11¾″ × 4½″

match A3

PIECE A

match A3

LAMB PAJAMA BAG

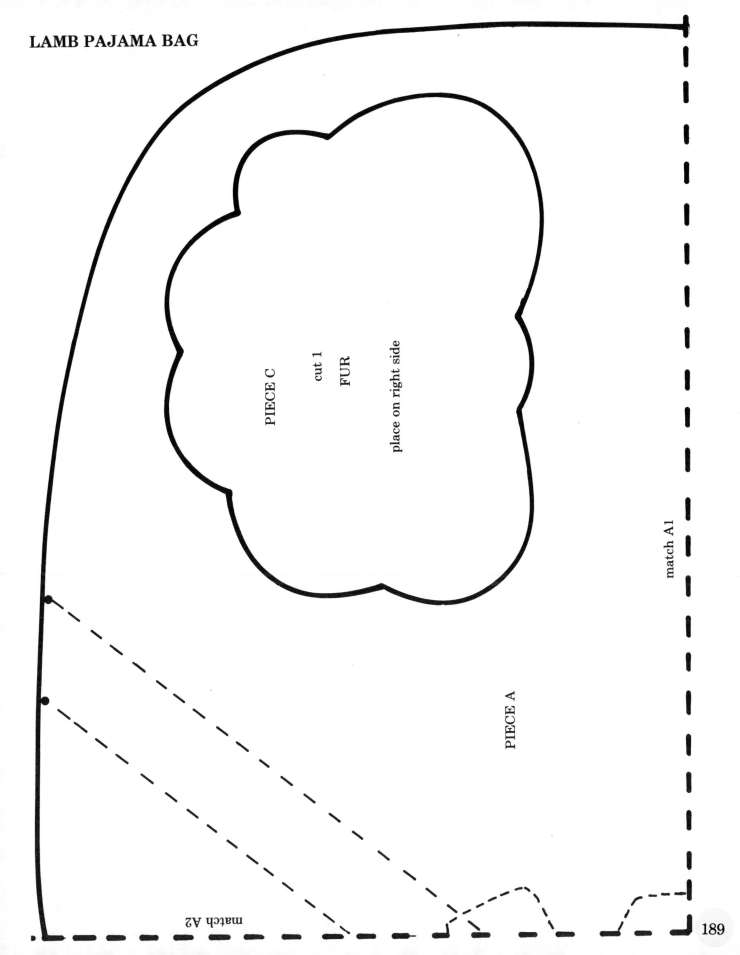

PIECE C

cut 1

FUR

place on right side

PIECE A

match A1

match A2

189

LAMB PAJAMA BAG

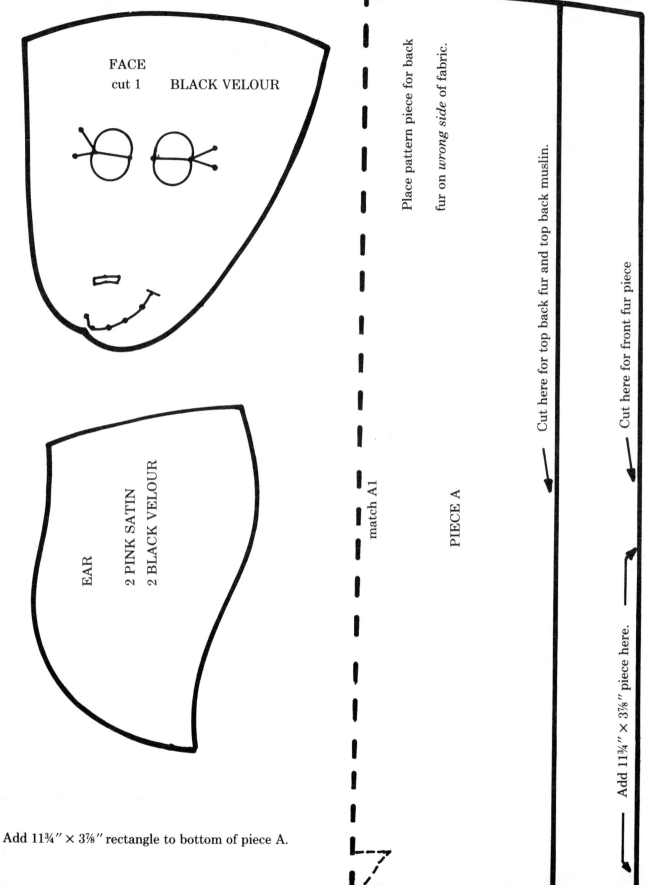

FACE
cut 1   BLACK VELOUR

EAR

2 PINK SATIN
2 BLACK VELOUR

Add 11¾″ × 3⅞″ rectangle to bottom of piece A.

Place pattern piece for back
fur on *wrong side* of fabric.

match A1

PIECE A

Cut here for top back fur and top back muslin.

Cut here for front fur piece

Add 11¾″ × 3⅞″ piece here.

LAMB PAJAMA BAG

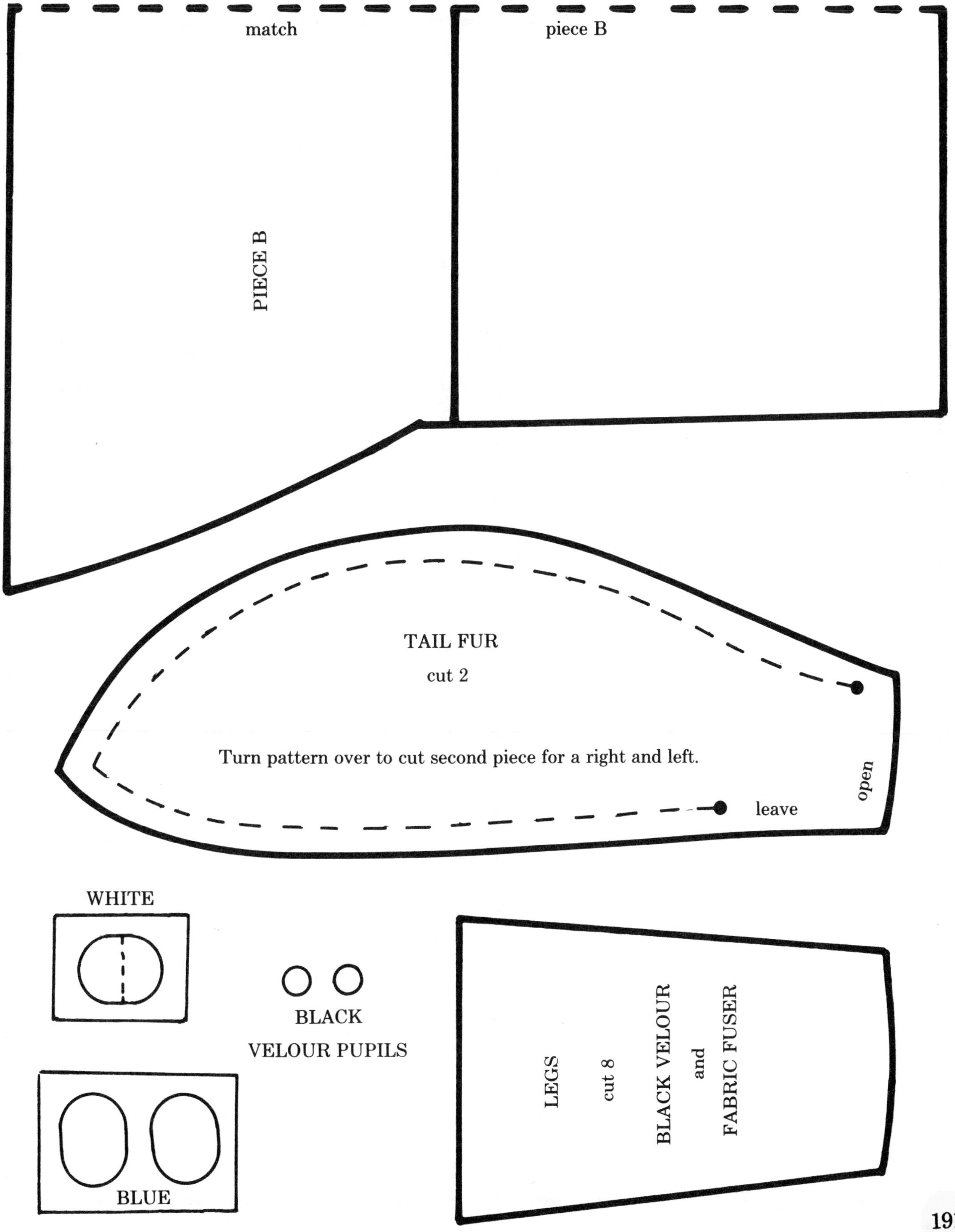

match   piece B

PIECE B

TAIL FUR

cut 2

Turn pattern over to cut second piece for a right and left.

open

leave

WHITE

BLACK
VELOUR PUPILS

LEGS

cut 8

BLACK VELOUR

and

FABRIC FUSER

BLUE

191

LAMB PAJAMA BAG

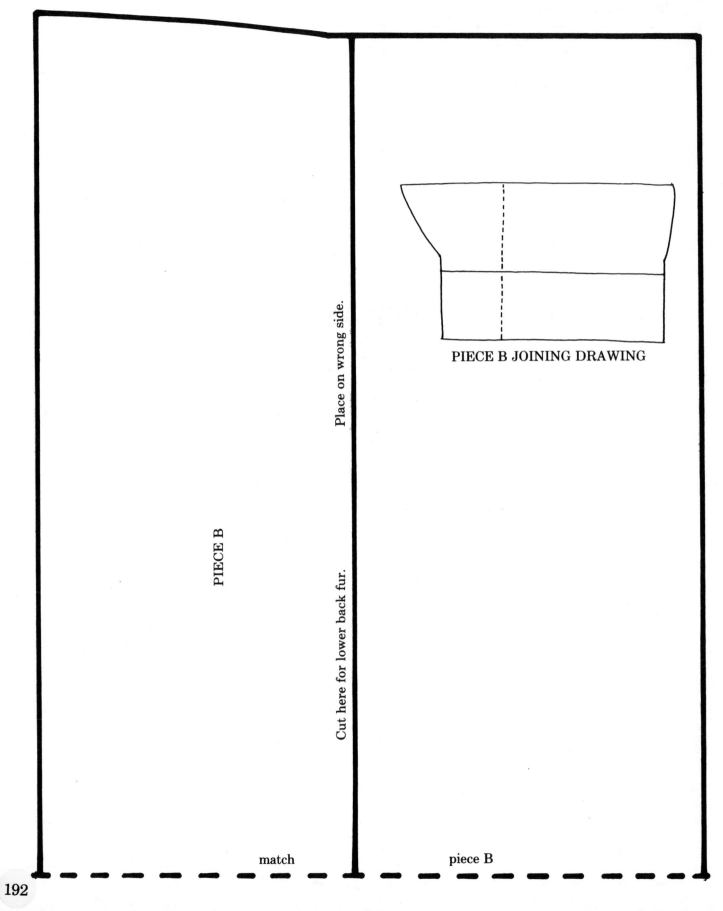

PIECE B

Place on wrong side.

Cut here for lower back fur.

PIECE B JOINING DRAWING

match   piece B